AF761409

Making Development Co-operation Work for Small Island Developing States

OECD
BETTER POLICIES FOR BETTER LIVES

This work is published under the responsibility of the Secretary-General of the OECD. The opinions expressed and arguments employed herein do not necessarily reflect the official views of OECD member countries.

This document, as well as any data and any map included herein, are without prejudice to the status of or sovereignty over any territory, to the delimitation of international frontiers and boundaries and to the name of any territory, city or area.

Please cite this publication as:
OECD (2018), *Making Development Co-operation Work for Small Island Developing States*, OECD Publishing, Paris.
http://dx.doi.org/10.1787/9789264287648-en

ISBN 978-92-64-28761-7 (print)
ISBN 978-92-64-28764-8 (PDF)

The statistical data for Israel are supplied by and under the responsibility of the relevant Israeli authorities. The use of such data by the OECD is without prejudice to the status of the Golan Heights, East Jerusalem and Israeli settlements in the West Bank under the terms of international law.

Photo credits: Cover © Izanbar/Dreamstime.com.

Corrigenda to OECD publications may be found on line at: *www.oecd.org/about/publishing/corrigenda.htm*.

© OECD 2018

You can copy, download or print OECD content for your own use, and you can include excerpts from OECD publications, databases and multimedia products in your own documents, presentations, blogs, websites and teaching materials, provided that suitable acknowledgement of OECD as source and copyright owner is given. All requests for public or commercial use and translation rights should be submitted to *rights@oecd.org*. Requests for permission to photocopy portions of this material for public or commercial use shall be addressed directly to the Copyright Clearance Center (CCC) at *info@copyright.com* or the Centre français d'exploitation du droit de copie (CFC) at *contact@cfcopies.com*.

Foreword

This report is part of the OECD work on "countries most in need" and contributes to international efforts to better tailor development co-operation to the specific circumstances of small island developing states (SIDS). The OECD has intensified its work on "countries most in need", with a view to maximising the full potential of development finance, particularly of scarce official development assistance (ODA), since the 2014 OECD Development Assistance Committee (DAC) High Level Meeting, where Ministers from DAC member countries decided to *"allocate more of total ODA to countries most in need, such as least developed countries (LDCs), low-income countries, small island developing states (SIDS), landlocked developing countries and fragile and conflict-affected states"*. At the Third International Conference on Small Island Developing States, the Chair of the DAC and the Administrator of the United Nations Development Programme, together with the Caribbean Community and the Pacific Islands Forum Secretariat, agreed to contribute new evidence to foster international dialogue and build international support for SIDS, including a focus on OECD work on "countries most in need" on SIDS. Tailoring financial instruments to different country needs is also at the heart of the concerns expressed during the 2016 and 2017 DAC High Level Meetings.

Previous OECD work documented the impacts of natural disasters and climate change in SIDS and the need to build resilience. This evidence was used to inform policy dialogue in partnership with SIDS governments and other international stakeholders, including during the 22nd Conference of the Parties to the UN Framework on Climate Change (COP22), the 2016 OECD DAC Senior Level Meeting, the 2016 Small States Forum and the 2017 UN High Level Conference to Support the Implementation of Sustainable Development Goal 14.

This new report draws upon a number of original sources and contributes new evidence to further efforts to tailor international co-operation and concessional finance to the specific circumstances of SIDS. It documents the economic and social performance of SIDS compared to that of other developing countries, pointing to specific challenges facing SIDS and suggesting that new development solutions and approaches are needed to chart the course to prosperity for their people and their environments. The report examines the financing for development resources - domestic and external - available to SIDS. It provides new evidence on sources, destination, and objectives of development finance in SIDS. It highlights innovative approaches and good practices that the international community could replicate, further develop, and scale up in order to make development co-operation work for SIDS, helping them set on a path of sustainable development.

The special development case of SIDS is internationally recognised. Yet, it is only recently that SIDS have more strongly advocated collectively for greater international support and that the international community has started to respond. The special challenges of SIDS were first recognised in the Rio Declaration, issued by the 1992 UN Conference on Environment and Development (also known as the Earth Summit) in the context of Agenda 21 (Chapter 17 G). The first UN Global Conference on Sustainable Development in SIDS took place in Barbados in May 1994. During the Conference, SIDS endorsed the Barbados Programme of Action, which served as the main policy framework addressing the economic, social and environmental vulnerabilities facing SIDS. The UN Third International Conference on Small Island Developing States held in 2014 in Apia, Samoa, provided further international impetus to the SIDS agenda, and focused the world's attention on the specific vulnerabilities of SIDS, calling for their adequate consideration. Most recently, in 2015, the Addis Ababa Action Agenda recognised the development constraints and vulnerability of SIDS, and acknowledged the need to look beyond per capita income as a criterion determining eligibility for concessional finance. Still in 2015, SIDS played a leading role in reaching the historic Paris Agreement, which acknowledged their acute vulnerability, and provided an international framework for ongoing financial and technical support as they seek to transition to climate-resilient green economies. The same year, the Sendai Framework for Disaster Risk Reduction also recognised the acute exposure of SIDS to natural disasters, and the need for greater investments in preparedness and risk reduction.

Acknowledgements

This report was written by Piera Tortora and Jonathan Barnes, under the overall supervision of Olivier Cattaneo and Haje Schütte. In Chapter 3, the section on triangular co-operation was co-authored with Nadine Piefer and the section on regional approaches with Gay Tejada (PARIS21 Secretariat). Statistical data support was provided by Cécilia Piemonte and Valérie Thielemans.

Members of the OECD Development Assistance Committee (DAC) are acknowledged for their useful feedback, namely Australia, Austria, Germany, Hungry, Ireland, Italy, Japan, New Zealand, Spain, United Kingdom and United States. Financial support and expert consultations with officials from Australia and New Zealand are kindly acknowledged.

The authors would like to acknowledge the following individuals and experts for their comments and advice on earlier versions of the report: Gail Hurley, United Nations Development Programme, Naresha Duraiswamy, World Bank Secretariat of Small States Forum, Natalie Cooke, (Cook Islands), and Kevin Hogan, as well as OECD colleagues: Wiebke Bartz, Juan Casado Asensio, Emilio Chiofalo, Paul Horrocks, He Yeon Ji, Antonia Leroy, Roger Martini, Rahul Malhotra, Rachel Morris and Cushla Thompson.

The report was prepared for publication under the direction of Henri-Bernard Solignac Lecomte and Stacey Bradbury with editorial support from Romy de Courtay. The report was designed by Corinne Hayworth and laid out by Stacey Bradbury and Maria Petit-Breuilh David. Stephanie Coic prepared the cover image. Anne-Lise Prigent from the Public Affairs and Communications Directorate provided editorial and content oversight.

Table of contents

Tables

Figures

Boxes

Abbreviations and acronyms

AAAA	Addis Ababa Action Agenda
ADB	Asian Development Bank
AIMS	Africa, Indian Ocean, Mediterranean and South China Sea
AML-CFT	Anti-money laundering and counter-terrorist financing
AOSIS	Alliance of Small Island States
AUD	Australian dollar
BPOA	Barbados Plan of Action
CARICOM	Caribbean Community
CCRIF	Caribbean Catastrophe Risk Insurance Facility
CDB	Caribbean Development Bank
COP22	Twenty-second Conference of the Parties to the United Nations Framework Convention on Climate Change
CRED	Collaborating Centre for Research on the Epidemiology of Disasters
CRS	Creditor reporting system
DAC	OECD Development Assistance Committee
EDF	European Development Fund
EEZ	Economic exclusion zones
EM-DAT	International disaster database
EU	European Union
EVI	Economic Vulnerability Index
FAO	Food and Agriculture Organization
FDI	Foreign direct investment
FERDI	Foundation for International Development Study and Research
GCF	Green Climate Fund
GDP	Gross domestic product
GEF	Global Environment Facility
GF	Global Fund
GNI	Gross national income
HDI	Human Development Index
HHI	Herfindahl-Hirschman Index

HIPC	Heavily Indebted Poor Countries
IBRD	International Bank for Reconstruction and Development
IDA	International Development Association
IDB	Inter-American Development Bank
IFAD	International Fund for Agriculture and Development
IMF	International Monetary Fund
ISDB	Islamic Development Bank
IUU	Illicit, unreported and unregulated fishing activities
LDC	Least developed country
LMICs	Lower middle-income countries
MDB	Multilateral development bank
MICs	Middle income countries
NDA	National Designated Authority
ODA	Official development assistance
PCRAFI	Pacific Catastrophe Risk Assessment and Financing Initiative
PIFS	Pacific Islands Forum Secretariat
SDG	Sustainable Development Goals
SDR	Special drawing rights
SIDS	Small island developing states
SME	Small and medium-sized enterprises
UMICs	Upper middle-income countries
UN	United Nations
UN-OHRLLS	UN Office of the High Representative for the Least Developed Countries, Landlocked Developing Countries and Small Island Developing States
UNCTAD	United Nations Conference on Trade and Development
UNDP	United Nations Development Programme
UNWTO	United Nations World Tourism Organization
USD	US dollar

Editorial: Helping small island developing states embark on sustainable development pathways

We are all affected by what happens to small island developing states. The strength of their economies, people, and land brings shared prosperity for everyone. Small island developing states are the custodians of the oceans that connect the world. At the same time, the families that live on these islands hold the frontline against the impact of natural disasters. These threats are increasing as a result of the climate change for which we all bear responsibility. Small island developing states are placed at the centre of a vicious cycle of high vulnerability and low growth. In response, development co-operation for this group of countries requires a unique strategy that is tailored to building long-term resilience against external blows.

We stand at a critical juncture, where action taken today can determine whether individual small island developing states are able to meet the 2030 Agenda goals. The devastating 2017 storms should be a catalyst for the international community to change the way it approaches development co-operation with small island nations. With and following the humanitarian response, attention should be turned to tackling the underlying drivers of vulnerability and reversing the broader challenges that hamstring development gains.

While development progress is fragile for all countries, small island states remain uniquely vulnerable. The paradox of developed small islands is a good example. Even islands that achieve relatively high income levels remain one exogenous shock away from a development crisis with long-lasting effects due to their size, remoteness and natural vulnerabilities. These factors mean that, as small island developing states achieve higher levels of national income, their access to the range and sources of development finance is reduced, yet their inherent vulnerability remains. Development co-operation must be tailored and strategic, to support approaches and instruments that reward small islands' upward economic trajectory.

The Organisation for Economic Co-operation and Development promotes an effective use of development finance globally, with a special focus on "countries most in need". These include small island developing states, fragile states and least developed countries, which can include middle-income countries. Building a body of evidence around what is needed to support these states is central to better understanding new distributions of need driven by fragility, climate change, inequality and other challenges.

This report, for the first time, draws upon a range of established and original statistics to quantify the specific development context of the small island developing states, the overall financing for development landscape and the allocation of concessional finance for the period 2000-2015. The international community mobilised an extraordinary amount of concessional finance in 2010 in response to the devastating earthquake in Haiti. After 2010 the volume of official development assistance to small island developing states decreased every year until 2014. In 2015, this volume increased for the first time above the 2009 level but it remains to be seen if this is a one-off or the beginning of an upward trend. The development co-operation landscape that has emerged for small island developing states includes a three-pronged mix of: a handful of OECD Development Assistance Committee (DAC) members providing the majority of ODA; a range of multilateral providers meeting critical needs; and, non-DAC sovereign providers that are increasingly meeting demands, especially for islands with relatively higher income levels as they lose access to concessional resources. To harness these financial flows in the most effective way for building resilience in small island states, the international community requires new ways of working. This report reviews the most promising ideas, best practices and new instruments for activating a broader range of public and private resources, as well as innovative approaches that can make a difference now, and mitigate future vulnerabilities in small island developing states.

Strengthening the blue economy, for example, has big potential for promoting resilience in small island developing states. Targeting development co-operation to focus on the sustainable management of oceans and coastal zones can boost production, serve as a route into global value chains, sustain more inclusive growth, and tackle debt burdens. In addition to driving national progress, fortifying blue and green economies will advance SDG14, to "conserve and sustainably use the oceans, seas and marine resources for sustainable development."

The governments and citizens in small island developing states are, and must remain, the driving force behind their development but they can't do this in isolation. We have a shared responsibility for promoting small islands' progress. The success of the 2030 Agenda, and the future prosperity of the planet, depends on healthy oceans that are supported by the small island states.

Jorge Moreira da Silva,

Director,
OECD Development Co-operation Directorate

Executive summary

Small island developing states have vulnerabilities, but opportunities for sustainable development lie ahead

Focusing on the 35 small island developing states (SIDS) that are currently eligible for official development assistance (ODA), this report provides evidence of SIDS' vulnerability stemming from their small populations and small landmasses, spatial dispersion and remoteness from major markets, and high exposure to external shocks, including severe climate-related events and natural disasters. While three fifths of SIDS are upper middle-income countries, they are among the most vulnerable developing countries. Compared to larger upper middle-income countries, SIDS in this same income group are 73% more vulnerable. The persistence of these vulnerabilities and of fragile growth patterns suggests that new development paradigms and solutions are needed to chart the course to sustainable development in SIDS.

Development opportunities to move closer to self-sufficiency lie ahead, at least for some SIDS: in technological innovations that could lift connectivity barriers to global markets; in the exploitation of renewable energies – sun, wind and ocean waves, all abundant in SIDS – which could break dependence on fossil fuels and create fiscal space to address critical development needs; in the development of the "blue economy" which, by connecting old and new sectors linked to the abundant marine resources of SIDS, could fuel economic growth and help address food insecurity, high unemployment and poverty.

For SIDS to seize these opportunities and embark on sustainable development pathways the international community needs to make development co-operation work better for them. Drawing upon new and original statistical sources, this report contributes evidence to the international efforts to tailor development co-operation and concessional finance to the specific circumstances of SIDS.

Financing for development landscape

SIDS face significant challenges in mobilising domestic resources and in accessing capital markets. They tend to have small and erratic domestic revenues, which combined with high costs for providing public services and the fiscal impacts of natural disasters, often result in limited fiscal space for development investments. The debt situation of the five SIDS that benefitted from the Heavily Indebted Poor Countries Initiative has drastically improved in the past 15 years, but for the remaining SIDS debt over gross national income (GNI) ratios have increased. Overall 20 SIDS are at "moderate" risk, "high" risk or "in debt distress" according to the International Monetary Fund. Foreign direct investments and other private finance flows are highly volatile and on average contribute little to SIDS' external financing: only 12% in 2012-15. This reflects the lack of creditworthiness to raise funds in capital markets for many SIDS (especially in the Pacific) and the recent deterioration in international capital-market ratings and debt sustainability issues for other SIDS (e.g. in the Caribbean). Owing to large diasporas, remittances represent the largest flow of external finance for SIDS: 52% in 2012-15.

Concessional finance (i.e. grants and concessional loans from bilateral and multilateral providers) **remains a vital source of financing for development in many SIDS,** accounting for the largest flow of external finance for three out of five SIDS in 2012-15 and for over 10% of GNI in 13 individual SIDS, reaching 90% in Tuvalu. Concessional finance to SIDS, which reached USD 7.08 billion in 2016, has been influenced by one-off increases to individual SIDS: to Haiti following the earthquake in 2010, and to Cuba in 2015-16 for debt relief. However, in between these two peaks, volumes decreased. SIDS receive 3% of global ODA. While, due to their small populations, in per capita terms SIDS receive 3.8 times more than other developing countries, the cost of delivering assistance in a SIDS context is estimated to be 4.7 times higher than in other developing countries.

SIDS receive the bulk of concessional finance by bilateral providers (79%), mainly influenced by proximity and geopolitical ties. Financing from multilateral providers was more modest (21%) but increasing and expected to further rise driven by the four-fold increase in resources allocated to SIDS decided during the IDA 18 Replenishment. Non-DAC sovereign providers have become important partners for SIDS, and China is estimated to be the largest provider to some. Private philanthropy has also increased (USD 54 million annually on average in 2013-15) as well as private finance mobilised through official interventions (USD 234 million per year on average).

Although more sources have become available, many SIDS struggle to access these, owing to low absorption capacity and the complex array of accreditation and application processes to access the global funds. Access to finance is further constrained by a complex web of eligibilities and that includes ad hoc exceptions, resulting at times in inconsistent treatment across SIDS. Consequently, SIDS rely on average on just a single provider for 46% of their concessional finance. Overall, concessional finance is strongly concentrated on a few providers and few recipients, scattered across small projects, and could be better used to address some of the major vulnerabilities and issues that hinder further development in SIDS, such as climate vulnerabilities, lack of fiscal space, energy and infrastructure.

Innovations and good practices for better co-operation with SIDS

Owing to their specific circumstances and development challenges, breaking dependence on international official assistance will not be easy for some SIDS; for others, it will remain a critical resource to meet specific development needs. In both cases, as they embark on a path of sustainable development, SIDS will need to mobilise more financing from a broader array of both public and private sources. Concessional funds will need to play a significant role in leveraging and catalysing those flows.

Promising innovative approaches and good practices have been rolled out by development partners in recent years to **catalyse new flows and tackle some of the fundamental impediments that keep SIDS from experiencing larger development gains**. Several of these approaches could be replicated, further developed or scaled up. They include: innovative countercyclical instruments (e.g. contingent borrowing and "hurricane" clauses), green and blue bonds and other blending arrangements to bring climate finance to scale; debt relief mechanisms, such as debt for nature swaps; fiscal reforms to expand tax coverage (especially to include high revenue-generating segments of the economy); and policies to reduce "leakages" from key sectors and expand the taxable production base. These innovations are presented in the report under three main clusters, building on which a set of recommendations is presented.

Infographic: Recommendations to make development co-operation work for small island developing states

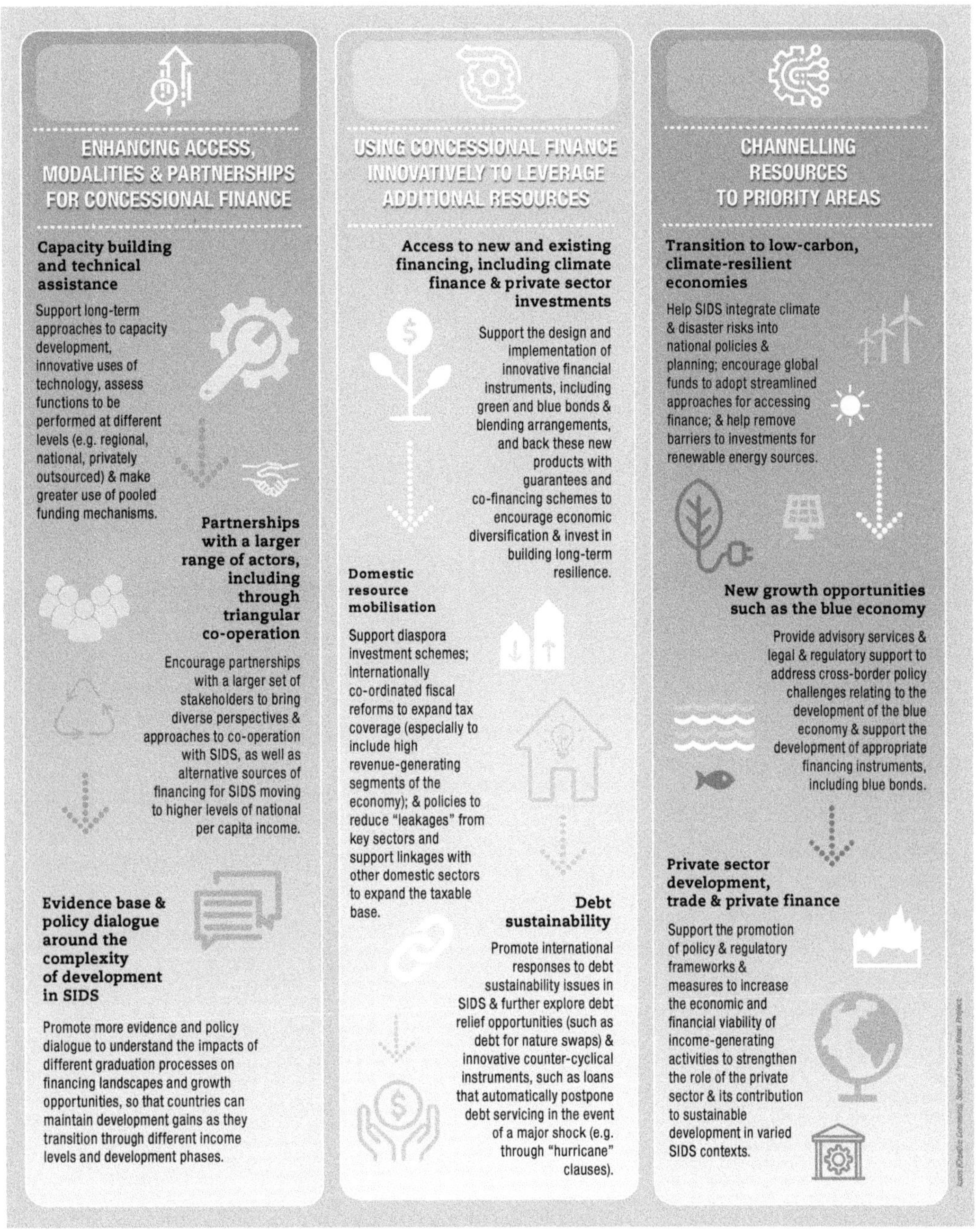

Chapter 1. Characteristics and vulnerabilities of small island developing states

Small island developing states (SIDS) have unique characteristics that contribute to their vulnerability to shocks and pose persistent challenges to their development. After reviewing definition issues, this chapter assesses the economic and development performance in SIDS compared to larger developing countries and unpacks geophysical and economic features that contribute to their vulnerability.

1.1. Small island developing states: a diverse group with strong commonalities

1.1.1. Definitions of SIDS

A number of lists of SIDS exist, including those established by: (i) the United Nations Office of the High Representative for the Least Developed Countries, Landlocked Developing Countries and Small Island Developing States (UN-OHRLLS) comprising 52 SIDS (38 of which are United Nations (UN) member states); (ii) the Alliance of Small Island States, comprising 39 SIDS; and (iii) the UN Conference on Trade and Development, comprising 29 SIDS. The World Bank Group defines small states as countries that: (a) have a population of 1.5 million or less; or (b) are members of the World Bank Group Small States Forum. Fifty small states fit this definition, including 27 of the 35 ODA-eligible SIDS considered in this report and landlocked states.

Given the focus of this report on financing for development and the role of concessional finance in SIDS in particular, this report considers the 35 SIDS that are eligible for official development assistance (ODA). These include: 9 least developed countries, 5 lower middle-income countries and 21 upper middle-income countries. [1] As illustrated in Figure 1.1, 7 of these SIDS are in the Africa, Indian Ocean, Mediterranean and South China Sea (AIMS) region, 13 are in the Caribbean and 15 are in the Pacific.

Figure 1.1. List of 35 ODA-eligible small island developing states by income group and by region

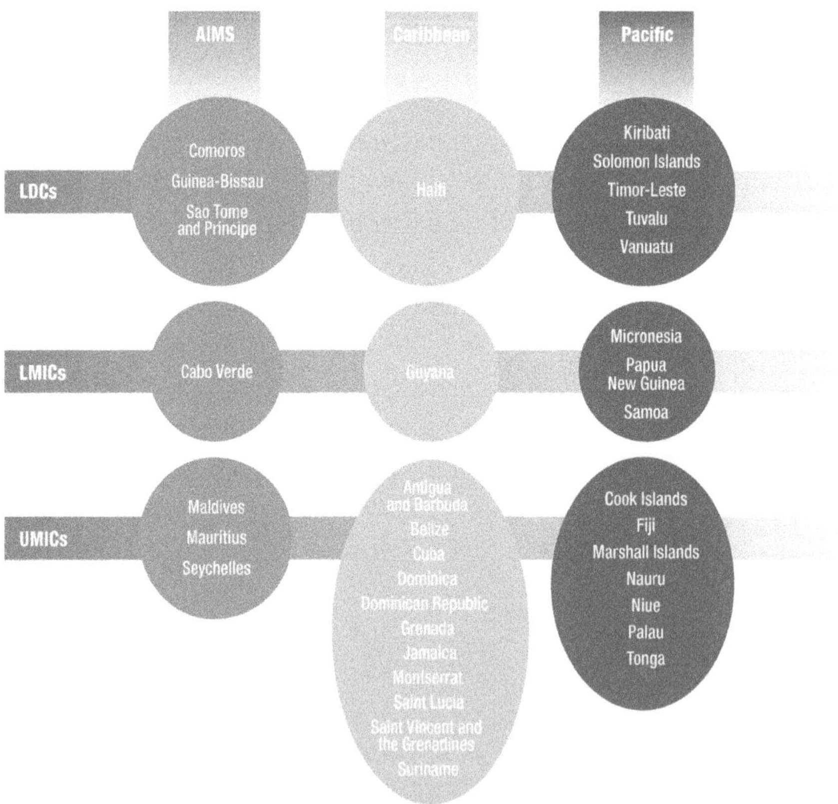

Source: Adapted from OECD DAC (2014), List of ODA Recipients, www.oecd.org/dac/financing-sustainable-development/development-finance-standards/daclist.htm and World Bank income classifications https://datahelpdesk.worldbank.org/knowledgebase/articles/906519-world-bank-country-and-lending-groups

The spread of SIDS across different regions and oncome categories suggests that they are a diverse and heterogeneous group of countries that nevertheless share strong commonalities. This report attempts to review both elements of heterogeneity and commonality, in particular in the light of economic growth, development performance, and vulnerability factors.

There are significant variations across SIDS

SIDS exhibit large variations in terms of population size and densities, geographical spread, natural resources endowments and relative development progress. Even among SIDS in the same region or belonging to the same income category, very distinct opportunities for growth and varied needs for support from the international community exist. Within the Pacific region, for instance, gross national income (GNI) per capita ranges from a low of USD 1 830 in the Solomon Islands to a high of USD 13 330 in Nauru (influenced by Nauru's small population size). Populations can range from under 1 600 inhabitants in Niue to over 7 million in Papua New Guinea. Remoteness from shipping lanes is highly pronounced in Nauru, Palau and Tuvalu,[2] and is lowest for Fiji,[3] which is a regional hub. In the Pacific, vulnerability to economic and natural shocks, as measured by the Economic Vulnerability Index (EVI),[4] is highest for Nauru (67.93) and Palau (69.65), but relatively lower for Papua New Guinea (31.67).

National income levels can also hide significant heterogeneity across SIDS. Some of the smallest SIDS in the Pacific with relatively higher national per capita income face significant challenges in finding a viable path towards sustainable growth. For example, Nauru, recorded sustained growth until 2011 when the main driver of growth – phosphate deposit extraction – became unavailable. Nauru is a microstate possessing no other natural resources, a population of only about 10 000, and a scarcely developed tourism and private sector. Although it has the highest GNI per capita among Pacific SIDS, its unemployment rate is estimated at 90%; and the Nauru government employs about 95% of the workforce.

Several middle-income SIDS – including Grenada, Jamaica, Mauritius, and the Seychelles – seem to enjoy better development prospects as they are better connected to international markets and shipping lanes and present a higher ease of doing business. However, they are often very reliant on top trading partners, which exposes them to "trade fragility"; they tend to have high levels of debt and strong vulnerability as measured by the EVI.

In addition, SIDS include countries that are in some form of free association compact with larger economies (e.g. Australia, New Zealand, United Kingdom or United States). Lacking in capacity and autonomy, more than other SIDS they depend on these larger economies for trade, tourism, and concessional finance, including for the financing of public services.

SIDS also share unique common challenges

As stated in Foreword, the special case of SIDS is internationally recognised, and it has received international attention. By analysing new data and performance against selected vulnerability factors, this report provides new evidence that, in spite of differences, SIDS face common economic and development challenges stemming from their small populations and small landmasses, their spatial dispersion and remoteness from major markets, and their high exposure to external shocks, including severe climate-related events and natural disasters.

While differences among SIDS point to the need for tailored development approaches across the group, they also point to scope for mutual learning and exchange of experiences among SIDS located in different geographical regions as well as among providers of concessional finance operating in different regions. Regional bodies, such as the Pacific Islands Forum Secretariat and the Caribbean Community (CARICOM) have so far been effective in bringing countries together to exchange views, build expertise, and develop policy options. More of this could be encouraged in the AIMS region as well as at the inter-regional level.

The challenge of making ODA work better for SIDS will be to strike the right balance between elements of heterogeneity – tailoring solutions to the specific needs of each country – and commonality – leveraging the political strength of the group and mutually beneficial experiences and good practices.

1.2. Economic and development performance of small island developing states

1.2.1. Economic growth is slow and volatile, owing to strong sensitivity to fluctuations in the global economy and natural disasters

Most SIDS[5] compare relatively well to other developing countries in terms of gross domestic product (GDP): three fifths of SIDS qualify as upper middle-income countries (see Figure 1.1). However, economic growth in most SIDS is fairly sluggish. It is also highly vulnerable to shocks in the global economy and to the impacts of climate change and natural disasters, owing to narrow production bases and undiversified economies, and strong reliance on the global economy for financial services, tourism, remittances and concessional finance.

Given the small size of SIDS economies, a single natural disaster can translate into losses of up to 200% of GDP (World Bank, 2005), wiping out entire economic sectors and eroding the development gains accumulated over decades (Box 1.1). Globally, SIDS make up two thirds of the countries that suffer the highest relative losses – between 1% and 9% of their GDP each year – from natural disasters (OECD-World Bank, 2016).

Box 1.1. Impacts of disasters and climate change will significantly increase the cost of sustainable development in small island developing states

SIDS are located in some of the world's most natural disaster-prone regions. Tropical storms and cyclones perennially afflict SIDS, whose dispersed and remote geographies, and small economies, make them poorly equipped to respond to these extreme events. Furthermore – as in other developing countries – rapid urbanisation, population growth and climate change are increasing the exposure of SIDS to disaster risk (Mimura et al., 2007). Pollution and ecosystem degradation, and the extraction of coastal aggregates for construction, are also compromising natural buffers, leaving the population and assets increasingly exposed. According to Mahul et al. (2014), the impacts of climate change will increase the severity and frequency of extreme weather events by 40-80%, and are posing additional challenges to the economic growth and sustainable development of SIDS. Many SIDS are low-lying or atoll nations, with key infrastructure and populations close to sea level, and hence acutely vulnerable to sea-level rises and storm surge events.

More than 335 major natural disasters have occurred in SIDS since 2000, resulting in an estimated USD 22.7 billion in direct damages. The occurrence of major natural disasters in SIDS has declined slightly since 2000; and yet the associated impacts of these events have increased (OECD-World Bank, 2016).

While absolute losses from natural disasters and climate-related events are dwarfed by those in larger economies, the relative impacts in SIDS are often far greater, causing widespread disruption to key economic sectors and service delivery resulting in significant costs as a share of national output (Figure 1.2). For example, tropical storm Erika caused widespread damage in Dominica in 2015. Landslides and flooding significantly damaged infrastructure, including highways financed with loans that had yet to be repaid. The Dominican government thus had to refinance to rebuild while also paying off debts for now defunct roads. The total cost was estimated at USD 483 million, roughly equivalent to 90% of GDP in 2015 (Government of the Commonwealth of Dominica, 2015).

The large exposure of SIDS to the impacts of climate change and natural disasters, combined with their limited ability to respond, means that SIDS are among the most vulnerable countries in the world. It also means that the cost of sustainable development in SIDS will be significantly higher than in other contexts. Short-term disaster response from humanitarian donors must be linked with long-term financial support for resilience building and, in turn, must be mainstreamed into development planning and financing. Therefore, while speed and low costs are important factors in carrying out reconstruction efforts in the wake of a disaster, taking into consideration the risks from climate change could require different standards and/or changes in planning processes to deliver cost effective, long-term development outcomes. Integrating the concept of resilience is critical to avoid locking out future development and creating new vulnerabilities.

Figure 1.2. Small island developing states suffer the largest relative losses from natural disasters, 2000-15

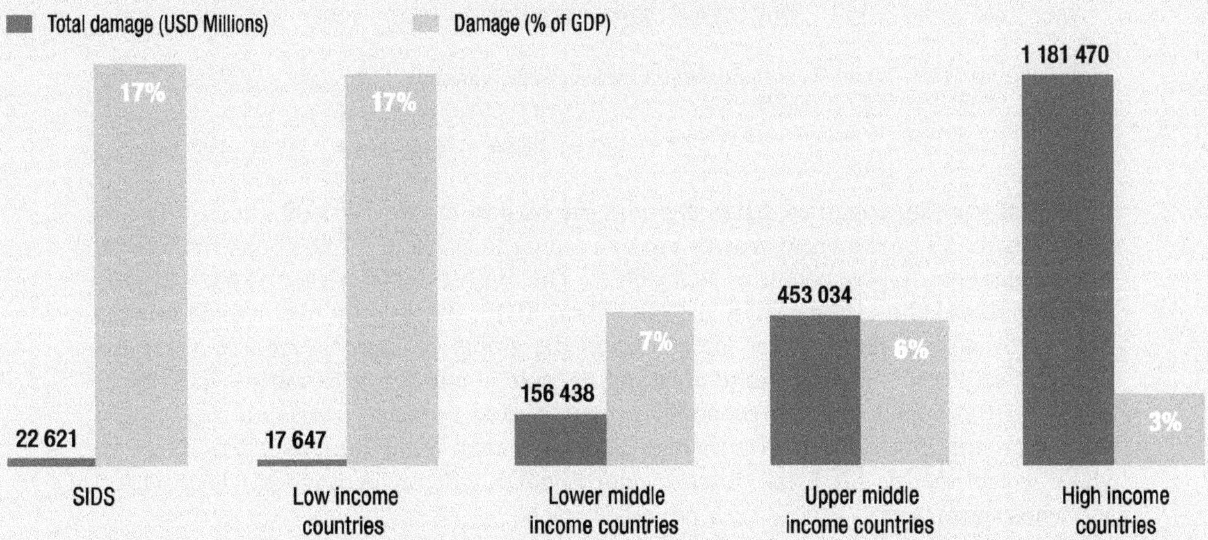

Source: OECD-World Bank (2016), Climate and Disaster Resilience Financing in Small Island Developing States, http://dx.doi.org/10.1787/9789264266919-en.

StatLink http://dx.doi.org/10.1787/888933645554/

Figure 1.3. Small island developing states were hit the hardest by the global financial crisis

GDP growth rates, 2000-15

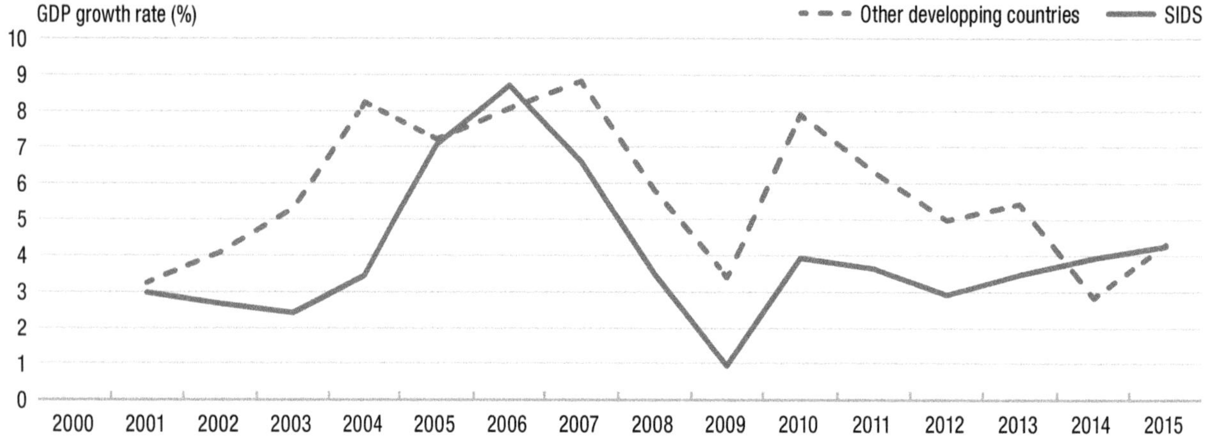

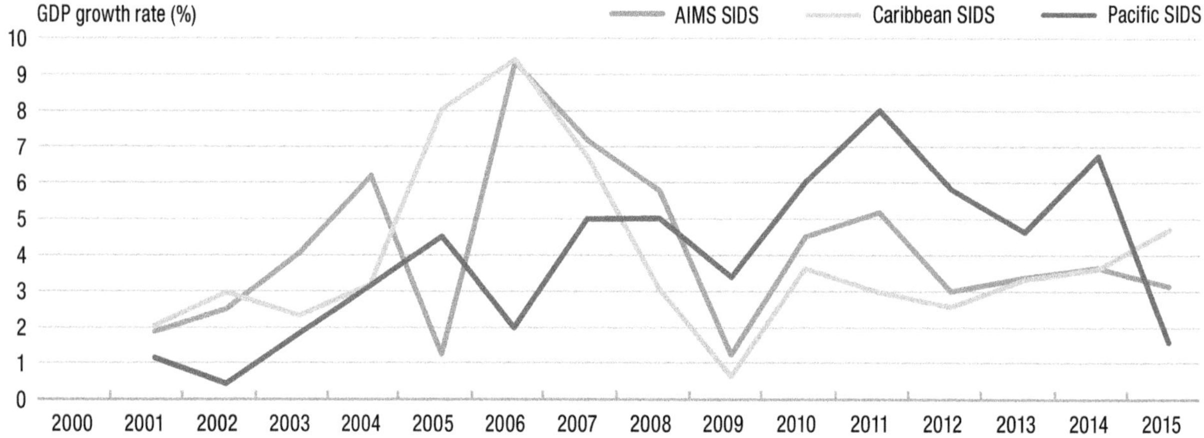

Source: Adapted from World Bank (n.d.), World Development Indicators, https://data.worldbank.org/data-catalog/world-development-indicators.

StatLink http://dx.doi.org/10.1787/888933645535

Among developing countries, SIDS were hit the hardest by the 2008-09 global financial crisis (Figure 1.3), with GDP growth rates slumping to 0.9% in 2009, compared to over 3% for other developing countries as a whole.[6] The impact of the crisis was most acutely felt in upper middle-income SIDS and Caribbean SIDS, two largely overlapping groups. This partly reflects their greater integration in the global economy – including through financial services, tourism, remittances and exports – compared to other SIDS. After SIDS' GDP dropped in 2009, economic growth picked up again across all regions and income groups. However, growth rates remain lower than in the pre-crisis period[7] for all SIDS, except Pacific SIDS and least developed SIDS, whose recovery has been faster, and whose growth rates exceed their pre-crisis levels.

Relying on income or geographic distinctions, however, can be at times misleading. Stronger economic performance of relatively larger SIDS economies, such as Papua New Guinea and Timor-Leste, leads to a rosier picture of performance in the Pacific after the crisis. The region's 3.4% growth in 2009 was mainly driven by 6.1% growth in Papua New Guinea and 13.0% growth in Timor-Leste; while six much smaller economies recorded negative growth, and the other nine Pacific SIDS saw lower growth rates. In general, trends in economic growth would also need to be assessed in per capita terms, as robust GDP growth in a few SIDS has not kept up with rapidly expanding populations, as it is the case of Papua New Guinea.

1.2.2. Human development lags behind and SIDS score as the most vulnerable among developing countries

While referring to GDP as a widely recognised and practical means of taking the pulse of a country's economy, its limitations as a measure of welfare and quality of life are well known.[8] When considering a country's achievements along a broader set of development dimensions (including health and standards of living) through the UN Human Development Index (HDI) (UNDP, n.d.), two fifths of SIDS display a low or medium level of development (Table 1.1). SIDS with low or medium HDI mainly comprise SIDS that are classified as least developed countries, but also some lower middle-income countries across different regions, such as Cabo Verde, Guyana, Federated States of Micronesia ("Micronesia") and Papua New Guinea.

Table 1.1. Over two fifths of small island developing states display a low or medium level of human development

HDI Rank	Country	HDI score	Human development group
60	Palau	0.79	High
62	Antigua and Barbuda	0.79	High
63	Seychelles	0.78	High
64	Mauritius	0.78	High
68	Cuba	0.77	High
79	Grenada	0.75	High
91	Fiji	0.74	High
92	Saint Lucia	0.74	High
94	Jamaica	0.73	High
96	Dominica	0.73	High
97	Suriname	0.72	High
99	Dominican Republic	0.72	High
99	Grenadines	0.72	High
101	Tonga	0.72	High
103	Belize	0.71	High
104	Samoa	0.70	High
105	Maldives	0.70	High
122	**Cabo Verde**	**0.65**	**Medium**
127	**Micronesia**	**0.64**	**Medium**
127	**Guyana**	**0.64**	**Medium**
133	**Timor-Leste**	**0.61**	**Medium**
134	**Vanuatu**	**0.60**	**Medium**
137	**Kiribati**	**0.59**	**Medium**
142	**Sao Tome and Principe**	**0.57**	**Medium**
154	**Papua New Guinea**	**0.52**	**Low**
156	**Solomon Islands**	**0.51**	**Low**
160	**Comoros**	**0.50**	**Low**
163	**Haiti**	**0.49**	**Low**
178	**Guinea-Bissau**	**0.42**	**Low**

Source: Adapted from UNDP Human Development Index Data for 2015, http://hdr.undp.org/en/content/human-development-index-hdi.

As a group, SIDS also score the highest among developing countries in terms of the EVI, a measure of the structural vulnerability of developing countries that takes into accounts the impacts of economic and natural shocks[9], as well as the determinants of exposure to shocks (including small population size and remoteness from world markets[10]). Vulnerability measured in terms of EVI is highest for least developed SIDS. When considering a measure of vulnerability, the largest gap between SIDS and other developing countries emerges for upper middle income countries: upper middle-income SIDS exhibit a 73% higher vulnerability than other upper middle-income countries (Figure 1.4).

Figure 1.4. Small island developing states are on average more vulnerable than other developing countries

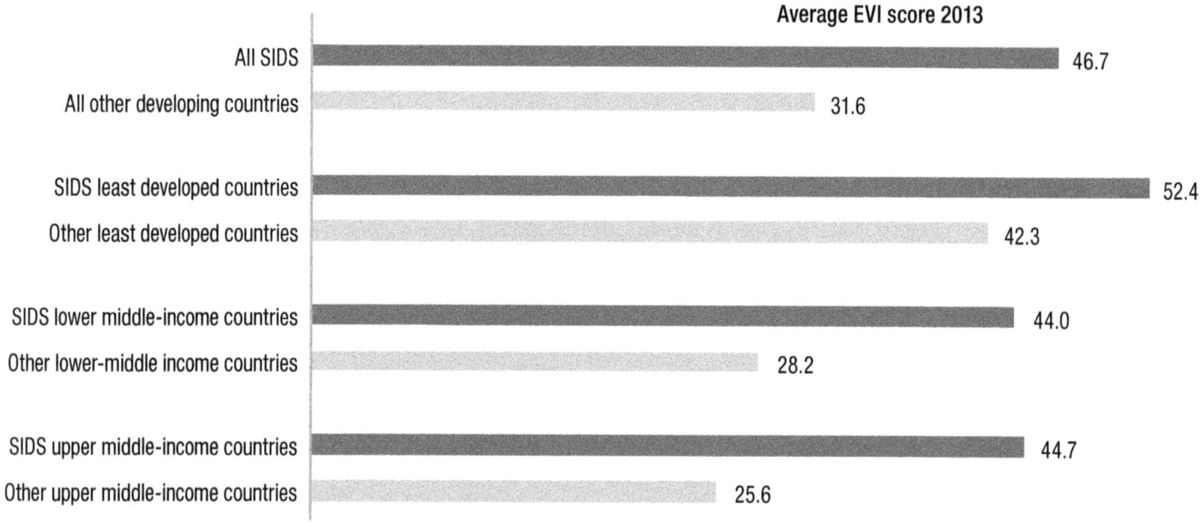

Source: Adapted from Ferdi (n.d.) Economic Vulnerability Index data, www.ferdi.fr/en/node/899.

StatLink http://dx.doi.org/10.1787/888933645573

1.3. Key drivers of vulnerability and structural characteristics

1.3.1. Small, dispersed populations hamper the creation of sizable domestic markets and lead to capacity constraints

Small, dispersed populations are a key driver of vulnerability in SIDS: they limit the scope for developing domestic markets and prevent SIDS from exploiting economies of scale in production. Hence, production costs tend to be higher in SIDS – particularly when populations are scattered across multiple distant islands, and transport costs significantly increase overall production costs. As a result, SIDS tend to focus their economic activities on a small number of sectors (most often tourism, services, agriculture and fishing and natural resource extraction) that capitalise on their natural and human resources. This concentration of activity, in turn, increases the impact of shocks on key sectors.

Small and scattered populations also entail high per capita costs to deliver essential public services, challenging governments' ability to provide education, health, security and other services. These costs have a significant impact on public finances, leading to larger public sector expenditures compared to other developing countries with a similar income level (see, for example, Horscroft, 2014) and to a larger share of public expenditure that is recurrent expenditure rather than capital investment (See also Chapter 2). Figure 1.5 shows that SIDS' average for both health and education public expenditure (as a share of GDP) is higher than for comparable income countries, with some countries spending up to four times the comparator average in health (Micronesia), and almost double in education (Timor-Leste).

Finally, human and institutional capital is hard to build and maintain in small states, and small populations often translate into relatively low numbers of qualified staff working in key capacities. Some SIDS face a shortage of skilled labour and rely heavily on expatriate labour, despite a high unemployment rate. In some SIDS, the skilled labour shortage partly stems from limited access to good quality secondary, tertiary and vocational education; in other SIDS, it mainly results from a lack of adequate job opportunities and the ensuing brain drain. For example, Grenada has an annual emigration rate of 2% and ranks among the top five developing nations in terms of the share of college-educated citizens leaving the country. Moreover, while some SIDS are experiencing considerable population growth (20% in Antigua and Barbuda, and 40% in Timor-Leste over 2000-15), some SIDS face large emigration flows, a phenomenon which might increase as a consequence of climate change. Diasporas can be significant, sometimes outnumbering resident populations. Grenada, for example, has a population of about 100 000, with an estimated 230 000 Grenadians living abroad.

Figure 1.5. Public expenditure in health and education as a share of GDP, 2014

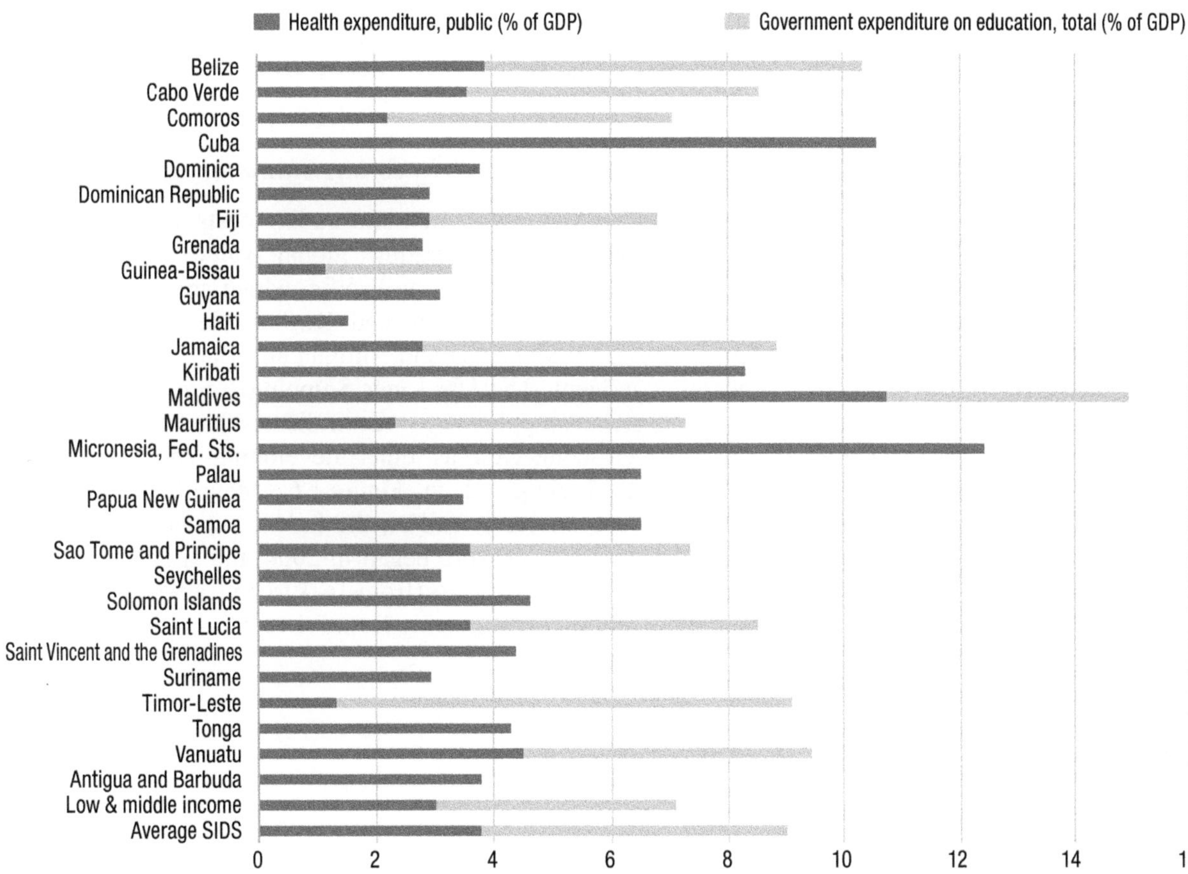

Note: Data is for 2014, except for Cabo Verde, Fiji, Guinea-Bissau for education (2013).

Source: World Bank (n.d.), World Development Indicators, https://data.worldbank.org/data-catalog/world-development-indicators.

StatLink http://dx.doi.org/10.1787/888933645592

According to de La Croix, Docquier and Schiff (2014), on average, emigration rates of SIDS are far above those of other developing countries and high-income countries. This is true for low-skilled workers (15.6 %, i.e. about 13 percentage points above the average level of other developing countries) and for college graduates (50.8 %, i.e. about 37 percentage points above the average level of other developing countries). Countries exhibiting the largest brain drain rates are Guyana (89.2 %), Jamaica (84.7 %), Grenada (84.3 %), Saint Vincent and the Grenadines (81.9 %), Haiti (79.0 %), Tonga (75.6 %) and Samoa (73.4 %). Migration flows can, however, also be a driver for development, which seems to be the case, for example, with labour arrangements with neighbouring countries, revolving migration, or remittances (See Chapter 3).

Overall, most SIDS (18 out of 35) are microstates numbering under 200 000 inhabitants; a further 11 SIDS have populations under 1.5 million (Niue is the smallest, with a population of 1 612); and six have populations between 1.5 and 12 million, with Cuba being the most populous. On aggregate, the total population of SIDS was estimated at 66 million in 2014, roughly 1% of the total global population. The extensive spatial dispersion of their island groupings is particularly pronounced for SIDS in the Pacific. Kiribati, for example, comprises 33 coral atolls scattered over 3.5 million square kilometres (km2) of ocean: an area larger than India. The Solomon Islands is geographically splintered, with 1 000 small islands and a population of 500 000 dispersed across 90 inhabited islands. In the Indian Ocean, the Maldives has a population of 341 200, scattered over 188 inhabited islands spanning an archipelago more than 800 km long and 130 km wide.

1.3.2. Long distances challenge access and connectivity to international markets

Coupled with small size, remoteness leads to high production and trading costs, limiting investment, competitiveness and the scope for integrating global value chains. Remoteness is an issue for most SIDS, especially those in the Pacific, which are among the most remote states on earth. Nauru, Marshall Islands and Kiribati are at least 3 000 km from the nearest continent, Australia. Mauritius and Antigua and Barbuda, are each over 1 000 km from the nearest continent. The UN Liner Shipping Connectivity Index, which measures connectedness to global shipping networks, indicates that SIDS as a group are less than one third as well connected as other developing countries (UNCTAD, 2010; UNCTAD, 2014). As highlighted in Figure 1.6, Mauritius, the Dominican Republic and Jamaica score comparatively well on the Index, but the other SIDS are very disconnected. Moreover, since the measure began in 2004, the aggregate score for the other developing countries has grown by 75% (from 14.3 to 25.0), whereas the improvement for SIDS has been more modest (40%), rising from 5.1 to 7.1.

Figure 1.6. Small island developing states are less than one third as well-connected as other developing countries

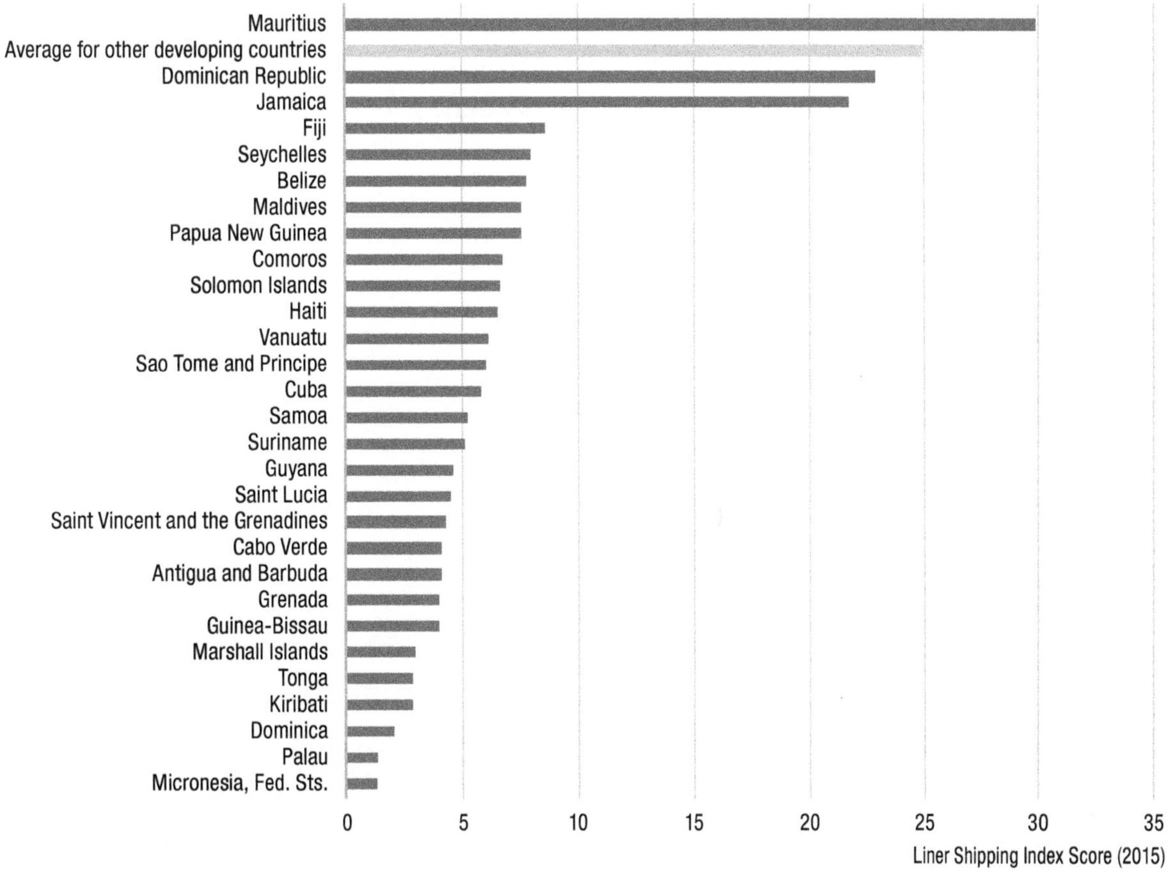

Source: Adapted from UNCTAD (n.d.), Liner shipping connectivity index, http://unctadstat.unctad.org/wds/TableViewer/tableView.aspx?ReportId=92.

StatLink http://dx.doi.org/10.1787/888933645611

Besides their remoteness from larger economies, some SIDS are also distant from each other, limiting the potential for intraregional SIDS trade integration. For example, Fiji is closer to Australia than to Papua New Guinea, and Palau is closer to Asia than to most other SIDS in the Pacific (IMF, 2016).

1.3.3. SIDS economies rely on narrow, undiversified production bases

Given high production costs, limited competitiveness and difficulties in integrating in global value chains, the economy of most SIDS relies on just a few products and sectors. Product concentration[11] is widespread and particularly high for several of the least developed SIDS, especially Guinea-Bissau, Timor-Leste, Kiribati, Vanuatu and Tuvalu (Figure 1.7). The economy of least developed SIDS is essentially based on agriculture (which represented 23% of GDP in 2015, compared to 7% in upper middle-income SIDS) and, in some cases, fisheries. Among least developed SIDS, Timor-Leste is an exception, due to its strong reliance on oil and natural gas, which account for about 80% of GDP and 90% of government revenues (IMF, 2016). While a handful of other SIDS rely strongly on natural resources, the economy of most SIDS largely relies on services, particularly tourism and financial services. Economic diversification usually is a path to resilience to external shocks.

Figure 1.7. The economies of most small island developing states rely on a narrow base of products and sectors

Product concentration as measured by the Herfindahl-Hirschman Index (Product HHI)
(High score indicates high reliance on one or few products)

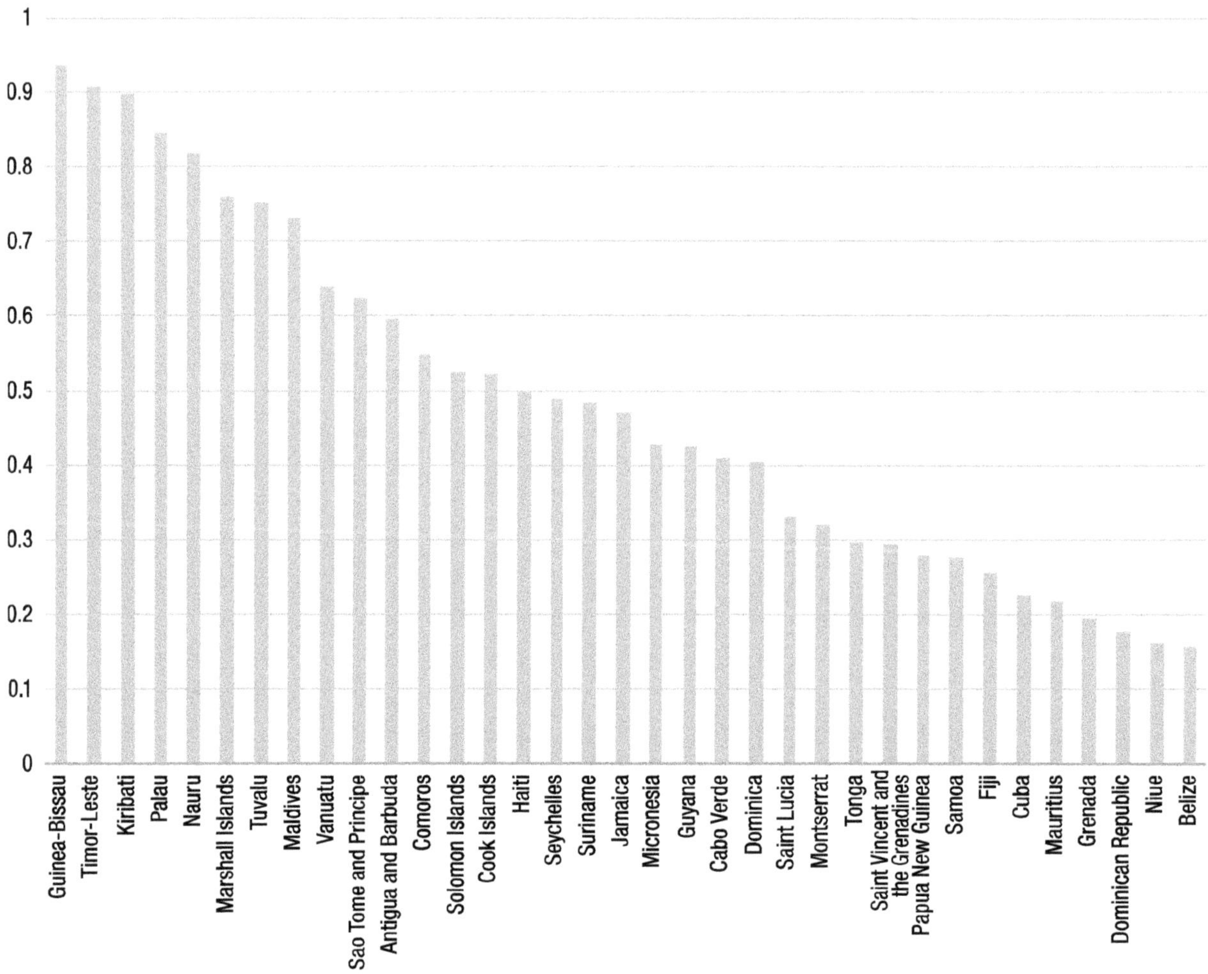

Source: Adapted from UNCTAD data for 2014, http://unctadstat.unctad.org/EN/.

StatLink http://dx.doi.org/10.1787/888933645630

1.3.4. Natural resources have been a driver of economic growth in a handful of SIDS

Besides Timor-Leste, other SIDS – such as Papua New Guinea, Guyana, Suriname, Solomon Islands and Guinea-Bissau – possess natural resources, including oil, gas, gold, nickel and bauxite. In 2000-15, natural-resource rents accounted for 10-40% of GDP in these SIDS, and over 140% in Timor-Leste. In the remaining SIDS, they represented less than 5% of GDP.

While natural resource-rich SIDS have benefitted from high commodity prices in recent years, the combined effect of falling commodity prices, China's economic slowdown and the rising cost of external debt may challenge the pace of their future economic growth. Other SIDS, which are large net importers of fuels and food, are instead likely to benefit from lower commodity prices (see end of Section 1.2). Overall, these SIDS grew slightly faster than other SIDS over 2000-15, recording an average annual growth rate of 4.3%, compared to 3.9% in other SIDS. Similarly to other natural resource-rich developing countries, however, the resource-rich SIDS are prone to suffering economically because of "Dutch disease": the increase in revenues from natural resources strengthens a country's currency, rendering its other exports more expensive, with a negative impact on the competitiveness of its manufacturing and agriculture sectors.

Several SIDS, especially in the Pacific, have well-established sovereign funds, which were created to ensure a stable stream of future revenue, to insure against fluctuations in domestic resource mobilisation, promote a wise use of public resources and earmark revenue for pre-approved long-term development expenditure. Kiribati and Timor-Leste successfully established sovereign funds to ensure a stable stream of natural resource revenues and reduce currency appreciation. Although phosphate deposits in Kiribati were depleted in the late 1970s, the Revenue Equalisation Reserve Fund, established in 1956 and financed through phosphate earnings, still represents over 200% of the country's GDP and significantly contributes to government spending. Timor-Leste's sovereign fund, established in 2005 to store and invest Timor-Leste's petroleum revenues, represents over 500% of the country's GDP (Drew, 2015). The global financial crisis had a strong impact on these SIDS, as it significantly reduced the value of their sovereign funds. Nevertheless, these funds still represent a significant source of wealth.

1.3.5. The economy of several SIDS strongly relies on tourism

Owing to their enchanting natural landscapes, beaches and cultural heritage, several SIDS rely on tourism as a significant source of income and foreign exchange. The tourism sector accounts for less than 5% of GDP in other developing countries, but represents over 20% of GDP for almost two thirds of SIDS, and between 58% and 65% for Palau and the Maldives (IMF, 2016). According to the World Travel and Tourism Council (WTTC, 2016), direct and indirect contributions to the Maldives economy amount to 78% of GDP and 62% of total employment. The tourism sector has been a main driver for graduation from least developed country status for Cabo Verde and Samoa, and represents a main source of revenue, especially for some upper middle-income SIDS (Figure 1.8).

Large financial "leakages" from the tourism sector, however, often diminish its positive impact on the domestic economies and livelihoods of SIDS. Spill over effects on the domestic economy can be limited by large food imports to meet foreign tourists' tastes, and the considerable imports of consumer goods and construction materials used in the tourism sector. In addition, the repatriation of profits earned by foreign investors and the land rents retained offshore can be considerable. For example, the expansion of the tourism sector in the Cook Islands led to a rapid growth in GDP figures; this, however, does not appear to match the population's stagnant living standards, likely because of the growing share of revenues flowing out of the economy and the falling share accruing locally (Bertram, 2016).

The risks stemming from the over reliance of SIDS economies on tourism became apparent during the 2008 global financial crisis, pointing again to the need to develop more diversified production bases. The tourism sector was, in fact, a key indirect channel of transmission for the 2008-09 global financial crisis, as visitor numbers fell considerably in many SIDS, with significant impacts on economic growth.

Large opportunities lie ahead for SIDS to both develop more sustainable tourism sectors, and integrate local value chains to foster better employment opportunities and inclusive development domestically. This would mean seizing the opportunities provided by the tourism sector to promote the sustainable use of oceans, to foster biodiversity conservation, and invest in green technologies to reduce energy and water consumption. It would also mean establishing policies to reduce the financial leakages currently experienced by several SIDS, mainly owing to the repatriation of profits earned by foreign investors, and the imports of consumer goods and construction materials used in the tourism sector.

Figure 1.8. Tourism represents over 20% of GDP for almost two thirds of small island developing states

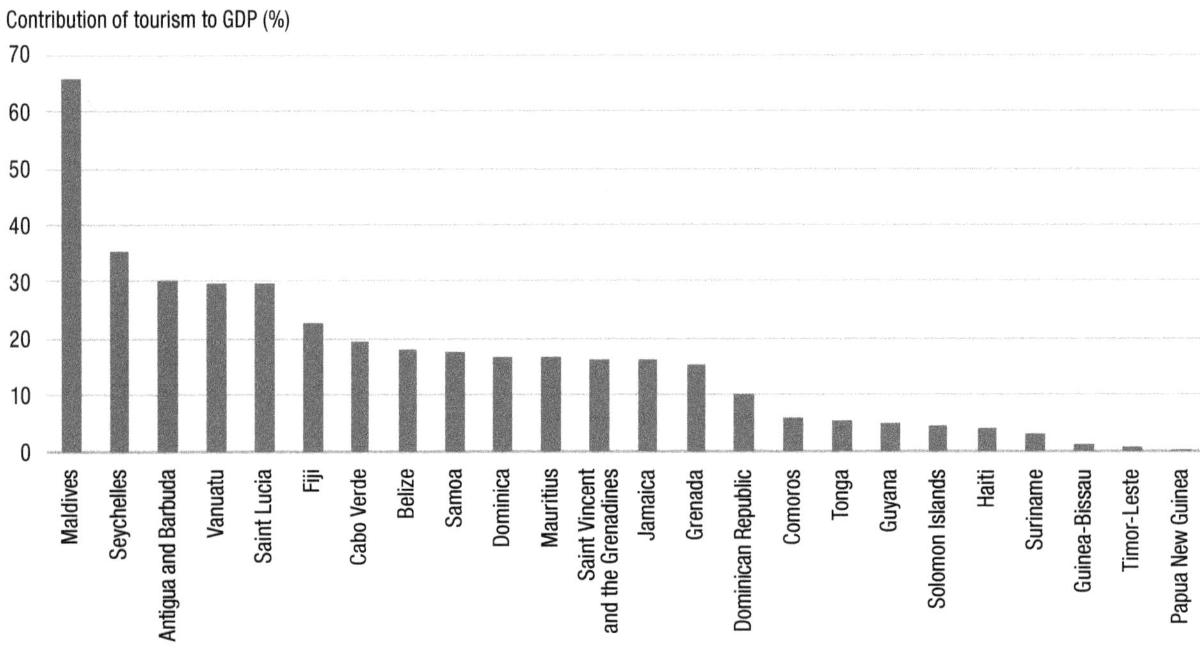

Source: Adapted from UN World Tourism Organization (2016), Statistics database www2.unwto.org/content/data.

StatLink http://dx.doi.org/10.1787/888933645649

The Seychelles provides a positive example in this regard. This atoll nation has introduced high standards in ecological sustainability, embedding them in its efforts to enhance its position in the global tourism market. Currently, 43% of the land – and much of the surrounding ocean – is protected for conservation. The Seychelles has also introduced policies and reforms aiming to enhance this sector's benefits to the domestic economy. For example, the University of the Seychelles is now providing tailored qualifications to raise the domestic capacity to meet the sector's demand for skilled labour. A number of initiatives have also been launched to integrate the tourism industry with other domestic sectors. For example, the Small Establishment Enhancement Programme is a local marketing initiative promoting smaller local accommodation under the brand "Secret Seychelles". Similarly, the use of local materials whenever possible, and advances in renewable energy, can reduce the leakage effect and contribute to more sustainable tourism.

1.3.6. SIDS' economies are very open to trade and reliance on a handful of trading partners exposes them to "trade fragilities"

SIDS are more open to trade than other developing countries, as signalled by a relatively higher share of trade in GDP (100.5% vs. 78.2% in 2000-15), in part due the small size of their domestic markets. Wide variations, however, are seen across SIDS. The highest level of trade openness is evident in the AIMS region (Figure 1.9), mainly due to the Maldives and the Seychelles, as well as in relatively higher income, tourism-dependent SIDS.

Figure 1.9. Small island developing states, especially in the AIMS region, are more open to trade than other developing countries

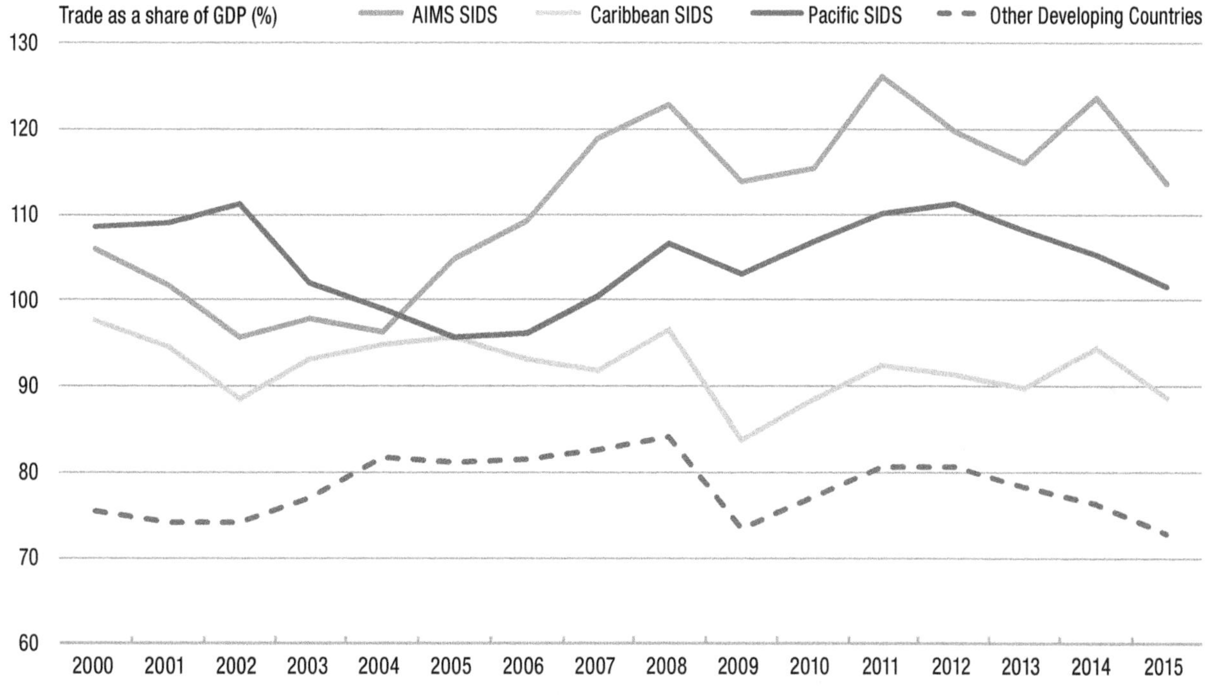

Source: Adapted from World Bank (n.d.), World Development Indicators, https://data.worldbank.org/data-catalog/world-development-indicators.

StatLink http://dx.doi.org/10.1787/888933645668

The large GDP share stemming from the value of trade, however, exposes SIDS to market fluctuations more than other developing countries. This fragility is exacerbated by their narrower selection of trade partners. On average, 60% of SIDS exports go to the top three trading partners and 87% to the top ten trading partners, compared to 52% and 77% in other developing countries (Figure 1.10). Key trading partners often coincide with the countries from which SIDS receive the largest flows of tourism, remittances and concessional finance, making development in the economies of those countries particularly impactful for SIDS.

Figure 1.10. SIDS trade is concentrated in fewer partner countries than for other developing countries

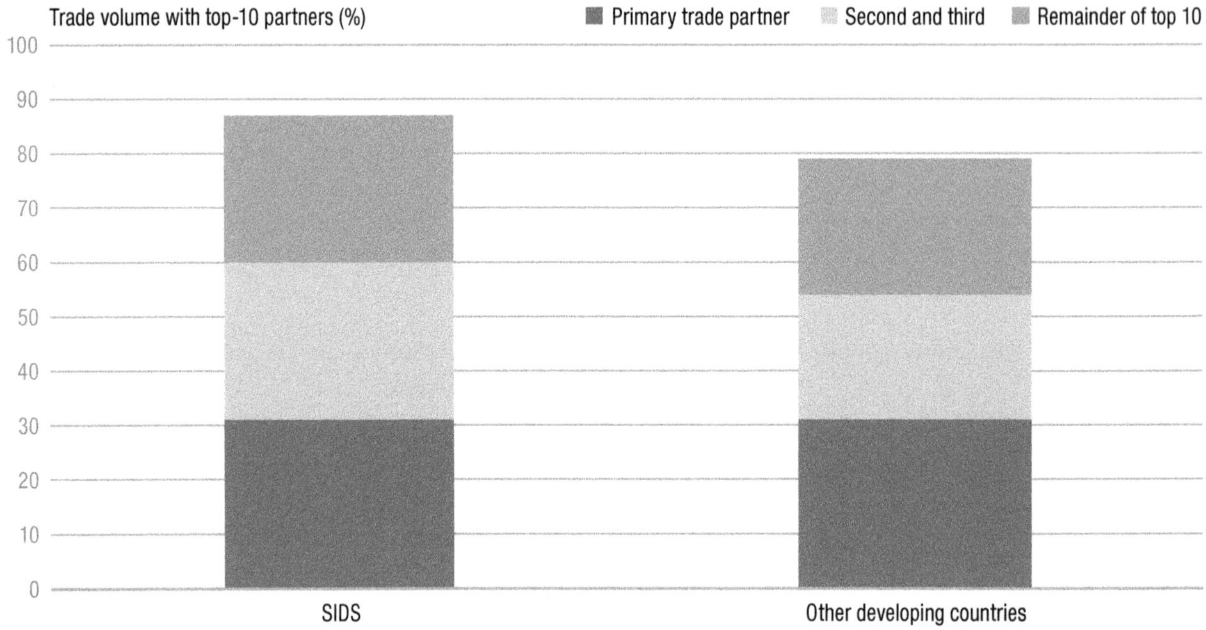

Source: Adapted from World Bank (n.d.), World Development Indicators, https://data.worldbank.org/data-catalog/world-development-indicators.

StatLink http://dx.doi.org/10.1787/888933645687

1.3.7. SIDS strongly depend on imported fossil fuels, but are demonstrating an ambition to transition to renewable sources of energy

The vulnerability of SIDS also stems from their strong reliance on strategic imports, again leaving them exposed to terms-of-trade shocks. Food and fuel imports are high due to high demand for these in key economic sectors, such as fisheries and tourism. Imported fossil fuels are used for electricity production and to transport commodities across geographically dispersed internal markets.

The reliance on imported fuel for electricity generation leads to particularly high energy production costs in SIDS, affecting consumers both directly and indirectly through higher commodity production costs. For example, electricity rates for residential customers in Micronesia are nearly four times as high (USD 0.48 per kilowatt hour) as the average residential rate in the United States (USD 0.13 per kilowatt hour) (United States Department of Energy, 2015). Retail electricity prices in the Solomon Islands are even higher: at an average of USD 0.85/kilowatt hour they are the highest in the Pacific and among the highest in the world.

Most SIDS allocate more than 30% of their foreign exchange reserves each year to cover the cost of fossil fuel imports.[12] At the same time, high debt burdens in some SIDS hamper investment in innovative sustainable energy technologies, perpetuating their dependence on imported fossil fuels and its negative effect on fiscal space.

SIDS continue to demonstrate ambition in the area of renewable energy: transitioning to low-carbon economies will heavily reduce fossil fuel import costs and free up fiscal space. In the past, this strong ambition strengthened the position of SIDS in the climate change negotiations. The Intended Nationally Determined Contributions (INDCs) of many SIDS contain some of the most ambitious renewable energy targets, with countries (including Samoa and the Cook Islands[13]) targeting 100% renewable energy for electricity generation by 2025 (UNFCCC, 2015). Guyana plans to increase its share of renewable energy by 100% by 2025, in keeping with its ambition to achieve a green economy and low-carbon development strategy. These targets come with caveats and conditions, provided they receive adequate technical and financial support to remove existing barriers.

Box 1.2. Small states, large ocean states: The potential of the blue economy

Smallness and other geophysical characteristics, such as exposure to extreme weather events and natural disasters, have challenged economic growth and development in SIDS. But while SIDS collectively occupy less than 1% of the global land area, they make up a vast share (14%) of the world's coastline and possess some of the largest economic exclusion zones (EEZs) in the world: their combined EEZ area covers nearly 23.2 million km^2. In Tuvalu, for example, the EEZ is approximately 28 000 times the size of the land mass. The largest EEZs are found in Kiribati (3.44 million km^2) Micronesia (2.99 million km^2), Marshall Islands (1.99 million km^2) and Seychelles (1.33 million km^2; the average size of a SIDS EEZ is nearly 724 km^2.

Possessing such vast ocean resources, many SIDS are increasingly looking to the oceans as the next frontier for economic development, and are determined to embark on a pathway toward sustainable "blue" growth. The value of the global ocean economy is estimated at USD 1.5 trillion per year (OECD, 2016). OECD projections suggest that the ocean economy could reach over USD 3 trillion between 2010 and 2030, more than doubling its contribution to global value added. The ocean economy is expected to account for around 40 million full-time equivalent jobs; the most rapid job growth should occur in offshore wind energy, marine aquaculture, fish processing and port activities.

Ocean-based industries (such as tourism and fisheries) are already key sources of income in SIDSs. Innovative investments to make sustainable use of existing sectors and create new sectors (integrating land-based, coastal and ocean-based activities) could boost sustainable, inclusive growth and tackle some of the critical challenges facing these economies, such as high unemployment, food insecurity and poverty. New economic sectors include improved aquaculture, ocean renewable energy and ocean biotechnology (Table 1.2.). The potential of ocean renewables is vast. Ever-improving technologies may open up new possibilities, although limitations in the infrastructure required to connect and distribute power, as well as limited finance, may hold back progress. While the potential of biotechnological resources is largely unknown, marine organisms could provide valuable resources to the chemical and pharmaceutical sectors (Day et al., 2016).

Table 1.2. Established and emerging sectors of the ocean economy

Established	Emerging
Capture fisheries and seafood processing	Marine aquaculture
Shipping and ports	Deep-water and ultra-deep water oil and gas
Shipbuilding and repair	offshore wind energy
Offshore oil and gas (shallow water)	Ocean renewable energy
Marine manufacturing and construction	Marine and seabed mining
Maritime and coastal tourism	Maritime safety and surveillance
Marine business services	Marine biotechnology
Marine research and development and education	High-tech marine products and services
Dredging	

Innovative approaches and a more sustainable use of resources also have great potential for boosting the economic and social benefits of existing sectors. For example, global demand for fish products is greatly benefiting the fishing sector in SIDS: exports of fish and fish products contribute between 30-80% of GDP in Pacific SIDS and there is scope to expand this (Ababouch, 2015). However, the sustainable management of fisheries will require designing a favourable policy and regulatory environment, and investing adequate resources. Fishery revenues could also increase through measures to curb illicit, unregulated and unreported fishing, as well as through fairer trade. For example, fishing agreements that provide access to an EEZ usually allow for a low appropriation of fishery export revenues by national operators and do not translate into knowledge transfer by foreign fishing companies to national stakeholders (World Bank Group and United Nations Department of Economic and Social Affairs, 2017).

Notes

1. In 2017, Samoa moved from lower middle income status to upper middle-income country, according to the updated World Bank income thresholds. As this report mostly covers in its analysis statistical data up to the year 2015 (when Samoa was still a lower middle income country), Samoa is consistently treated as a lower middle income country throughout this report.

2. Nauru, Palau and Tuvalu have a liner shipping index of 1.32.

3. Fiji has a liner shipping index of 8.56.

4. The EVI is the simple arithmetic average of 2 sub-indexes: the exposure sub-index, which is a weighted average of five component indexes: population size (25%), remoteness from world markets (25%), exports concentration (12.5%), share of agriculture, forestry and fishery in GDP (12.5%) and the share of population living in low elevated coastal zone (25%), and the shocks sub-index, which is a weighted average of 3 component indexes: the victims of natural disasters (25%), the instability in the agricultural production (25%), and the instability in exports of goods and services. The EVI is calculated by Ferdi (Fondation pour les Études et recherches sur le

Développement International), a French foundation for international development studies (www.ferdi.fr/en).

5. As highlighted in Chapter 1 of this report, the SIDS considered here are the 35 ODA-eligible SIDS.

6. In this report, the term "other developing countries" refers to all other ODA-eligible countries that are not identified as SIDS.

7. The pre-crisis period under consideration is 2000-08, while the post-crisis period is 2010-15.

8. The criticisms towards GDP concerns even its ability to capture economic development. Simon Kuznets, who developed GDP back in the late 1930s, warned it was not a suitable measure of a country's economic development. He highlighted that *GDP is not a welfare measure, it is not a measure of how well we are all doing. It counts the things that we're buying and selling, but it's quite possible for GDP to go in the opposite direction of welfare*. See National income and its composition 1919-1938 (Kuznets,1941), The Trouble with GDP (The Economist, 2016).

9. Victims of natural disasters; instability of agricultural production; and instability of exports of goods and services.

10 The full list of indicators regarding the determinants of exposure to shocks is: small population size; remoteness from world markets; export concentration; share of agriculture, forestry and fisheries in GDP; and share of population living in low-elevation costal zones.

11. This is based on the Concentration Index published by UNCTAD annually. The index is a Herfindahl-Hirschmann Index (Product HHI) measuring the degree of product concentration. A HHI value closer to 1 indicates that a country's exports or imports are highly concentrated in a few products. On the contrary, values closer to 0 reflect exports or imports are more homogeneously distributed among a series of products.

12. http://unctad.org/meetings/en/SessionalDocuments/cimem7d8_en.pdf.

13. The timeframe indicated by the Cook Islands is 2020.

References

Ababouch, L. (2015), *Fisheries and Aquaculture in the Context of Blue Economy*, background paper from "Feeding Africa, High Level Conference on Agricultural Transformation" UN Economic Commission for Africa, Dakar, Senegal, 21-23 October 2015, www.afdb.org/fileadmin/uploads/afdb/Documents/Events/DakAgri2015/Fisheries_and_Aquaculture_in_the_Context_of_Blue_Economy.pdf.

Bertram, G. (2016), *Implications of the Cook Islands' Graduation from Development Assistance Committee (DAC) Eligibility*, Ministry of Finance and Economic Management, Government of the Cook Islands, www.mfem.gov.ck/images/documents/DCD_Docs/Development-Resources/Implications_of_the_CKI_Graduation_from_DAC_Eligibility.pdf.

Day, J., A. Hughes, L. Greenhill and M.S. Stanley (2016), "Blue Biotechnology" *Commonwealth Blue Economy Report Series, No. 5*, Commonwealth Secretariat, London, http://thecommonwealth.org/sites/default/files/inline/Blue%2BBiotechnology_UPDF.pdf.

De la Croix, D., F. Docquier, M. Schiff (2014), "Brain Drain and Economic Performance in Small Island Developing States", *in* Artal-Tur, A. & G. Peri & F. Requena-Silvente (eds), *The Socio-Economic Impact of Migration flows - Effects on Trade, Remittances, Output, and the Labour Market*, Springer International Publishing, www.springerprofessional.de/en/brain-drain- and-economic-performance-in-small-island-developing-/2078340.

Drew, A (2015), *The Role of Sovereign Funds in Pacific Island Nations*, New Zealand Institute for Pacific Research, University of Auckland, Auckland, https://nzipr.blogs.auckland.ac.nz/files/2017/07/theroleofsovereignfundsinpacificislandsnations-1etr6ol.pdf.

Ferdi (n.d.), *Economic Vulnerability Index* (database), Fondation pour les études et recherches sur le développement international, Clermont Ferrand, France, http://byind.ferdi.fr/en/indicator/evi/results/0bad6ab7965ccca0e81a70ddbe010754ff774aa4.

Government of the Commonwealth of Dominica (2015), *Rapid Damage and Impact Assessment Tropical Storm Erika – August 27, 2015*, A report by the Government of the Commonwealth of Dominica, Roseau, Dominica, http://documents.worldbank.org/curated/en/142861467995411564/pdf/104251-WP-PUBLIC-Rapid-Damage-and-Needs-Assessment-Final-Report-Oct5.pdf.

Horscroft, V. (2014), "Public Sectors in the Islands: Are They 'Too Big' and Do They 'Crowd Out' the Private Sector?" *Policy Research Working Paper* Series, No. 7102, World Bank, Washington, D.C., http://documents.worldbank.org/curated/en/986481468098052675/pdf/WPS7102.pdf.

IMF (2016), *Resilience and Growth in the Small States of the Pacific*, (eds.), H. Khor, R. Kronenberg, and P. Tumbarello, published Spring 2016, International Monetary Fund Publications, Washington, D.C., www.elibrary.imf.org/staticfiles/misc/excerpts/small_states_pacific_excerpt.pdf.

Kuznets (1941), *National income and its composition 1919–1938*, National Bureau of Economic Research, New York.

Mahul, O., B. Signer, L. Boudreau, H. Yi, S. Atamuratova, D. Clarke, E. White, (2014), *Financial Protection against Natural Disasters: From products to comprehensive strategies - an operational framework for disaster risk financing and insurance*, World Bank Group, Washington, D.C., http://documents.worldbank.org/curated/en/523011468129274796/Financial-protection-against-natural-disasters-from-products-to-comprehensive-strategies-an-operational-framework-for-disaster-risk-financing-and-insurance

Mimura, N., L. Nurse, R.F. McLean, J. Agard, L. Briguglio, P. Lefale, R. Payet and G. Sem, (2007), "Small islands. Climate Change 2007: Impacts, Adaptation and Vulnerability". Contribution of Working Group II to the *Fourth Assessment Report of the Intergovernmental Panel on Climate Change*, pp 687-716, M.L. Parry, O.F. Canziani, J.P. Palutikof, P.J. van der Linden and C.E. Hanson, Eds., Cambridge University Press, Cambridge, www.ipcc.ch/pdf/assessment-report/ar4/wg2/ar4-wg2-chapter16.pdf.

OECD (2016), *The Ocean Economy in 2030*, OECD Publishing, Paris, http://dx.doi.org/10.1787/9789264251724-en.

OECD DAC (2014), *DAC List of ODA Recipients*, OECD, Paris, www.oecd.org/dac/financing-sustainable-development/development-finance-standards/daclist.htm.

OECD-World Bank (2016), *Climate and Disaster Resilience Financing in Small Island Developing States*, OECD Publishing, Paris, http://dx.doi.org/10.1787/9789264266919-en.

The Economist (2016), "The Trouble with GDP", *The Economist,* April 2016, London, www.economist.com/news/briefing/21697845-gross-domestic-product-gdp-increasingly-poor-measure-prosperity-it-not-even.

UNCTAD (2014), *Small Island Developing States: Challenges in transport and trade logistics*, United Nations Convention on Trade and Development, Geneva, http://unctad.org/meetings/en/SessionalDocuments/cimem7d8_en.pdf.

UNCTAD (2010), *Review of Maritime Transport*, United Nations Convention on Trade and Development, Geneva, http://unctad.org/en/docs/rmt2010_en.pdf.

UNCTAD (n.d.), *Shipping Liner Connectivity Index* (database), United Nations Convention on Trade and Development, Geneva, http://unctadstat.unctad.org/wds/TableViewer/tableView.aspx?ReportId=92.

UNDP (n.d.), *Human Development Index* (database), United Nations Development Programme, New York, http://hdr.undp.org/en/content/human-development-index-hdi.

UNFCCC (2015), *Samoa's Intended Nationally Determined Contribution, September 2015*, United Nations Framework Convention on Climate Change, New York, http://www4.unfccc.int/ndcregistry/PublishedDocuments/Samoa%20First/Samoa%20INDC_Submission%20to%20UNFCCC.pdf.

United States Department of Energy (2015), *Energy Transition Initiative: Island Energy Snapshot - Federated States of Micronesia*, NREL (National Renewable Energy Laboratory), National Renewable Energy Initiative, U.S. Department of Energy, Washington, D.C., www.nrel.gov/docs/fy15osti/64294.pdf.

World Bank (2005), *Grenada: A Nation Rebuilding An assessment of reconstruction and economic recovery one year after Hurricane Ivan,* World Bank Group, Washington D.C., http://documents.worldbank.org/curated/en/538951468030331426/pdf/355660GD0rebuilding0hurricane0ivan.pdf.

World Bank (n.d.) *World Development Indicators* (database), World Bank Group, Washington D.C., https://data.worldbank.org/data-catalog/world-development-indicators.

World Bank and United Nations Department of Economic and Social Affairs (2017), *The Potential of the Blue Economy: Increasing long-term benefits of the sustainable use of marine resources for small island developing states and coastal least developed countries*, World Bank, Washington D.C., http://www.climateactionprogramme.org/images/uploads/documents/World_Bank.pdf.

WTO (2016), *UNWTO Statistics* (database), United Nations World Tourism Organisation, Madrid, http://statistics.unwto.org/.

WTTC (2016), *Economic Impact Reports*, World Travel and Tourism Council, London, www.wttc.org/research/economic-research/economic-impact-analysis/.

Annex 1.A. Data sources and coverage

This report focuses on the 35 SIDS currently eligible for ODA (as per the OECD DAC List of ODA-Eligible Countries (OECD, 2014). When referring to "other developing countries", the report considers all remaining ODA-eligible countries that are not the 35 SIDS.

In this chapter, a number of statistical sources are used, the coverage of which varies across SIDS. In general, data quality and availability remains a challenge in SIDS, largely owing to limited national capacity. For several SIDS the lack of data is linked to the fact that they are not members of the Bretton Woods institutions. This is the case for three SIDS: Cook Islands, Montserrat and Niue. Nauru joined the International Monetary Fund and World Bank in 2016. Annex Table 1.A.1 details the data sources and coverage of the statistical data used in this chapter.

Annex Table 1.A.1. Data sources and coverage

Variable	Source	Coverage (%)	Missing SIDS	Notes
GDP per capita	World Bank, World Development Indicators	100		
Trade Openness (the sum of exports and imports of goods and services measured as a share of gross domestic product)	World Bank, World Development Indicators	84	Micronesia, Marshall Islands, Sao Tome and Principe, Tuvalu, Nauru	
GNI per capita	World Bank, World Development Indicators	88	Cuba, Maldives, Nauru, Sao Tome and Principe	
GNI current	World Bank, World Development Indicators	97	Nauru	
GDP growth (%)	World Bank national accounts data, and OECD National Accounts data files.	97	Nauru	
External debt stock % of GNI	World Bank, World Development Indicators	63	Antigua and Barbuda, Cuba, Kiribati, Marshall Islands, Micronesia, Nauru, Palau, Seychelles, Suriname, Tuvalu, Timor-Leste	
Total debt service % of GNI	World Bank, World Development Indicators	69	Antigua and Barbuda, Cuba, Kiribati, Marshall Islands, Nauru, Palau, Seychelles, Suriname, Timor-Leste , Tuvalu	
Natural resource rent	World Bank, World Development	63	Antigua and Barbuda, Cabo Verde, Comoros, Grenada, Guinea-Bissau, Marshall Islands,	

Variable	Source	Coverage (%)	Missing SIDS	Notes
	Indicators		Micronesia, Nauru, Palau, Tuvalu, Sao Tome and Principe, Seychelles	
Exports % GDP	World Bank, World Development Indicators	81	Marshall Islands, Micronesia, Nauru, Papua New Guinea, Sao Tome and Principe, Tuvalu	
Fuel imports	World Bank, World Development Indicators	47	Antigua and Barbuda, Cuba, Dominica, Grenada, Guinea-Bissau, Haiti, Kiribati, Marshall Islands, Micronesia, Nauru, Palau, Papua New Guinea, Solomon Islands, Saint Lucia, Timor-Leste, Tuvalu, Vanuatu	
Public expenditure in health and education as a share of GDP, (2014)	World Bank, World Development Indicators	100		Data for Cabo Verde, Fiji and Guinea-Bissau refer to 2013.
Brain drain	La Croix, Docquier and Schiff, 2014			
Liner shipping index	UNCTAD	91	(Series starts in 2004). Nauru, Timor-Leste, Tuvalu	
Ease of doing business	World Bank, World Development Indicators	91	Cuba, Nauru, Tuvalu	
Debt composition	World Bank Debt Statistics	66	Antigua and Barbuda, Cuba, Kiribati, Marshall Islands, Micronesia, Nauru, Palau, Seychelles, Suriname, Timor-Leste, Tuvalu	
HDI (2015)	UNDP	83	Marshall Islands, Nauru, Tuvalu, Cook Islands, Montserrat and Niue	
EVI (2013)	FERDI	100		
Product Concentration (2014)	UNCTAD	100		
Inbound tourism/GDP	UNWTO	75	Cuba, Kiribati, Marshall Islands, Micronesia, Palau, Nauru, Sao Tome and Principe, Tuvalu	
Top 3 Trading Partners (2015)	UNCTAD	100		
Food imports	World Bank, World Development Indicators WDI	88	Haiti, Marshall Islands, Micronesia, Nauru	
Gross Debt/GDP (2014)	World Economic Outlook	100		

Chapter 2. Financing for development in small island developing states: A focus on concessional finance

To what extent does financing for development address the specific needs and challenges identified in the previous chapter that are associated with the vulnerability of small island developing states (SIDS)? This chapter attempts to answer this question. It illustrates the financing for development landscape for SIDS: it analyses the composition and evolution of the full range of external financial flows (e.g. remittances, foreign direct investments, private grants, as well as concessional finance) and highlights some of the challenges relating to domestic resource mobilisation and debt sustainability. The chapter then focuses on concessional finance from the international community. It explores the scope and nature of flows and approaches to SIDS: the array of development partners involved, the articulation between bilateral and multilateral concessional sources, the sectoral focus and the prevailing co-operation modalities in different SIDS contexts. The analysis in the chapter capitalises on the wealth of OECD Development Assistance Committee (DAC) statistics and on new statistical sources.

2.1. The big picture: elements of the "financing for development" landscape

The international community identified, through the Addis Ababa Action Agenda of the Third International Conference on Financing for Development (UN, 2015), a comprehensive and integrated global framework to support sustainable development around the world. This framework includes both domestic and international resources, both public and private finance. This section analyses these flows, and key policy issues in relation to them, in the context of small island developing states.

SIDS tend to have small and erratic domestic revenues, which combined with high costs for providing public services and the fiscal impacts of natural disasters, often result in limited fiscal space for development investments. The debt situation of the five SIDS that benefitted from the Heavily Indebted Poor Countries (HIPC) Initiative has drastically improved in the past 15 years, but the remaining SIDS have seen on average an increase in their debt to gross national income (GNI) ratios, which, at 57%, is currently above the average for other developing countries (47%). Foreign direct investments and other private finance flows are highly volatile and on average contribute little to SIDS' external sources of financing: only 12% in 2012-15. Owing to large diasporas, remittances represent the largest flow of external finance for SIDS: 52% in 2012-15. Concessional finance (i.e. grants and concessional loans from bilateral and multilateral providers) is the second largest flow of external finance on aggregate, and the largest for 22 out of 35 individual SIDS. For this reason the second part of this chapter focuses squarely on concessional finance to examine its sources and destinations, its modalities and reach.

2.1.1. Domestic resources

Erratic domestic revenues and the high unit cost of public services contribute to precarious fiscal positions for many SIDS. Domestic revenues can be volatile in SIDS given the relatively narrow productive bases concentrated in sectors that are exposed to external fluctuations. SIDS that rely on natural resource rents or tourism as their primary export sectors are especially prone to fluctuating domestic and tax revenues. In Timor-Leste, for example, tax revenues accounted for 103% of gross domestic product (GDP) in 2010, rising to 133% in 2012 before falling to 40% in 2015.

Besides limited domestic revenue generation, the high unit costs of services have a significant effect on public finances, leading to larger public sector expenditures than in other developing countries. This is especially true in Pacific SIDS, where small populations are often scattered across a multitude of islands, compared to developing countries of a similar income level (see, for example, Horscroft, 2014). Government expenses accounted for 29% of GDP in SIDS, compared to 22% in other developing countries in 2014. Compared to other countries, a larger share of public expenditure is also current expenditure and not capital investment.

Severe climate events and natural disasters tend to have heavy fiscal impacts (OECD-World Bank, 2016; World Bank, 2016a): financing humanitarian responses, recovery and reconstruction can divert scarce public resources from essential social and economic development investments, compromising the pace and scope of future growth and development. Grenada, located on the southern tip of the Caribbean hurricane belt, was hit by hurricanes Ivan in 2004 and Emily in 2005. The hurricanes damaged or destroyed 90% of the country's housing stock, and devastated its nutmeg and tourism industries, as well as much of its coastal infrastructure. The cost of the hurricanes was estimated at 200% of Grenada's GDP. In their aftermath, the country experienced a sharp economic downturn, making it impossible to service its debt. The global financial crisis compounded Grenada's already acute debt situation: lost income from lower tourism receipts spurred low growth, resulting in insufficient government revenues and an inability to keep up debt servicing costs. Even after tourists returned and income rebounded, the Government of Grenada was unable to reduce its fiscal deficit (World Bank, 2015). In 2015, the country embarked on a debt restructuring programme and obtained debt relief from its Paris Club creditors, as well as from some of its non-Paris Club bilateral creditors. However, fiscal deficits and public debt accumulation remain an issue, together with the limited fiscal space for development investments resulting from the austerity imposed by Grenada's 2015 Fiscal Responsibility Act.

High levels of public debt remain a challenge for many SIDS, especially in the Caribbean

High levels of debt reduce the fiscal space for governments to make critical investments for development. A country's total debt and its ability to repay a loan also impact on creditworthiness, affecting access to capital markets. Besides commercial loans, even concessional borrowing is affected by a country's debt sustainability: the outcomes of the Debt Sustainability Analysis (DSA) directly affect the cost of concessional borrowing from the International Development Association (IDA) (with improving external debt sustainability translating into hardening terms). Given the large fiscal impacts that natural disasters can have in SIDS, it is positive that DSA increasingly integrate natural disaster risks, therefore accounting for some of the vulnerabilities of SIDS. DSA that consider natural disaster risks include the 2015 DSA of Haiti and the 2016 DSA of the Solomon Islands.

According to the International Monetary Fund (IMF, 2017), 20 of the 35 SIDS considered in this report are assessed as being at "moderate" risk, "high" risk or "in debt distress" in 2017[1]: 1 country (Grenada) is currently in debt distress, 11 are at high risk, 8 are at moderate risk. Only one SIDS (Papua New Guinea) is considered at low risk of debt distress. Since 2016, three SIDS – Cabo Verde, Haiti and Samoa – moved from a moderate to a high-risk level of debt distress.

SIDS have, on average, higher ratios of external debt to GNI than other developing countries, 57% compared to 47% in 2015. Debt-to-GNI ratios are particularly high in upper middle-income countries and lower middle-income countries, largely in the Caribbean. The largest debt-to-GNI ratio is found in Mauritius, where debt stood at 128% of GNI in 2015 (and annual servicing costs represented 29% of GNI), followed by: Jamaica (103%), Cabo Verde (98%), Belize (82%), Grenada (73%), Dominica (63%) and Samoa (60%).

Some SIDS, especially least developed countries, have been supported by the international community to bring down debt, but further measures are not forthcoming

Five SIDS – Comoros, Haiti, Guinea Bissau, Guyana, and Sao Tome and Principe – benefitted from the HIPC Initiative, which contributed to bring down their debt from an average of 196% of GNI in 2000 to 35% in 2015. Debt-to-GNI ratios for the remaining SIDS, are instead on the rise, having reached 62% in 2015, up from 44% in 2000. The HIPC Initiative was designed to support only the poorest and most indebted countries, and other SIDS are instead called upon to reduce expenditures, raise taxes and work with individual creditors to address debt issues, despite their numerous calls to the international community for broader support to alleviate their debt burdens and create fiscal space. Chapter 3 discusses successful and innovative approaches (such as debt-for-nature swaps) that may contribute to address debt issues in SIDS.

Figure 2.1. Impressive reductions in the level of debt in the small island developing states that benefitted from the Heavily Indebted Poor Countries Initiative

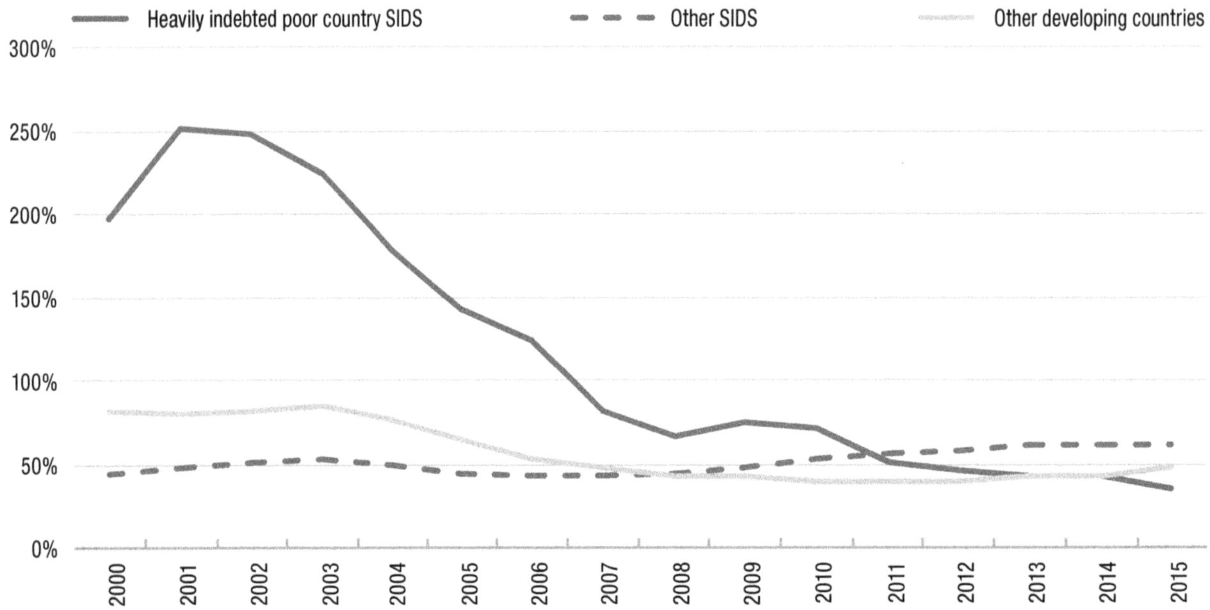

Source: Adapted from World Bank (n.d.), World Development Indicators, https://data.worldbank.org/data-catalog/world-development-indicators.

StatLink http://dx.doi.org/10.1787/888933645706

Debt-servicing costs account for a high share of public expenditure in many SIDS

The composition of the debt portfolios of SIDS – specifically the extent of concessional debt and the repayment schedules – dictates their debt servicing levels. Borrowing countries incur debt at different conditions depending on whether they borrow from private, official, bilateral or multilateral sources. Private credit entails higher and volatile interest rates, pro-cyclicality and shorter repayment schedules. By contrast, concessional debt owed to official bilateral or multilateral creditors usually involves longer and less expensive repayment schedules. Lower income SIDS, which have access to concessional finance from bilateral and multilateral sources, tend to have a greater share of concessional debt. Middle-income countries, instead, have more developed domestic credit markets and greater access to international capital markets and, as a result, a larger share of debt from private creditors and higher debt-servicing costs. Figure 2.2 shows that the highest level of commercial debt was in Jamaica, weighing in at 50% of its public debt in 2014. Reliance on commercial debt was also significant for other upper middle-income SIDS in the Caribbean – Belize (40%), Dominican Republic (35%), Grenada (34%), Saint Lucia (23%), and for one upper middle-income country in the Pacific, Fiji (29%).

Figure 2.2. Commercial debt represents a significant share of public debt for some upper middle-income small island developing states

Composition of public debt in 2014

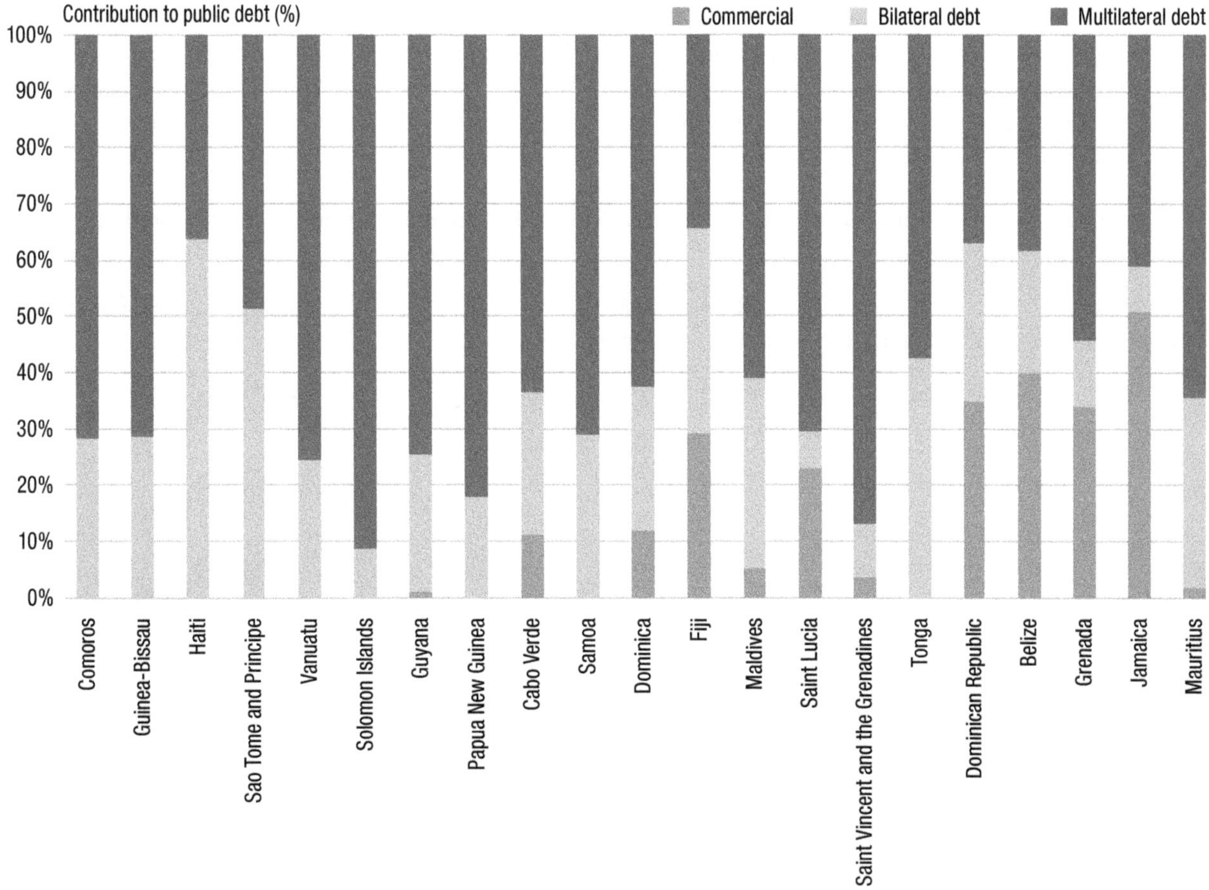

Source: Adapted from World Bank (2017), International Debt Statistics (database), https://data.worldbank.org/data-catalog/international-debt-statistics.

StatLink http://dx.doi.org/10.1787/888933645725

2.1.2. External flows for development

Several external financial flows reach SIDS. These flows include: (i) remittances, (ii) private flows at market terms (e.g. foreign direct investments, and total bank and non-bank purchases of bonds and other securities, including equities), (iii) private grants, (iv) non-concessional flows from bilateral and multilateral providers (i.e. official flows that do not meet the ODA definition) and (v) concessional finance from bilateral and multilateral providers (gross bilateral ODA and concessional flows from multilateral organisations meeting the ODA definition). This section examines the composition and evolution of these flows in SIDS.

Remittances account for the largest share of external finance to SIDS

Remittances are the largest external financial flow to SIDS, accounting for 52% (i.e. a total of USD 36.1 billion) of external finance in 2012-15 (Figure 2.3). New international anti-money laundering/combating the financing of terrorism (AML/FCT) regulations, however, could have a significant impact on vital remittance flows in the future. Over the 2012-15 period, remittances represented over 50% of total external financial flows for seven SIDS: Grenada (50%), Fiji (56%), Belize (59%), Tonga (60%), Dominican Republic (75%), Jamaica (90%), and Antigua and Barbuda (126%, due to negative net private flows at market terms). Significant data gaps on remittances for some of the smallest SIDS could mean that the real figure could be much higher. Remittances also make for a large share of GDP in many SIDS (World Bank, 2016b): Cabo Verde (10%), Tuvalu (11%), Marshall Islands (14%), Jamaica (16%), Samoa (18%), Comoros (20%), and Haiti (23%).

Figure 2.3. Remittances account for the bulk of external financing to small island developing states

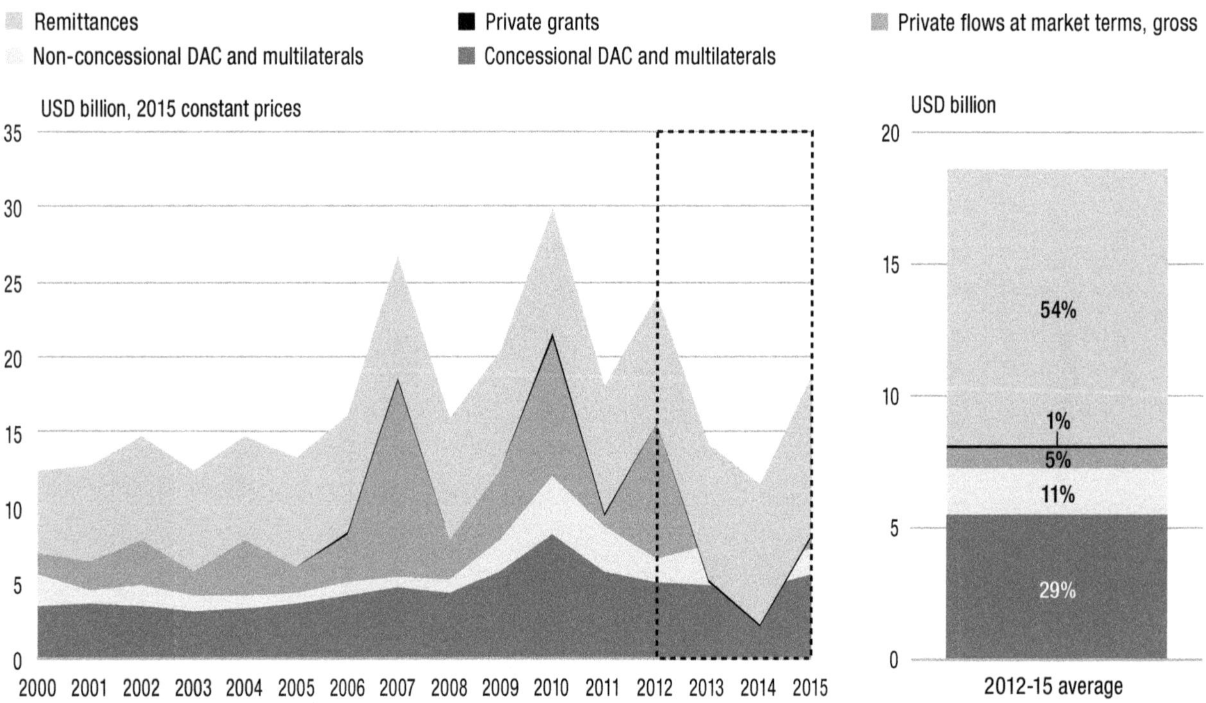

Note: Composition of external flows to SIDS, 2000-15 (constant prices).
Source: OECD DAC Statistics, and IMF and World Bank data.

StatLink http://dx.doi.org/10.1787/888933645744

Non-concessional official flows[2] are less significant (USD 5.8 billion in 2012-15, i.e. 8% of the total). Across SIDS, these flows are highly concentrated, as they are primarily channelled to more developed or larger markets: in 2012-15, three SIDS – the Dominican Republic, Papua New Guinea and Jamaica – received over 70% of total non-concessional finance, and represented more than 20% of total external finance only in four SIDS: Antigua and Barbuda (116%), Suriname (41%), Papua New Guinea (21%) and Cook Islands (20%). Concentration is strong also on the provider side, with three providers accounting for over 70% in 2012-15: the Inter-American Development Bank (38%), United States (21%), and the International Bank for Reconstruction and Development (13%).

Private flows at market terms can be very volatile: in 2007 they represented 49% of total external flows but became recently negative (years 2013 and 2014). The volatility of market-term flows became particularly visible after the global financial crisis, with several extreme peaks and troughs. In 2012-15, these flows represented on average 12% of the external financial flows reaching SIDS and less than 20% for 18 individual SIDS out of 35. In addition, private finance re-flows exceeded the inflows in nine SIDS, resulting in negative net private flows in this period.

Concessional finance from bilateral and multilateral providers represents the second-largest external flow for SIDS as a whole, at 27% of total external financing in 2012-15 (USD 18.8 billion). However, they represent the largest external financial flow for most individual SIDS: for 22 out of 35 in 2012-15 (Figure 2.4).

Figure 2.4. Concessional finance is the largest flow of external finance for three out of five small island developing states, 2012-15

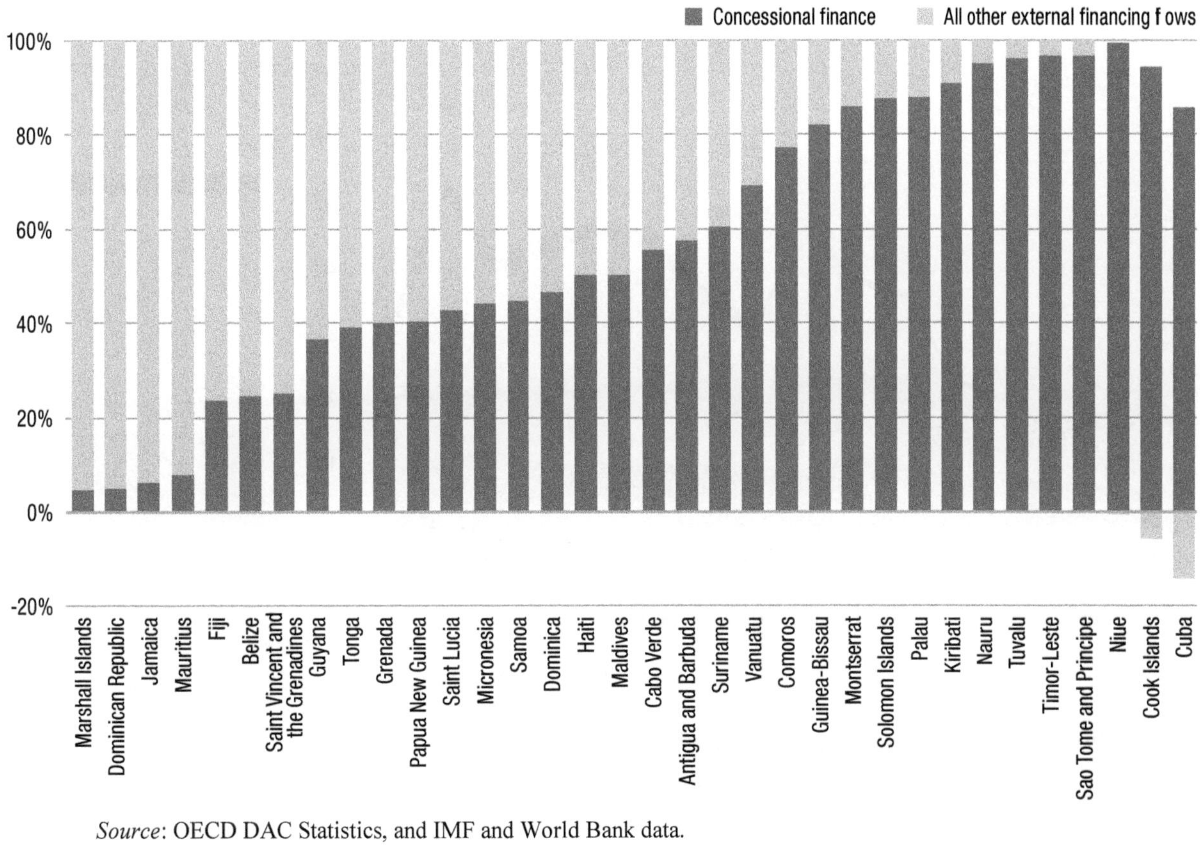

Source: OECD DAC Statistics, and IMF and World Bank data.

StatLink http://dx.doi.org/10.1787/888933645763

The composition of external financial flows to SIDS is quite distinct from that in other developing countries, and flows are more erratic

As Figure 2.5 illustrates, external finance to other developing countries displays much less volatility than in SIDS. Even private flows at market terms, which fluctuated over the full period in other developing countries, still exhibit a less erratic pattern than for SIDS.

In terms of the relative weight of different flows of external finance, SIDS tend to face, more than other ODA-eligible developing countries, significant challenges in attracting a significant and more stable flows of private finance: in 2012-15, these flows weighed only 12% in the total of external finance to SIDS, compared to a much larger 35% in other ODA-eligible developing countries. Compared to other developing countries (27% in 2012-15), SIDS are on average also more reliant on remittances (54%). Non-concessional flows have a similar weight in the external financing of SIDS (8%) and in that of other developing countries on average (9%). Concessional finance represents a slightly larger share of external finance for SIDS (27%) than for other developing countries on average (23%).

Figure 2.5. External finance is less volatile, and the weight of remittances is smaller, for other developing countries than for small island developing states

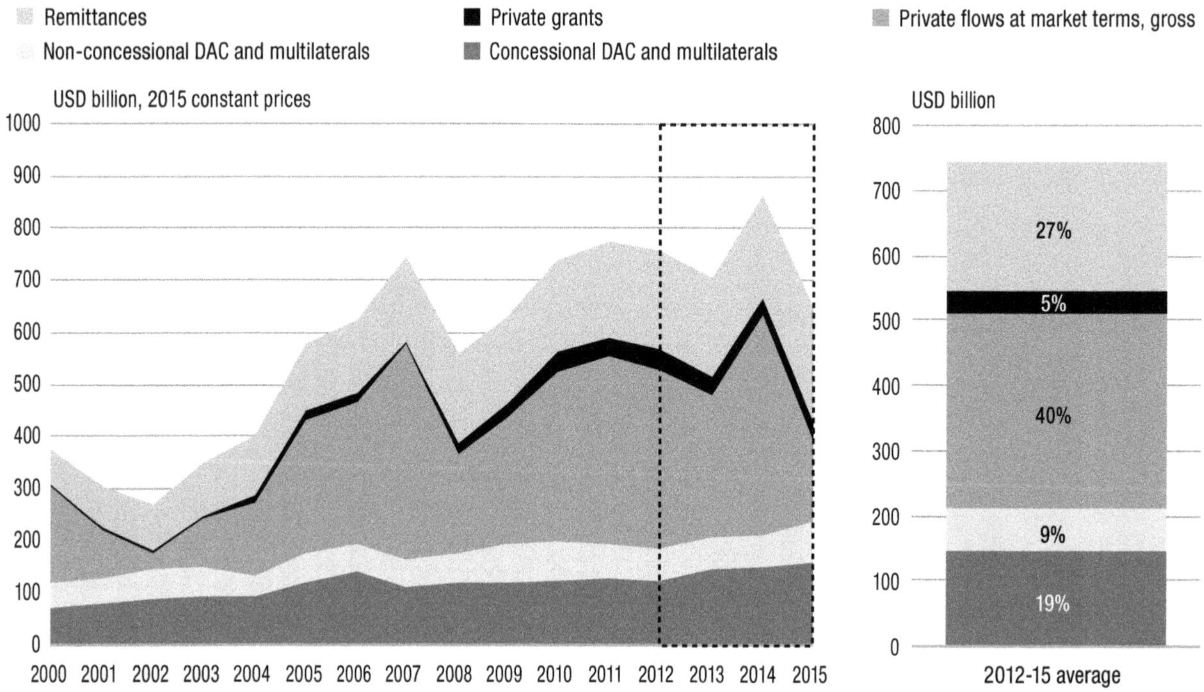

Source: OECD DAC Statistics, and IMF and World Bank data.

StatLink http://dx.doi.org/10.1787/888933645782

Philanthropy is becoming a relevant resource for development

The OECD has recently started to collect statistical data on philanthropy for development, through the 2016 OECD DAC Survey on Global Private Philanthropy for Development, which covers financing from the most active and influential philanthropic foundations[3], trusts and corporations in the years 2013-15. These are generally cross-border (i.e. external) flows, although the survey also covers foundations based in developing countries, in which case the activities captured do not necessarily represent cross-border flows.

According to data from this survey, 30 out of 35 SIDS were beneficiaries of support from private foundations, with a total of USD 161 million allocated to the benefit of SIDS. The bulk of support was concentrated on a few countries, with Haiti receiving nearly half of the total (48%) and Cuba the second-largest share (13%). All other SIDS received much smaller amounts: less than 6% of the total each. Around 5% of the total was allocated to regional initiatives in the Caribbean or the Pacific. Three foundations provided half of the total: the Bill and Melinda Gates Foundation (25%), the W.K. Kellogg Foundation (16%)

and Atlantic Philanthropies (9%). Philanthropic giving primarily targeted health (42%), partly owing to the weight of the Bill and Melinda Gates Foundation and its strong focus on this sector. The next largest sectors benefitting from philanthropic giving were the environment (18%), agriculture (11%) and education (9%) (Figure 2.6).

Figure 2.6. The bulk of the philanthropic resources supporting SIDS targeted health interventions, and over half was allocated to Haiti

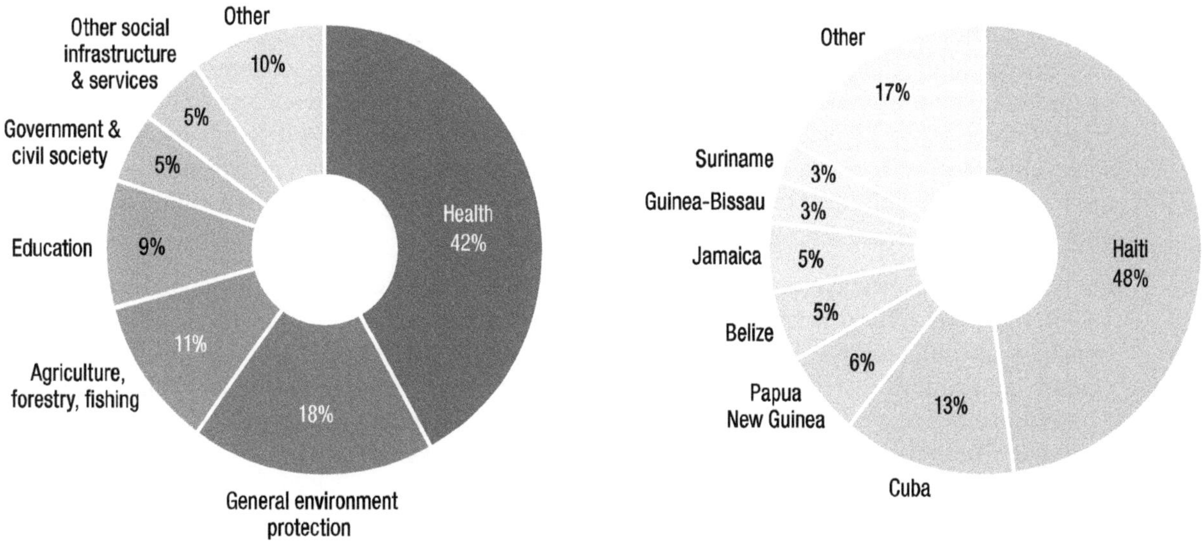

Source: OECD DAC (2016), Survey on Global Private Philanthropy for Development data, www.oecd.org/development/beyond-oda-foundations.htm.

StatLink http://dx.doi.org/10.1787/888933645801

2.2. Zooming in on concessional finance: the scope and nature of development co-operation in small island developing states

Concessional finance[4] provided by the international community as part of international development co-operation remains a vital source of financing for development in SIDS. In aggregate, it accounted for 27% of total external flows reaching SIDS in 2012-15, and represents the largest flow of external finance for three out of five SIDS. On average, concessional finance represents only 2.1% of the GNI of SIDS, but over 10% of GNI in 13 individual SIDS. In Tuvalu, it accounts for as much as 90% of GNI[5]. In some SIDS, concessional finance makes for a considerable part of public budgets, contributing significantly to the financing of public functions and public services. Concessional finance often targets vital sectors – such as health, education, water and sanitation – where investments have large net social returns, yet domestic resources may be insufficient.

Concessional finance is particularly important for the financing of resilience to climate and natural disasters. This stems from the high cost of coping with natural disasters and building resilient economies, which largely exceeds national resources of SIDS. It also derives from the general recognition that SIDS are bearing the brunt of the impacts of climate change, and that their limited fiscal space may prevent them from using domestic resources or borrowing to meet the additional costs of investing in climate and disaster resilience (OECD-World Bank, 2016).

SIDS receive the bulk of concessional finance by bilateral providers (79%), mainly influenced by proximity and geopolitical ties, and often in connection to emergency responses or one-off interventions. Five providers accounted for 58% of all concessional finance to SIDS in 2012-15, although providers totalled 72, signalling that several providers spread themselves thinly across SIDS and projects. The bulk of allocations tend to be concentrated on a few SIDS, with Haiti alone still receiving 25% of the total and the top seven recipients 64%. The use of budget support, which has been declining globally, has increased in SIDS, especially in the Pacific and in 2012-15 it represented more than 20% of concessional finance for 11 SIDS. Otherwise, however, a proliferation of small project-type interventions prevails, with 70% of transactions in SIDS accounting for 2% of the total value of concessional finance. In terms of targeting of resources, while the broad nature of development needs in several SIDS can make prioritisation difficult, some areas and sectors that would seem vital – and even appear as prerequisites – to promoting sustainable development in SIDS receive relatively little support, including climate, energy, infrastructures, and debt.

Owing to their specific circumstances and development challenges, breaking dependence on international official assistance will not be easy for some SIDS; for others, it will remain a critical resource to meet specific development needs. In both cases, as they embark on a path of sustainable development, SIDS will need to mobilise more financing from a broader array of both public and private sources. Concessional funds will need to play a significant role in leveraging and catalysing those flows.

2.2.1. Recent trends in concessional finance

Concessional finance to SIDS is largely driven by allocations to a few countries and in response to emergences and one-off interventions

Since 2000, in aggregate terms, concessional finance has represented for SIDS a fairly stable source of financing for development, increasing at an average rate of 9%. This aggregate trend, however, has been largely driven by temporary increases to few countries: concessional finance to SIDS reached an historical peak in 2010 in response to the devastating earthquake in Haiti, and it increased again in 2015 and peaked in 2016 (at USD 7.07 billion, in 2015 prices) mostly due to debt relief to Cuba (Figure 2.7). When the increase to Cuba is excluded, the 2016 figure represents a 4% decline compared to the 2015 level, continuing to fall short of the 2009 pre-"Haiti" peak level. In between these two peaks instead, concessional finance declined at an average rate of 13% per year.

SIDS receive a fairly stable share of global concessional finance

In 2012-15, concessional finance to SIDS accounted for 3.1% of concessional finance to all developing countries[6]. Although SIDS receive just a fraction of the total volume of concessional finance to developing countries, allocations to SIDS are fairly higher in per capita terms compared to other developing countries (USD 96 per capita on average compared to USD 25 per capita in 2012-15). These high per capita levels of concessional finance stem from the dis-economies of scale associated with providing development assistance to a small country – the so called "small country bias" (OECD, 2013), which in SIDS is exacerbated by the challenges and additional costs of delivering assistance to remote and dispersed populations. Hence, any consideration of per capita allocations to SIDS should take into account the higher per capita costs of assistance in this context: transaction costs for development activities are an estimated 4.7 times higher in SIDS than in other developing countries (IFAD, 2014).

Figure 2.7. Concessional finance to small island developing states peaked in 2010 and 2016 in response to emergencies in Haiti and Cuba

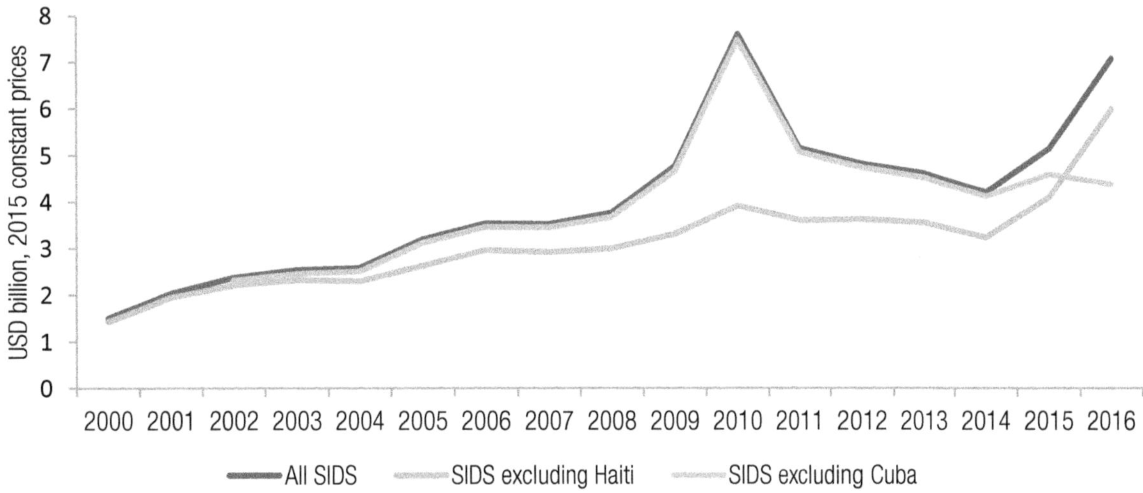

Source: OECD (n.d.), Creditor Reporting System (database), https://stats.oecd.org/Index.aspx?DataSetCode=CRS1.

StatLink http://dx.doi.org/10.1787/888933645820

DAC members account for the bulk of concessional finance to SIDS

In 2012-15, 72 providers[7] extended concessional finance to SIDS, of which 42 bilateral and 30 multilateral. The bilateral sources comprised all DAC members, as well as other high-income economies (such as Russian Federation ("Russia"), United Arab Emirates and Kuwait), some South-South providers (such as Thailand, Kazakhstan and Azerbaijan) and even Timor-Leste[8]. Multilateral providers included regional and global multilateral development banks, United Nations agencies and funds, and global funds such as the Global Environment Facility; the Global Fund to Fight AIDS, Tuberculosis and Malaria, and the Adaptation Fund.

Over 2012-15, DAC members accounted for the bulk of concessional financing to SIDS (77%), extending an average annual amount of USD 3.6 billion, for a total of USD 14.4 billion in the period (Figure 2.8). When including all other bilateral providers, this figure reaches 79% of total concessional finance to SIDS.

Concessional finance from bilateral sources increased by 4% between 2012 and 2015, mainly due to considerable increases by Spain (+USD 100 million), Japan (+ USD 63 million), New Zealand (+USD 35 million), Korea (+USD 20 million) and the United Kingdom (+ USD 20 million). The overall increase between 2012 and 2015 was recorded despite significant temporary decreases in 2013 and 2014 by some large providers, such as Australia, Canada and the United States.

Multilateral providers are stepping up support to SIDS

Multilateral providers accounted, in 2012-15, for a smaller share of total financing to SIDS: 21%, extending a yearly average of nearly USD 1 billion (for a total of USD 3.9 billion). However, financial support to SIDS from multilateral sources has increased faster than support from bilateral sources, rising by 22% from 2012 to 2015.

While several multilateral organisations increased their support, the largest increase by far came from the International Development Association (IDA, + USD 47 million), which accounts for 23% of multilateral concessional finance to SIDS and is therefore the largest multilateral provider. IDA allocations to SIDS are expected to increase even further in light of the outcomes of the IDA 18 Replenishment, but not all SIDS will benefit. IDA will almost quadruple the resources allocated to SIDS, including because of the increase in the base allocation for small states from Special Drawing Rights (SDR) 4 million (SDR) in IDA 17 to SDR 15 million in IDA 18[9]. Only the IDA-eligible SIDS, 21 out of the 35 considered here, will benefit from this increase.

The global funds[10] have played an increasingly important role in the development finance landscape of SIDS. In 2012-15, they collectively accounted for about 19% of multilateral financing to SIDS (for a total of USD 731million in 2012-15). Although the overall volume of their contributions fluctuated, it grew by 11% over this period.

Figure 2.8. Bilateral providers account for the bulk of concessional financing to small island developing states

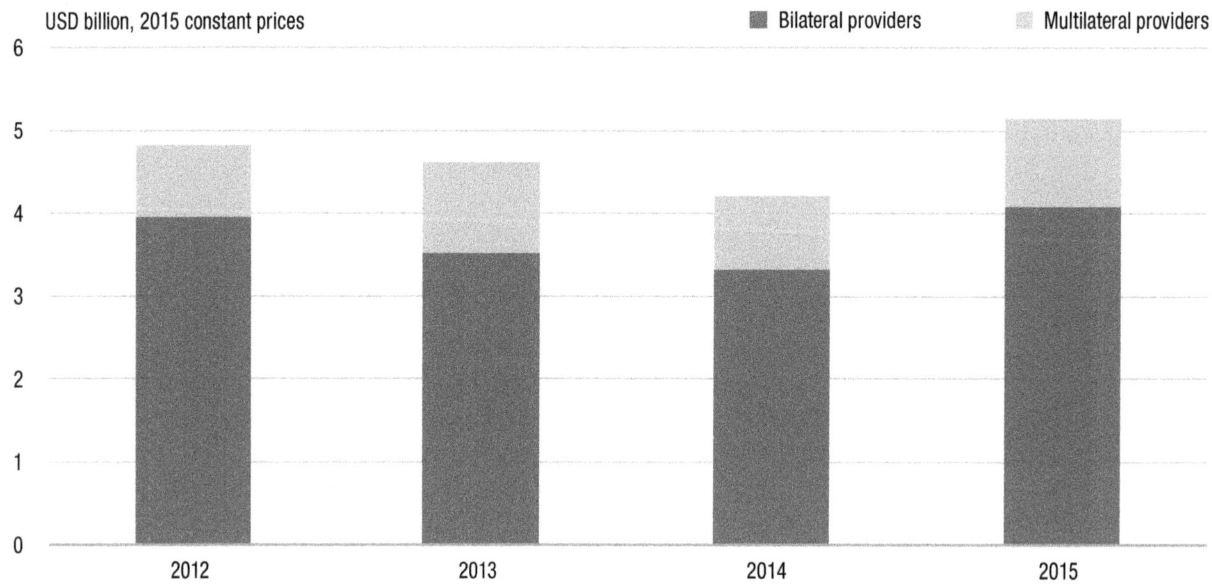

Source: OECD (n.d.), Creditor Reporting System (database), https://stats.oecd.org/Index.aspx?DataSetCode=CRS1.

StatLink http://dx.doi.org/10.1787/888933645839

The importance of development finance from the People's Republic of China and other sovereign states beyond "traditional donors" is growing

The People's Republic of China ("China") and other emerging providers[11] – including Chinese Taipei, India, Indonesia, Malaysia, Morocco, Russia, United Arab Emirates and Venezuela – are becoming key partners for SIDS. Resources from a larger number of providers can mean more financing options for SIDS, as well as greater and more varied opportunities for mutual learning and partnerships. In the future, as SIDS graduate from ODA, the importance of concessional finance from these providers – whose financing allocations do not rely on ODA criteria – could further increase.

The Lowry Institute estimates that China provided USD 1.8 billion[12] to Pacific SIDS in 2006-14, becoming an important provider of development finance in the region (UNDP, 2017a). For some Pacific SIDS, China is estimated to be already a larger provider of development finance than some important "traditional" providers. It is estimated that China's largest share of financing in the Pacific went to Papua New Guinea, which received USD 632 million in 2006-14. China is an active development partner in several other Pacific SIDS, including the Cook Islands, Fiji, Papua New Guinea, Samoa, Timor-Leste, Tonga and Vanuatu (Dornan and Brant, 2014). The main focus of Chinese financing in this period was infrastructure, accounting for 42% of the total; followed by governance (13%) and education (9%). Chinese support has also focused on addressing capacity constraints in the region: the China-Pacific Islands Countries Economic Development Cooperation Forum, established in 2006, helped train over 2 500 SIDS officials by 2012 (UNDP, 2017a).

Twelve non-DAC providers[13] that report their ODA spending to the OECD Creditor Reporting System allocated concessional finance to SIDS in 2012-15, including two South-South providers: Thailand and Timor-Leste. Concessional finance from these providers averaged USD 121 million a year, totalling USD 483 million in 2012-15, and representing 2.6% of all financing to SIDS over the period. Similarly to financing from DAC members and multilateral providers, concessional finance from non-DAC providers dropped in 2011-14 and picked up again in 2015, largely due to large debt relief Russia provided to Cuba (USD 351 million). Russia accounted for 74% of total concessional finance to SIDS from non-DAC providers over 2012-15, although, besides Cuba, it only provided concessional finance to Vanuatu (USD 2.6 million) in 2015. The second largest provider was the United Arab Emirates (USD 85 million to 27 SIDS, or18% of total financing by non-DAC providers in 2012-15), which extended the largest contributions to the Seychelles (26%), Comoros (15%) and the Maldives (12%). Among the South-South providers, Thailand extended a total of just under USD 1 million in 2012-15 to 18 SIDS, mainly Timor-Leste (25%), the Maldives (20%), Fiji, Tonga and Vanuatu (10% each). Timor-Leste extended a total of USD 1.5 million across Cabo Verde, Guinea Bissau, Tonga and Vanuatu, mainly as humanitarian support.

2.2.2. Recipients

Caribbean SIDS receive the largest share of concessional finance in volume terms

Over 2012-15, SIDS in the Caribbean received the largest share of concessional flows to SIDS: 44% of the total, or USD 8.4 billion. A similar share reached SIDS in the Pacific: 42% (or USD 7.9 billion), while SIDS in the Africa, Indian Ocean, Mediterranean and South China Sea (AIMS) region received 14% (USD 2.6 billion), the smallest share (Figure 2.9). While these shares have not fluctuated much over time, Caribbean SIDS received a larger share in 2015 (48%) while SIDS in the AIMS region saw a progressive decrease in concessional financing over 2012-15.

Figure 2.9. Caribbean SIDS received the largest share of concessional finance, followed by SIDS in the Pacific, 2012-15

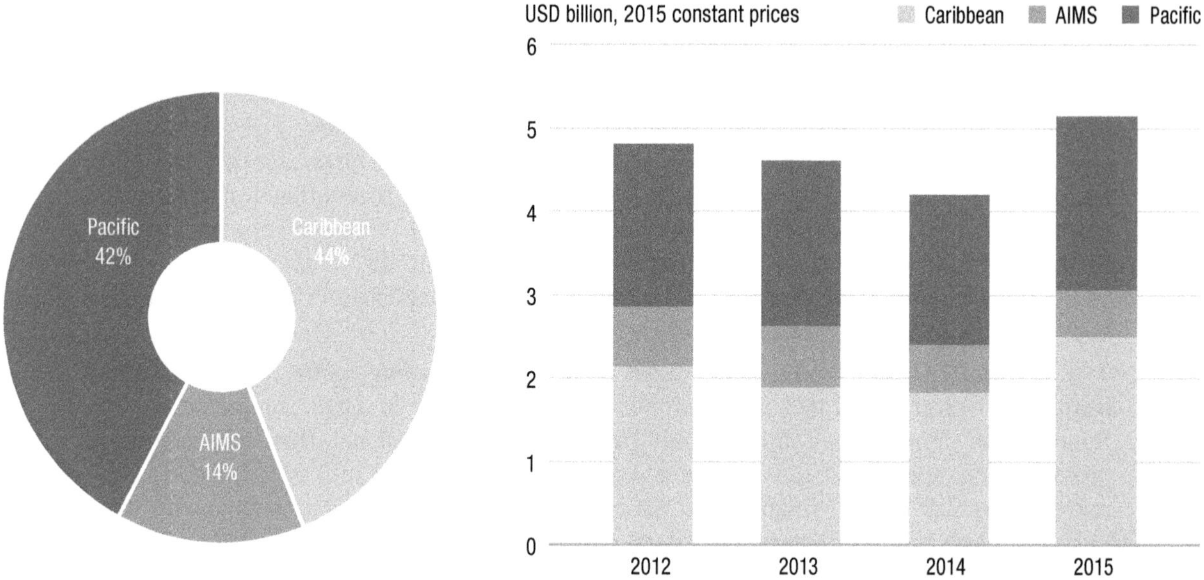

Source: OECD (n.d.), Creditor Reporting System (database), https://stats.oecd.org/Index.aspx?DataSetCode=CRS1.

StatLink http://dx.doi.org/10.1787/888933645858

However, regional allocations hide important trends

Regional aggregations can hide important differences in the distribution of concessional finance across SIDS. In fact, while the Caribbean as a region receives the largest shares overall, several of the SIDS in the region are actually among the smallest recipients. The strong concentration of concessional financing in the region is greatly affected by large allocations to Haiti and the Dominican Republic, which together account for 64% of total allocations to the Caribbean.

While the Caribbean and Pacific regions receive similar shares of total concessional financing, per capita allocations are much higher in the Pacific, given the smaller populations in this region. Per capita allocations to Pacific SIDS average USD 186, compared to USD 66 in the Caribbean, and USD 111 in the AIMS region, and USD 96 for SIDS overall. Niue, the SIDS with the smallest population (around 1 190 inhabitants), received the largest per capita amounts of concessional finance (USD 12 135) in 2015, together with other microstates (Figure 2.10). Several of the microstates retain a special constitutional relationship with advanced economies, which may also influence these allocations.

Overall, the largest volumes were directed to seven SIDS which collectively accounted for 64% of the total concessional finance allocated to SIDS over 2012-15. Haiti alone accounted for more than 48% of total concessional finance to SIDS in the 2010 peak year. Although its weight in total concessional finance has since decreased, it still accounted for over 20% of the total in 2015, and for 25% of all concessional finance to SIDS in 2012-15. The remaining top six SIDS recipients were: Papua New Guinea (13% of the total in 2012-15, or USD 2.3 billion), the Dominican Republic (6%, or USD 1.1 billion), Timor-Leste (5%, or USD 882 million) Cabo Verde (5%, or USD 869 million), Solomon Islands (5%, or USD 842 million) and Cuba (5%, or USD 815 million).

These top five recipients of concessional finance are spread across regions and income groups. Two are located in the Caribbean, Haiti and Dominican Republic; two in the Pacific, Papua New Guinea and Timor-Leste; and one in the AIMS region, Cabo Verde. Two, Haiti and Timor-Leste, are least developed countries; two, Papua New Guinea and Cabo Verde, are lower middle-income countries and one, the Dominican Republic, is an upper middle-income country.

The remaining 30 SIDS collectively received 46% of concessional finance over 2012-15 (USD 7.9 billion), with the bottom 10 SIDS together accounting for only 4%. The smallest volumes mainly targeted upper middle-income SIDS, largely in the Caribbean region: Suriname, Grenada, Cook Islands, Saint Lucia, Seychelles, Dominica, Palau, Niue, Saint Vincent and the Grenadines, and Antigua and Barbuda (Figure 2.10).

Figure 2.10. Concessional finance is strongly concentrated in a few small island developing states

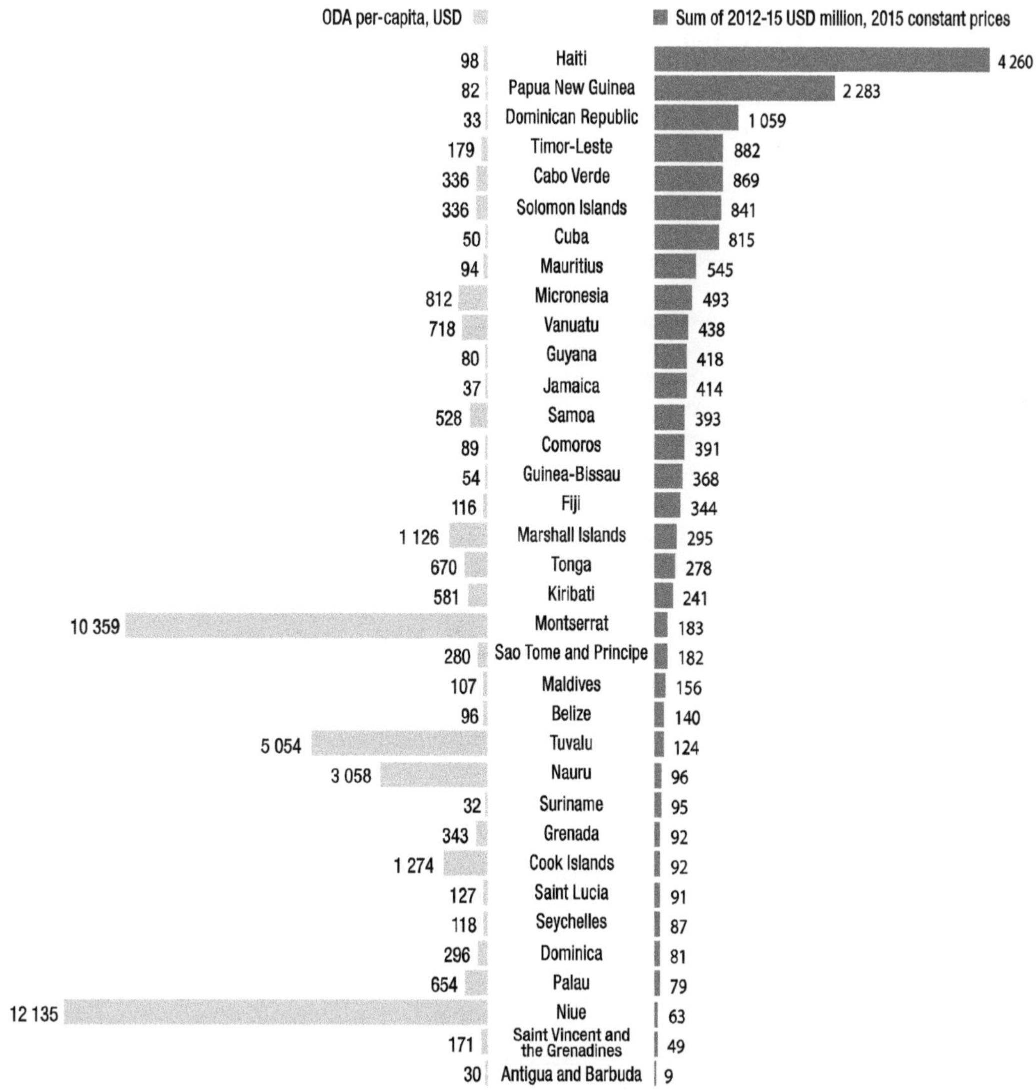

Source: OECD (n.d.), Creditor Reporting System (database), https://stats.oecd.org/Index.aspx?DataSetCode=CRS1.

StatLink http://dx.doi.org/10.1787/888933645877

2.2.3. Providers

Five providers account for over half of the concessional finance to SIDS

Of the 72 bilateral and multilateral providers extending concessional finance to SIDS in 2012-15, the five largest in volume terms were Australia, United States, the European Union, France and the IDA (Figure 2.11), together accounting for 58% of the total (i.e. nearly USD 11 billion over the period, or an average of USD 2.7 billion per year). Allocations from Australia and the United States were particularly significant, amounting to nearly four times the volume of the fifth-largest provider, IDA; this is largely due to Australia's development co-operation focus on the Indo-Pacific region, and to the massive interventions of the United States in Haiti following the 2010 earthquake. Contributions from several other providers were particularly small and scattered, with the smallest 40 providers accounting for less than 1% of total financing.

Figure 2.11. Top 25 providers of concessional finance, 2012-15

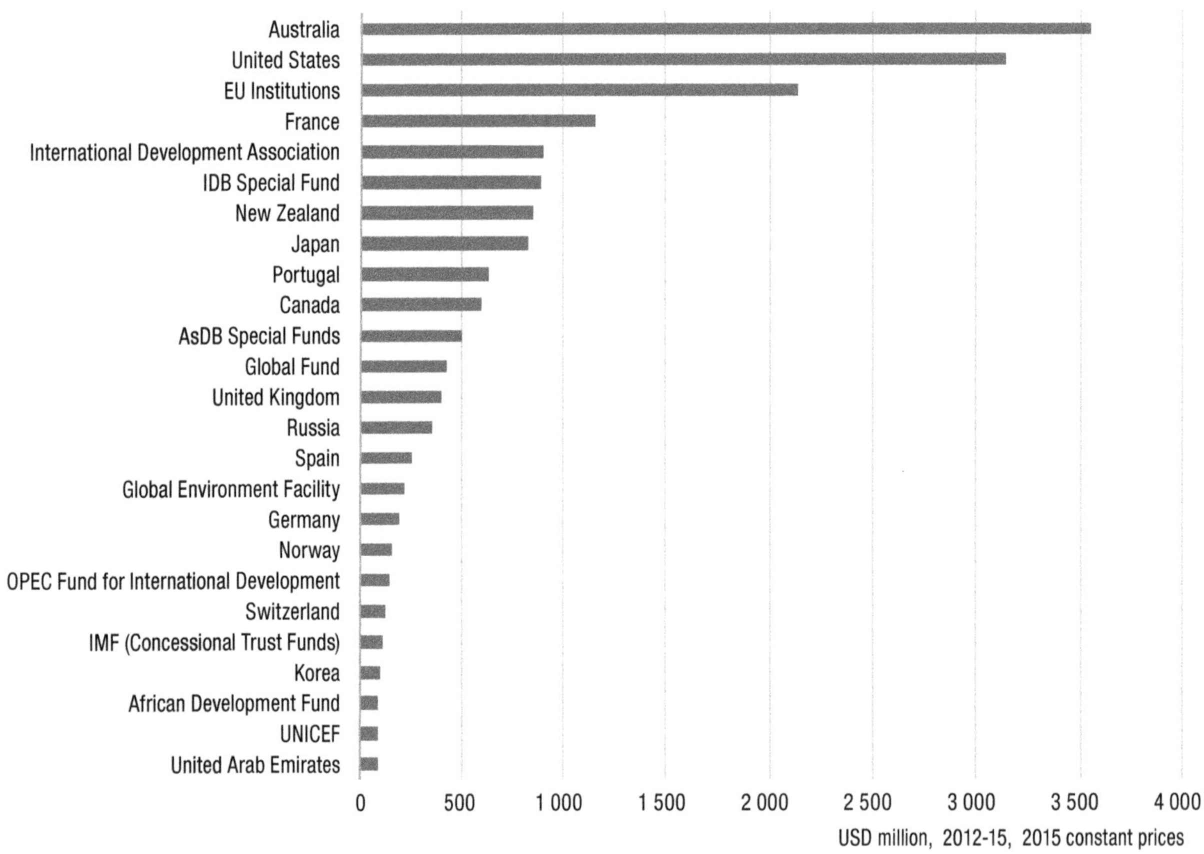

Source: OECD (n.d.), Creditor Reporting System (database), https://stats.oecd.org/Index.aspx?DataSetCode=CRS1.

StatLink http://dx.doi.org/10.1787/888933645896

The geographic spread of concessional finance from bilateral providers is largely influenced by proximity and geopolitical ties

Geographical and historical connections, as well as political, strategic and economic interest, and the provider's comparative advantage, dictate focus. Australia concentrates 96% of its support on the Pacific region, as does New Zealand (99%). Canada focuses 97% of its support, and the United States 71% of its support, in the Caribbean. The European Union splits its resources between the Pacific, 20%, the AIMS region, 21% and the Caribbean, 58%. Japan, for its part, directs 65% of its support to the Pacific, 15% to the AIMS region and 21% to the Caribbean. Multilateral providers' geographic allocation is largely determined by each organisation's mandate and allocation models. IDA for example works globally, supporting eligible SIDS across all regions. The IMF, which has the same membership, supported three AIMS, four Caribbean and three Pacific SIDS. The multilateral development banks work along regional lines, while the UN agencies and the global funds all support SIDS from each region quite equally.

Only a few bilateral providers prioritise SIDS in their global portfolios

Relatively smaller bilateral providers with strong historical ties and geographical proximity with SIDS display the strongest focus on these countries, to which they allocate a significant share of their global concessional finance. In 2012-15, concessional finance to SIDS represented 53% of New Zealand's ODA, 48% of Portugal's and 24% of Australia's. Some larger bilateral providers – such as the United States, the European Union, France and Japan – extended considerable volumes of concessional financing to SIDS that still amounted to only a tiny fraction of their total ODA portfolios. For instance, allocations to SIDS represented only 1% of Japan's ODA portfolio, and only 3% of the ODA portfolios of the United States and the European Union.

With the exception of the Caribbean Development Bank (100%) and the Adaptation Fund (30%), financing to SIDS represents a small share (up to 15%) of most multilateral providers' overall concessional portfolio. No significant differences in terms of SIDS prioritisation can be found between regional organisations and institutions with a universal mandate. Among the ten largest multilateral providers to SIDS in volume terms, the weight of allocations was largest for the IDB (which allocated 11% of its concessional flows to SIDS), the Organization of the Petroleum Exporting Countries Fund for International Development (OPEC Fund) (9%) and the Global Environment Facility (7%). IDA allocated 2% of its 2012-15 disbursements to SIDS (Figure 2.12).

Figure 2.12. The concessional finance portfolio of just a few providers has a strong focus on small island developing states, 2012-15

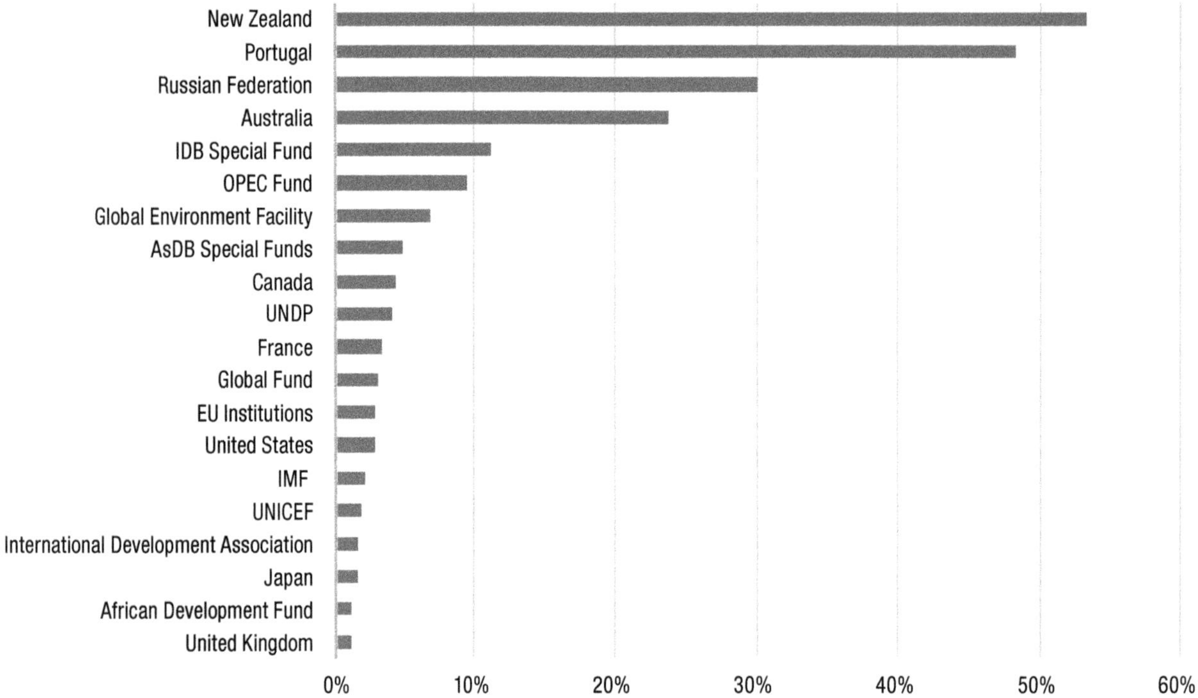

Source: OECD (n.d.), Creditor Reporting System (database), https://stats.oecd.org/Index.aspx?DataSetCode=CRS1.

StatLink http://dx.doi.org/10.1787/888933645915

SIDS feature in the development narratives of most bilateral providers, but donors do not have specific resource allocation targets or strategies to engage with SIDS

Most DAC members mention SIDS in their development co-operation policies or development narratives.[14] Some refer to them in their overarching development strategies, identifying SIDS as an explicit focus group for their co-operation efforts (e.g. Australia, New Zealand, Portugal, etc.). Others acknowledge SIDS more broadly, or in the context of their climate engagements: for instance, the United States Agency for International Development cites SIDS as a category of vulnerable countries in its Climate and Development Strategy. Others do not acknowledge SIDS as a specific group in their development policies, but do have instruments and policies in place benefitting SIDS. For instance, while the European Union does not explicitly refer to SIDS as a grouping in its development co-operation strategy, all SIDS benefit from its development co-operation instruments, either through the bilateral programmes, the regional programmes (Pacific, Caribbean or intra-African, Caribbean, and Pacific Group) or the thematic programmes. The European Union also considers the special situation and vulnerability of SIDS in the context of the EU Budget Support Guidelines.

However, even those DAC members whose development policies explicitly refer to SIDS as a distinct group of countries do not have specific policies for engaging with them, or tailored instruments to partner with them. Most DAC members adopt a case-by-case approach. Given a lack of field presence in SIDS, several DAC members mainly channel support through regional initiatives and institutions, or partnerships with other (especially multilateral) providers (see section on "approaches and modalities" in this chapter).

Collectively, DAC members are committed to "allocate more of total ODA to "countries most in need", such as least developed countries (LDCs), low-income countries, small island developing states (SIDS), land-locked developing countries and fragile and conflict-affected states" (OECD DAC, 2014a). While there is an international target of allocating 0.15-20% of ODA/GNI to least developed countries, no similar international target exists for SIDS or for "countries most in need" as a whole. Moreover, while some DAC members have adopted specific internal targets for allocating concessional resources to fragile states or other groups of countries, none have a target for SIDS.

Providers, especially bilateral ones, can spread themselves thinly

Bilateral providers tend to have a broader reach than multilateral providers. The largest 25 bilateral providers extended concessional finance to an average of 22 SIDS in 2012-15, with only Portugal, Netherlands, and Ireland providing financing to fewer SIDS (6 or 7). While the top five bilateral providers – i.e. Australia, United States, the European Union, France and New Zealand – were still able to extend significant volumes of concessional finance to each SIDS they support (above an annual average of USD 7 million per country), for smaller providers this wide reach resulted, for the most part, in small allocations per country (less than USD 1 million per year on average in each of the SIDS where they were operating).

The breadth and reach of concessional finance from multilateral organisations is more varied, largely hinging on the scope of these organisations' memberships and mandates. With their (quasi) universal membership and reach, several UN agencies and funds provide the widest coverage of SIDS among multilateral organisations (e.g. in 2012-15, the United Nations Development Programme covered 34 SIDS; the Food and Agricultural Organization 32 SIDS; and the International Labour Organization 30 SIDS). These organisations often provide capacity building and policy advice services, which translate into small dollar amounts (an average of slightly over USD 2 million per year for the United Nations Development Programme; and below USD 1 million per year for the International Labour Organization, and Food and Agricultural Organization). Among global funds, the reach of concessional finance ranges from 30 SIDS for the Global Environment Facility to 17 for the Global Fund, 13 for the Caribbean Investment Facility and 6 for the Adaptation Fund. The average volume allocated per country also varies, from a high annual average of USD 25 million (Global Fund) to a low of USD 0.5 million (Climate Investment Fund) in 2012-15. Multilateral development banks tend to allocate larger volumes per country – USD 149 million (Inter-American Development Bank) on average per year, USD 43 million (IDA) and USD 31 million (Asian Development Bank) – well above the volumes extended by bilateral providers. IDA has the largest coverage (21 SIDS), while Inter-American Development Bank and Asian Development Bank's memberships restrict the scope of their interventions to 6 and 16 SIDS, respectively.

No correlation exists between the total volumes allocated to SIDS and the number of SIDS with which they engage (Figure 2.13) and financing is often spread thinly across SIDS. The last section in this chapter explores the consequences of such an allocation pattern, which gives rise to a significant fragmentation of efforts in SIDS.

Figure 2.13. No strong correlation exists between the total volumes a provider allocates to small island developing states and with how many it engages

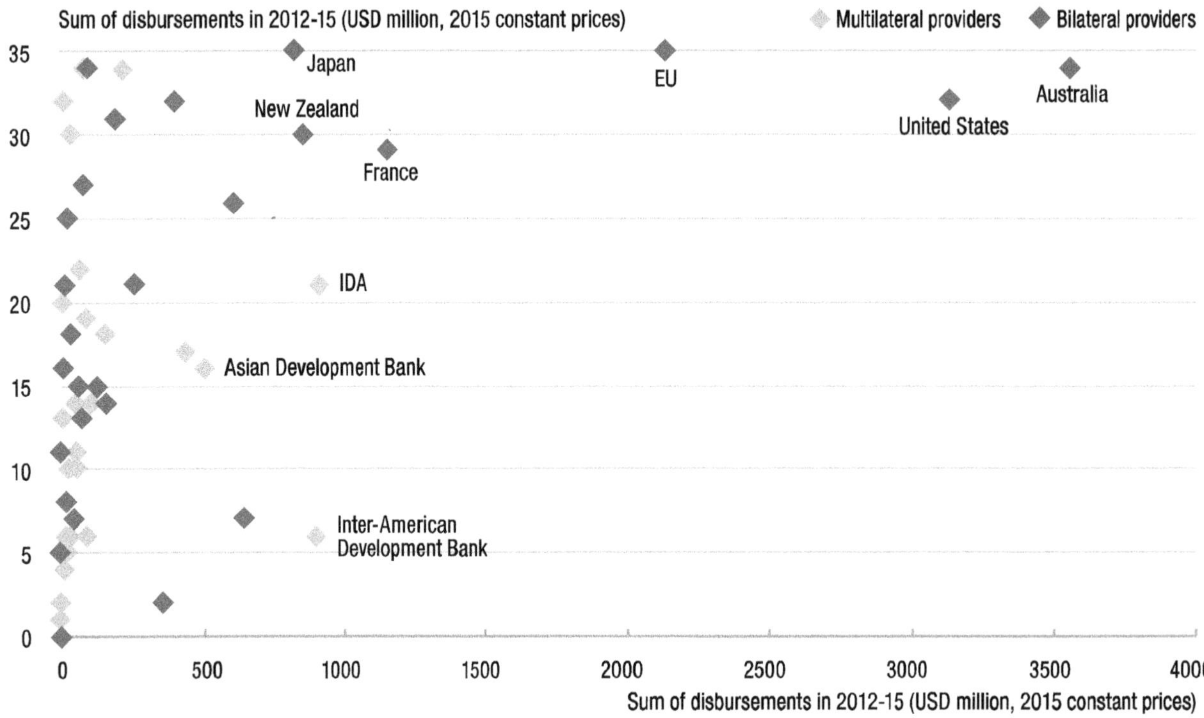

Source: OECD (n.d.), Creditor Reporting System (database), https://stats.oecd.org/Index.aspx?DataSetCode=CRS1.

StatLink http://dx.doi.org/10.1787/888933645934

The nature and focus of providers' development support for SIDS differ greatly

As for other developing countries, bilateral providers primarily extend concessional finance to SIDS in the form of grant financing[15] and project interventions, largely prioritising social sectors. Unlike in other developing countries, providers have revived the use of budget support in SIDS, especially in the Pacific region, as a way to address institutional challenges and strengthen public governance. Among the bilateral providers to SIDS, France, Japan and Portugal direct significant grant financing towards social sectors, but also make extensive use of concessional loans, largely for infrastructure development and technical support. Overall, eight bilateral providers used concessional loans in SIDS in 2012-15: these represented 6-15% of concessional financing to SIDS by the European Union, United Arab Emirates, Japan and Korea, and a much higher share for Portugal (64%), France (60%) and Kuwait (89%). Spain also used concessional loans (10% of total allocations), but the greatest share of its support was in the form of debt relief (47%).

The sectoral focus of concessional finance by the largest bilateral providers resembles the allocation focus to other developing countries, suggesting that providers' development co-operation with SIDS broadly reflects their comparative advantages and sectoral specialisation. For instance, some DAC members focus on the following sectors in both SIDS and other developing countries: Japan in infrastructure and energy; France in education and infrastructure; the United States in health and governance; and New Zealand in education and governance. The European Union engages in slightly different sectors than in other developing countries (where it mainly supports banking and financial services), targeting instead general budget support (19%), agriculture (13%) and governance (12%) (Figure 2.14).

Multilateral providers' development support has fairly distinct forms and focuses. Multilateral development banks mainly invest in infrastructure. Concessional loans represent over 60% of financing to SIDS by most multilateral providers (e.g. the International Monetary Fund, the Islamic Development Bank, the Caribbean Development Bank and the Asian Development Bank). Only the International Fund for Agriculture and Development (47%), the International Development Association (55%) and the Inter-American Development Bank (83%) extend a larger share of financing to SIDS as grants. The IDA consistently allocated resources to all 21 IDA-eligible SIDS in 2012-15, although amounts vary year on year, partly due to large one-off payments for infrastructure projects.

Global funds and United Nations agencies, on the other hand, exclusively extended grant financing, with the exception of the Climate Investment Fund, which provided the bulk (62%) of its concessional financing to SIDS as loans. Global funds have specialised areas of intervention, while UN agencies supported SIDS in a wider array of sectors. Multilateral funders differ from bilateral donors in that the vast majority of the activities financed are project type interventions; 75% of IDA and 100% of the Global Environment Facility and Global Fund resources. Nevertheless, both the Global Environment Facility and the Global Fund provided support quite consistently year on year to SIDS partners.

Figure 2.14. Several providers prioritise the same areas of intervention in small island developing states and other developing countries

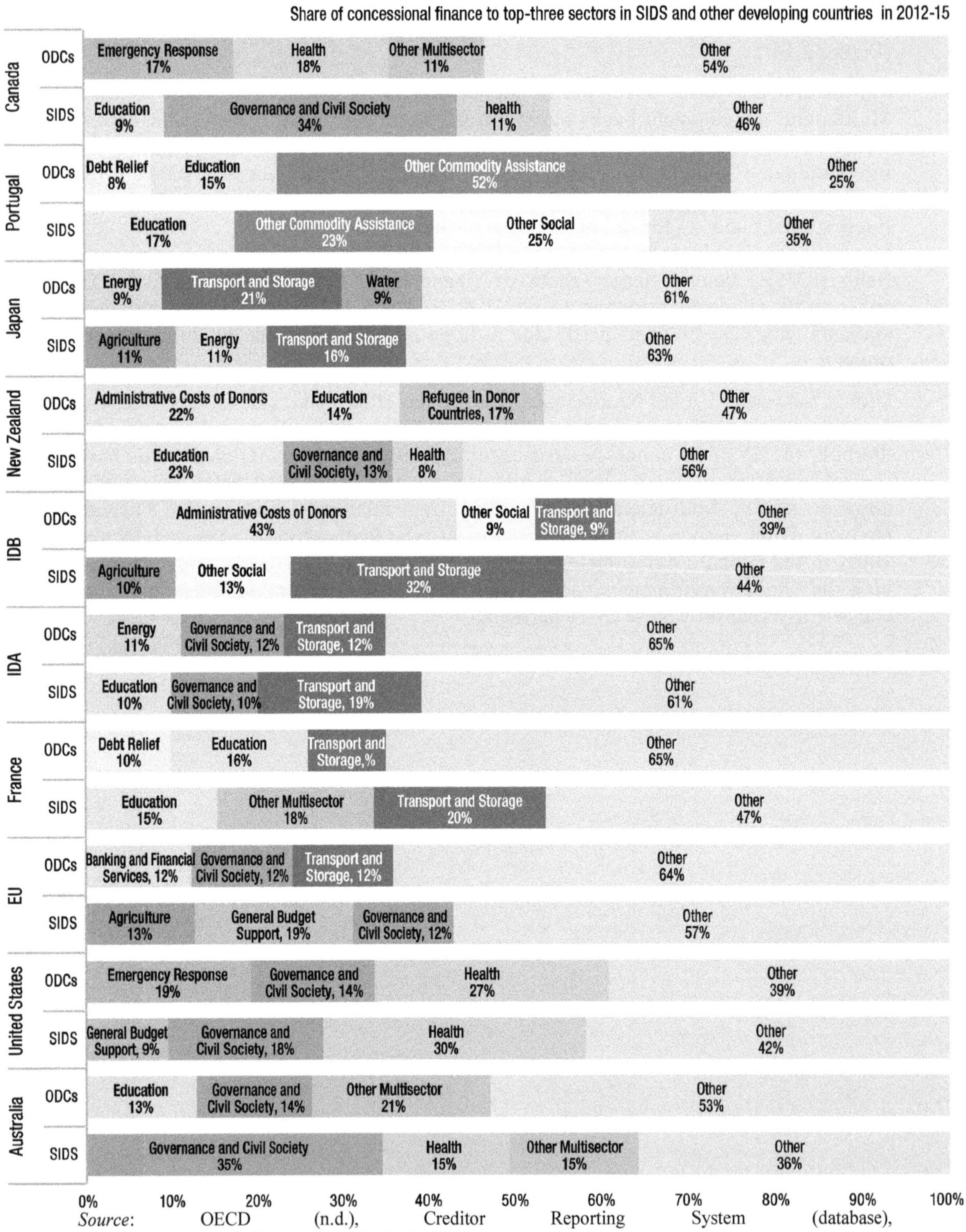

Source: OECD (n.d.), Creditor Reporting System (database), https://stats.oecd.org/Index.aspx?DataSetCode=CRS1.

StatLink http://dx.doi.org/10.1787/888933645953

2.2.4. Looking at allocations through a sectoral lens

Allocations concentrate on governance, health and infrastructures, with some differences between bilateral and multilateral providers

In 2012-15, concessional finance from bilateral and multilateral sources targeted 29 different sectors, with the largest volumes channelled to governance and civil society (16%), the health sector (15%) and infrastructure (10%) (Figure 2.15). This breakdown largely reflects allocations in the largest SIDS recipients (e.g. Haiti, Papua New Guinea, Timor-Leste). As described in the previous section, sectoral allocations of bilateral and multilateral providers display some differences: bilateral providers, for example, focus on improving governance and institutions (18%), whereas multilateral providers only channelled 7% to this sector in 2012-15. Multilateral concessional finance targets infrastructure development (21%), compared to 7% from bilateral providers. A large share of both bilateral (13%) and multilateral (18%) sectoral allocations targets health initiatives, mainly stemming from the focus of the global health funds and the United States on this sector (see also Box 2.1).

Figure 2.15. Concessional finance mainly targets governance, health and infrastructures (2012-15)

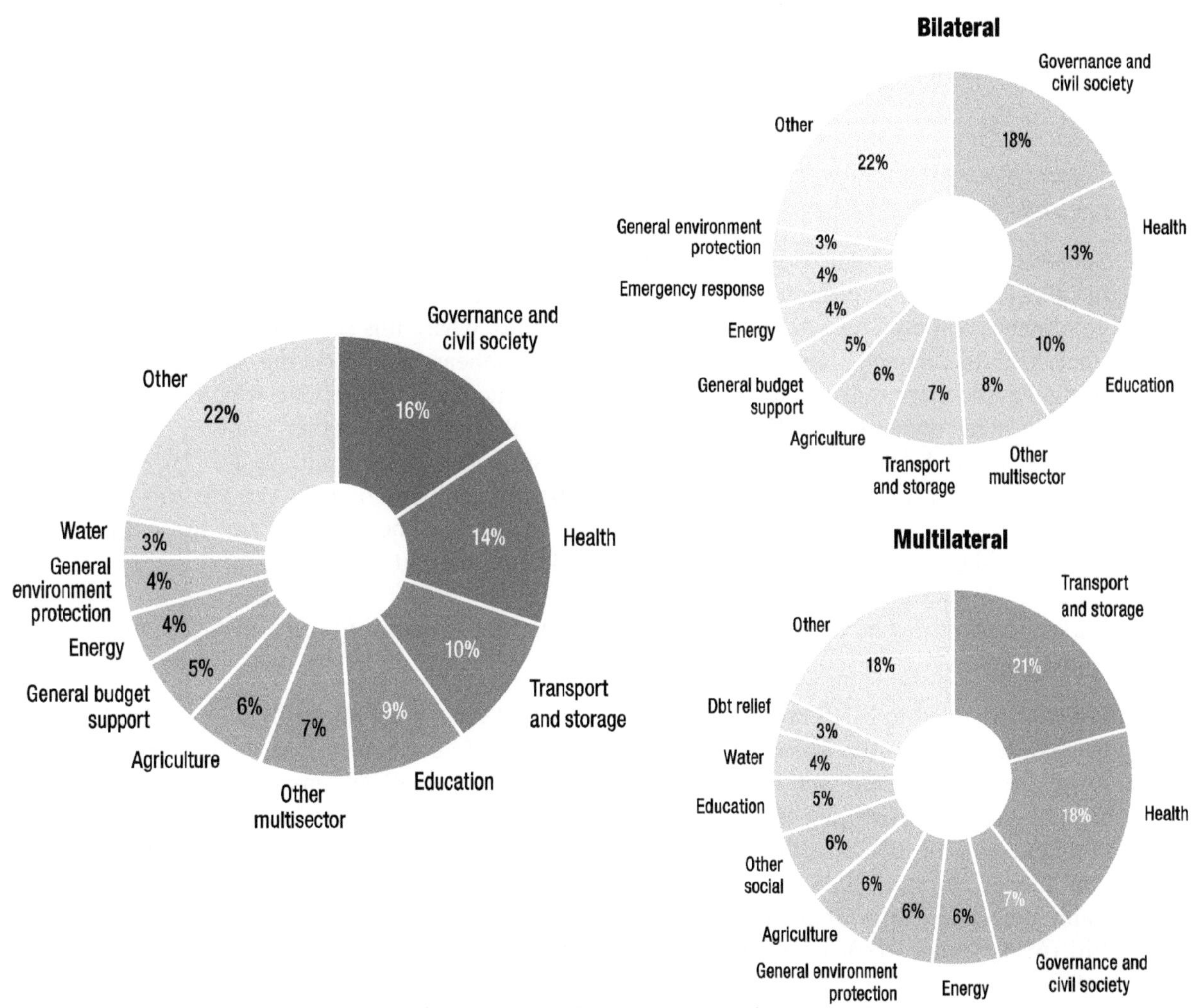

Source: OECD (n.d.), Creditor Reporting System (database), https://stats.oecd.org/Index.aspx?DataSetCode=CRS1.

StatLink http://dx.doi.org/10.1787/888933645972

Box 2.1. The Global Partnership for Education and small island developing states

The Global Partnership for Education was launched in 2002 as the Education For All – Fast Track Initiative (FTI). It is a multi-stakeholder partnership of bilateral and multilateral donors, developing countries, civil society and the private sector. Its goal is to provide quality basic education to all children.

Since 2002, it has mobilised USD 4.7 billion in grants to partner countries, including 18 SIDS. Pacific Island countries have a regional allocation of USD 5.4 million in implementation grants as follows: Federated States of Micronesia (USD 0.4 million), Kiribati (USD 0.4 million), Marshall Islands (USD 0.4 million), Samoa (USD 0.48 million), Solomon Islands (USD 1.3 million), Tonga (USD 0.4 million), Tuvalu (USD 0.4 million) and Vanuatu (USD 0.6 million).

From 2018, it will implement a new financing and funding framework that includes range of funding options to meet the diverse range of needs in its partner countries. It allocates its funding to countries using a needs-based formula. Its funding model incentivises results, with 70% of its financing to a country being conditional on meeting requirements regarding domestic resource mobilisation and other standards, and the remaining 30% on the achievement of demonstrated results.

Source: Adapted from the Global Partnership for Education website.

Different sectoral prioritisations prevail in the Pacific, Caribbean and AIMS regions

Sectoral allocations[16] across geographic regions vary, with the distribution in the Pacific, in particular, fairly different than in the other two regions. The prioritisation of governance and civil society is strongest in the Pacific, where this sector received 21% of total 2012-15 financing, compared to 13% in the Caribbean and 7% in the AIMS region. In the Pacific there is also a stronger focus on infrastructure development, which received 13% of total concessional finance, compared to 9-10% in the other regions. In the Caribbean and AIMS regions, the largest share of support is to the health sector (16% and 11%, respectively). A greater concentration of concessional finance on the top-five sectors exists in the Pacific (74%) as compared to the Caribbean (53%) and the AIMS region (51%), even though all 29 sectors received some support in 2012-15[17].

Humanitarian aid has not driven allocations of concessional finance to SIDS on aggregate

Humanitarian aid to SIDS recorded a peak in 2010 (USD 1.6 billion, or 21% of the total) as a consequence of the international response to the Haiti earthquake. On the longer run, however, humanitarian aid has not been a key driver of allocations of concessional finance to SIDS, averaging at 6% in the 2012-15 period and at 5% before the 2010 peak (Figure 2.16). In 2012-15, the weight of humanitarian aid in total concessional finance was highest for the SIDS hit by hurricanes and other natural disasters in the period: Saint Vincent and the Grenadines (24%), Vanuatu (19%), Grenada (12%), Samoa (6%), Fiji (6%), Tonga (6%). Humanitarian aid represented 4% or less for the remaining 28 SIDS.

Figure 2.16. Humanitarian aid peaked in 2010 but has not driven allocations of concessional finance

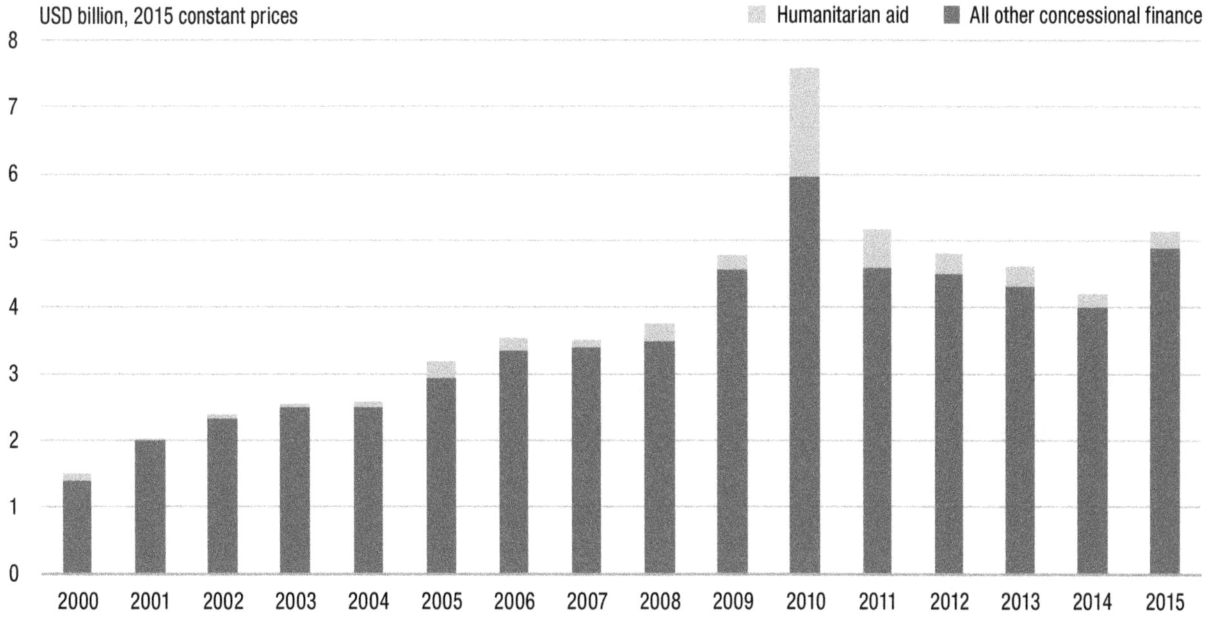

Source: OECD (n.d.), Creditor Reporting System (database), https://stats.oecd.org/Index.aspx?DataSetCode=CRS1.

StatLink http://dx.doi.org/10.1787/888933645991

Providers increasingly mainstream gender equality in their interventions

Gender equality and empowerment is either a significant (22%) or principal (2%) component of concessional finance allocated to SIDS between 2012 and 2015[18], increasing by 5% on average per year over the period. Given the large gender inequalities prevailing in many SIDS, this is an important area of future focus for development partners.

Among the larger providers, Australia (51% of whose financing activities included a gender component), New Zealand (56%) and Canada (68%) have made the greatest progress in this area, while the multilateral development banks in particular have not reported a significant focus on gender equality. Partly as a result of Australia and New Zealand's involvement, the share of concessional finance with a gender component is highest in the Pacific SIDS (36% in 2012-15) compared to 12% in AIMS SIDS and 16% in Caribbean SIDS. Papua New Guinea received the highest gender prioritisation (49% of activities with a gender component in 2012-15), followed by a 44% in Fiji and 43% each in Timor-Leste and Vanuatu.

As Figure 2.17 shows, a little over one quarter of activities in the governance and civil society sector include either a significant or primary gender component, compared to 33% in the health sector and 51% in the education sector.

Figure 2.17. Gender mainstreaming of development activities in the health and education sectors is promising, but providers need to consider it in all areas, 2012-15

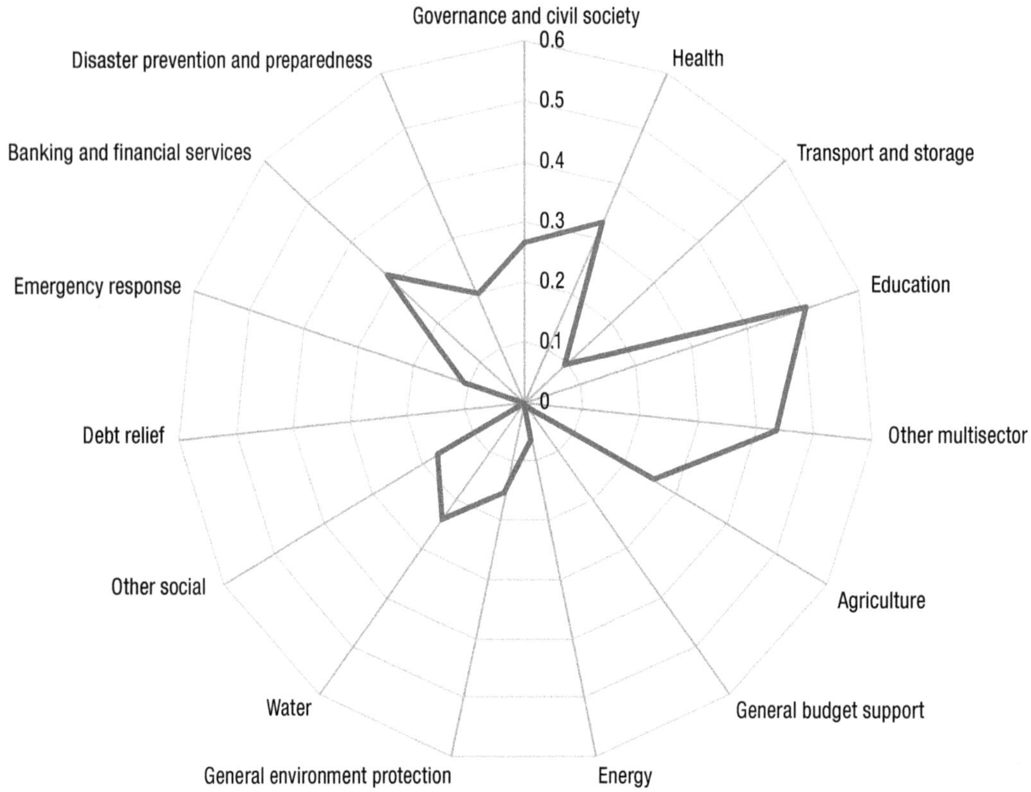

Source: OECD (n.d.), Creditor Reporting System (database), https://stats.oecd.org/Index.aspx?DataSetCode=CRS1.

StatLink http://dx.doi.org/10.1787/888933646010

Some sectors and areas may be receiving insufficient international attention

As is widely acknowledged internationally, SIDS face a number of specific challenges, including strong vulnerability to the impacts of climate change and natural disasters, high debt levels and reliance on a handful of sectors as the main drivers of their economies (OECD-World Bank, 2016; UNDP, 2017b; UNDP and UNOHRLLS, 2015) – see Chapter 1. While the broad nature of development needs in several SIDS can make prioritisation difficult, some areas and sectors that would seem vital – and even appear as prerequisites – to promoting sustainable development in SIDS receive relatively little support.

For instance, concessional finance to foster development that is resilient to the impacts of climate change and natural disasters only made up 14% of concessional finance to SIDS over 2011-14 (OECD-World Bank, 2016). Concessional finance from bilateral providers that includes a climate component decreased in 2014-15, to USD 1.08 billion, from USD 1.14 billion on average per year in 2012-13. Over the same period, the overall share of climate action in bilateral ODA decreased from 15.3% to 14.5%. Likewise, high costs and limited access to energy constrain development in SIDS, yet the energy sector received less than 5% of the total concessional finance to SIDS in 2012-15.

Despite the considerable infrastructure gap faced by SIDS, only 11% of concessional finance targeted infrastructure. The natural resource-rich SIDS saw a slightly greater focus on infrastructure development (17%), as there is a clear economic case for developing infrastructures to allow exploiting resources. Conversely, only 7% of concessional finance to some of the smallest SIDS in the Pacific targeted infrastructure improvements, despite the considerable needs to improve connectivity in the smallest and most remote SIDS.

Tourism, although a key economic sector in many SIDS, received less than 1% of all concessional finance to SIDS, suggesting that private sector resources and non-concessional finance could be used to meet needs. Allocations supporting tourism were limited (1%) even in SIDS that mainly have service-oriented economies.

Despite persistent debt issues in several SIDS, only 4% (USD 857 million) of all ODA flows targeted action relating to debt relief over 2012-15. Together, Cuba (78%) and Comoros (18%) received 96% of the total support in this area.

2.2.5. Approaches and modalities in concessional finance

Concessional finance to SIDS is largely provided as grants

In 2012-15, grants accounted for 83% of concessional finance to SIDS, slightly more than in other developing countries (73%). Concessional loans accounted for 14%, and the remaining 3% was debt relief. Bilateral providers accounted for the majority of grants (83%), while they extended just over half of all concessional loans (Figure 2.18). Although grants represent the bulk of concessional financing to SIDS, their level has been stagnating overall as a result of declining bilateral grants (-5% per year on average in 2012-15). In 2015, growth in concessional finance was mainly driven by a rise in concessional loans and debt relief from bilateral providers (soaring from USD 9 million in 2014 to USD 476 million in 2015). Bilateral providers accounted for 60% of the increase in concessional loans, which was concentrated on the Dominican Republic.

Figure 2.18. The bulk of concessional finance to small island developing states is provided as grants

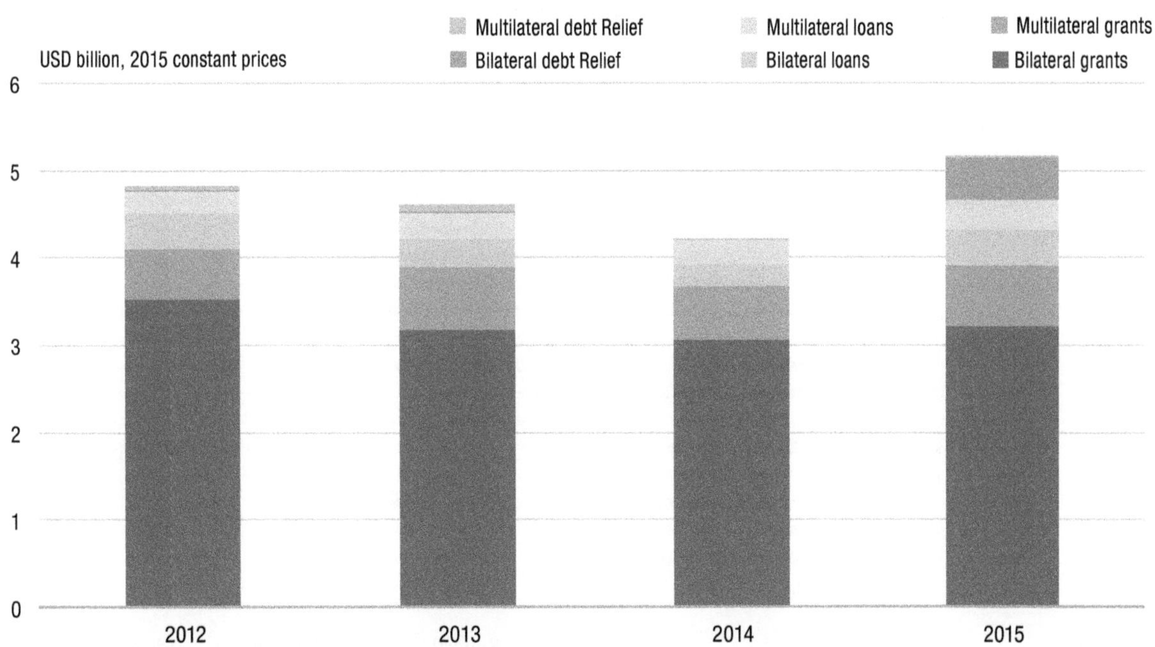

Source: OECD (n.d.), Creditor Reporting System (database), https://stats.oecd.org/Index.aspx?DataSetCode=CRS1.

StatLink http://dx.doi.org/10.1787/888933646029

Across SIDS there are large differences in the relative weight of grants and for some there could be scope for increasing concessional loans

For individual countries, increasing the volume of concessional loans could present viable opportunities to expand financing, provided that loans are provided at an adequate level of concessionality. As Figure 2.19 shows, in 2012-15, four SIDS, in both the Pacific and the Caribbean, received no concessional loans, relying exclusively on grants. These are all upper middle-income countries, and include three microstates: Fiji, Nauru, Niue, and Antigua and Barbuda. For another 20 SIDS, concessional loans contributed less than 10% of the total concessional finance in 2012-15. Conversely, loans represented over 50% of the total concessional finance allocated in 2012-15 to four SIDS: Mauritius, Dominica, Cabo Verde and Grenada, reaching a high of 72% in the case of Grenada.

Figure 2.19. Concessional loans represented less than 10% of the concessional finance to most small island developing states, 2012-15

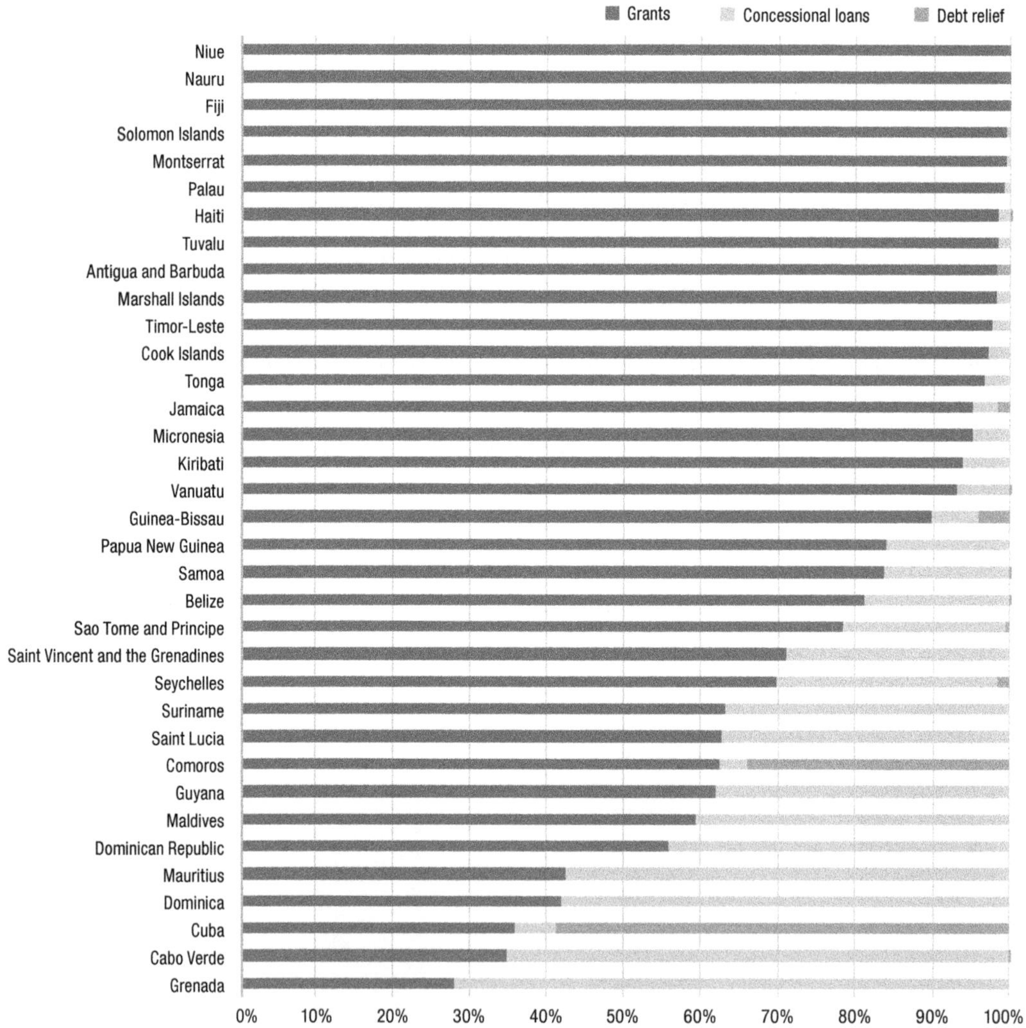

Source: OECD (n.d.), Creditor Reporting System (database), https://stats.oecd.org/Index.aspx?DataSetCode=CRS1.

StatLink http://dx.doi.org/10.1787/888933646048

Budget support accounts for a small share of financing overall, but was highly prioritised in a number of SIDS

Globally, the rise of the aid effectiveness agenda popularised the use of programmatic approaches to development assistance in the 2000s, including a greater use of budget support. While several providers have since moved away from providing budget support, others have stepped up its use in SIDS in recent years, seeing it as a powerful tool for reducing transaction costs and increasing the level of co-ordination commonly lacking in project-based support.

Budget support has also been used to help reform public financial management, meet spending targets in specific sectors, or achieve overall economic reform (Dornan and Brant, 2017). In the Solomon Islands, for example, budget support is contingent on at least 22% of the domestically sourced government recurrent budget being spent on education, and 10% being spent on healthcare. As highlighted in Section 2.2.6, SIDS rely strongly on one or several providers for the bulk of their financing. Hence, while budget support can be a useful instrument to reduce administrative burdens, and foster a meaningful policy dialogue between the government and the international community, care should be taken to avoid the largest providers becoming overly influential in the policy choices of SIDS governments.

The use of budget support has increased especially in the Pacific, but in 2012-15 it represented more than 20% of concessional finance for 11 SIDS across all regions, mainly upper middle-income countries: Marshall Islands (63%), Micronesia (61%), Grenada (47%), Niue (46%), Mauritius (33%), Cook Islands (27%), Jamaica (26%) and Nauru (26%), Samoa (25%), Dominica (23%), Palau (21%) (Figure 2.20). No use of budget support was made in 2012-15 in seven SIDS: Antigua and Barbuda, Belize, Cuba, Fiji, Maldives, Saint Vincent and the Grenadines, and Suriname.

Overall, 11% of total concessional finance to SIDS was either general or sector-specific budget support in 2012-15, compared to 7% as the global average in other developing countries. In total, SIDS received USD 2.0 billion in budget support, of which USD 0.9 billion went to general budget support and USD 1.1 billion was sector-specific budget support. General budget support increased in 2012-13, but its level more than halved in 2014-15; while the volume of sector-specific budget support in 2014-15 was 8% higher than its 2012-13 level.

Budget support is provided by both bilateral providers (80% of the total) and multilateral providers (20%). The European Union (31%), United States (25%) and Australia (12%) are the largest providers of combined general and sector-specific budget support. The largest multilateral provider is the World Bank (7%).

Figure 2.20. For 11 small island developing states budget support represents over 20% of concessional finance, 2012-15

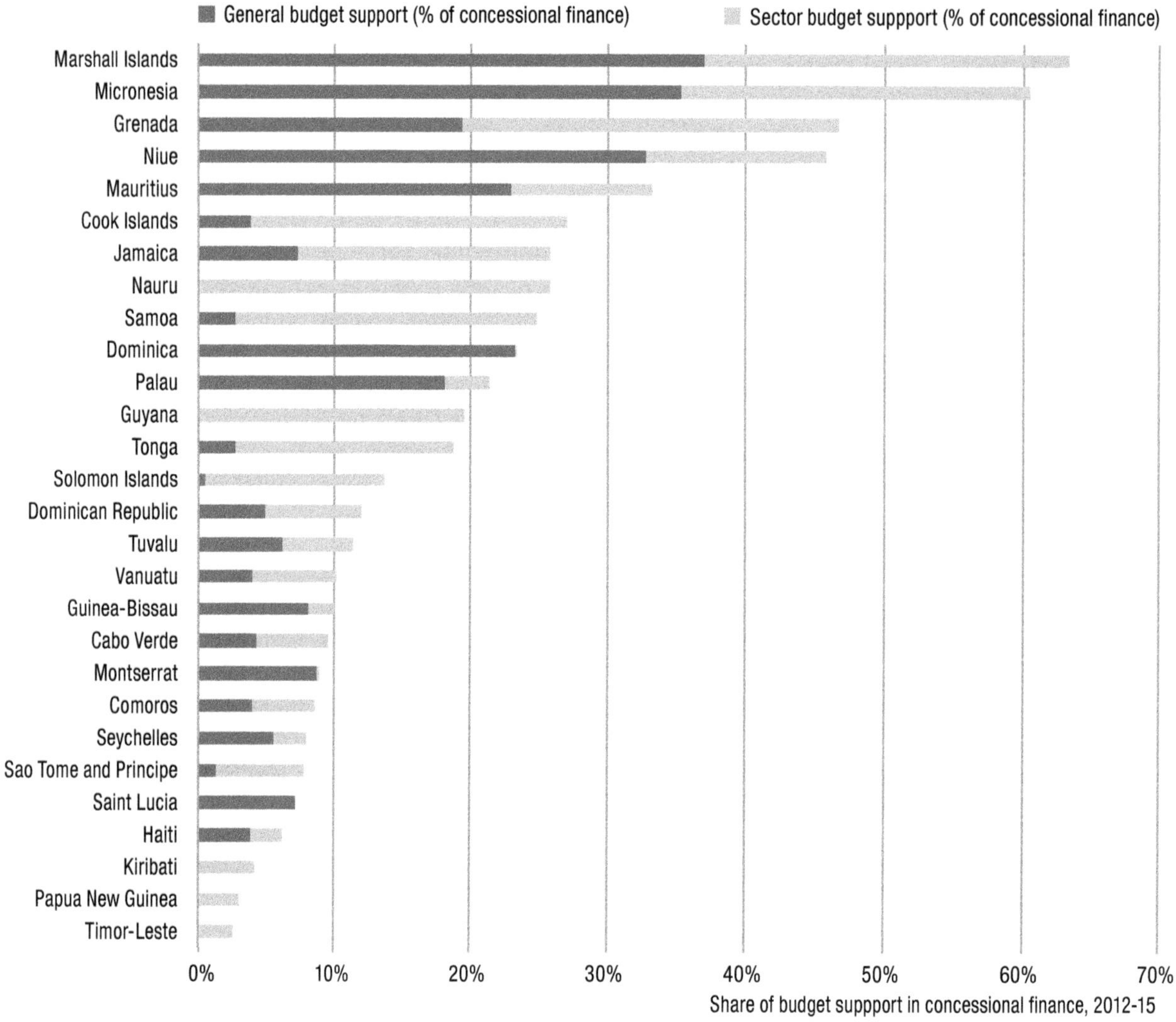

Source: OECD (n.d.), Creditor Reporting System (database), https://stats.oecd.org/Index.aspx?DataSetCode=CRS1.

StatLink http://dx.doi.org/10.1787/888933646067

Regional initiatives account for a small part of the financing reaching SIDS

The relatively expensive nature of development co-operation in SIDS and the need to take advantage of regional economies of scale make regional projects and initiatives a sensible approach for extending concessional finance to SIDS. In 2012-15, however, only 8% of the concessional financing to SIDS reached these countries through regional initiatives (USD 1.5 billion), suggesting that there could be scope for making further use of such approaches[19]. The main contributors were bilateral providers, which channelled 10% of their concessional financing to SIDS through regional initiatives, compared to 3% for multilateral providers. Australia, United States and the European Union accounted for the bulk of the regional initiatives (53%).

Providers largely focus on governance and health both when partnering directly with individual SIDS and at the regional level. At the regional level they provide a greater share of concessional finance to environmental projects (12%, compared to 3% directly to SIDS in 2012-15), as well as banking and financial services (8%, compared to 2% in individual SIDS) (Figure 2.21). The World Bank has recently approved two projects for the eastern Caribbean countries of Saint Vincent and the Grenadines, and Grenada, for a total of USD 19 million, which aim to address key constraints in human development and agriculture sectors. The Human Development Service Delivery Project (USD 10.7 million) targets improved quality of primary and secondary education, a more efficient social protection system and improved access to skills training in Saint Vincent and the Grenadines. The OECS Regional Agriculture Competitiveness Project (USD 8.3 million) aims to increase market access and sales for farmers, fishers and agro-processors in both Saint Vincent and the Grenadines, and Grenada by linking them to larger markets for their products[20].

Figure 2.21. Sectoral prioritisation varies between regional and country-specific allocations (2012-15)

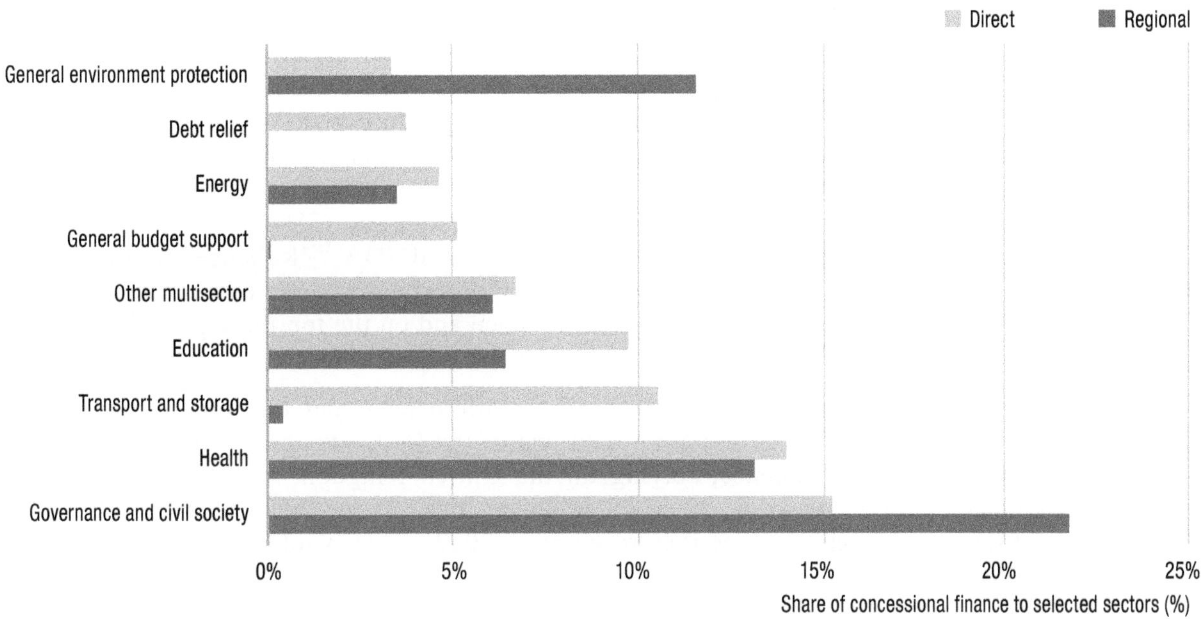

Source: OECD (n.d.), Creditor Reporting System (database), https://stats.oecd.org/Index.aspx?DataSetCode=CRS1.

StatLink http://dx.doi.org/10.1787/888933646086

Bilateral providers channelled 12% of their support through multilateral organisations

Of the total concessional finance extended to SIDS in 2012-15, 12% (USD 1.7 billion, amounting to USD 435 million on average per year) was channelled through multilateral organisations. This financing modality enables bilateral partners to enhance multilateral organisations' presence in regions of interest (for example, Australia and New Zealand in the Pacific).[21] It also allows providers without a strong field presence to still support individual SIDS or regional initiatives. For instance, several bilateral providers contributed in this manner to the international response supporting Haiti, which received 23% of these flows.

Twenty seven bilateral providers allocated earmarked funding to multilateral organisations in 2012-15, with three providers accounting for 68% of the total: Australia (USD 466 million, or 27%); the European Union (USD 418 million, or 24%) and Canada (USD 296 million, or 17%). Canada earmarked over 49% of its total concessional finance, Australia 13% and the European Union 19%.

This financing was channelled through 65 different multilateral organisations, including 22 UN agencies in 2012-15. UNDP received the largest share of this financing (USD 225 million, or 13%). Bilateral providers channelled financing through multilateral organisations to support governance and civil society activities (16%), general environment protection (11%) and health programmes (10%).

2.2.6. Reliance on a single or few sources of financing for the bulk of concessional finance and fragmentation

A previous report (OECD-World Bank, 2016) found that many SIDS rely on a handful of providers for the bulk of their financing for climate and disaster resilience while the remainder of this support is splintered across several small projects from various sources. This combination makes SIDS extremely vulnerable to shifts in the priorities of the dominant provider(s), while also burdening their limited administrative capacity. This finding is still valid when considering the full spectrum of concessional finance to SIDS. In aggregate, over half of concessional finance reaching SIDS was provided by just five providers (58% in 2012-15): Australia, United States, European Union, France, and IDA.[22] Reliance on top providers is even more extreme for individual SIDS, which rely on average on a single provider for 46% of their concessional finance and on the top three providers for 74% thereof.

This phenomenon is particularly pronounced for microstates and for some of the SIDS in a Compact of Free Association with one of the DAC members. Montserrat exhibits the highest dependence, relying on the United Kingdom for 90% of its concessional finance.[23] Overall, 12 SIDS relied on the top provider for 50% (or more) of the concessional finance they received in 2012-15. Dependence on the top three 3 providers is high across the board: over 2012-15, all but 2 SIDS[24] relied on only 3 providers for over half of their concessional financing, while 20 SIDS relied on the top 3 providers for over 70% of their financing (Figure 2.22).

SIDS generally depend on a bilateral provider as their primary provider. Australia is the top provider for ten SIDS in the Pacific, the European Union is the main finance supplier for six SIDS[25] (four in the Caribbean and two in the AIMS region), and France and the United States are the main providers for four SIDS (mainly in the Caribbean). Other primary providers include Portugal and New Zealand, IDA, Japan, United Kingdom, Russia, the Inter-American Development Bank and the Asian Development Bank.

While the bulk of concessional finance is provided by a single provider, the remainder is spread across a myriad of small projects financed by multiple sources. Small, capacity-constrained administrations in SIDS struggle to meet the competing demands to programme and manage so many low volume transactions.

Figure 2.22. Eleven SIDS relied on a single provider for over half of their concessional finance in 2012-15

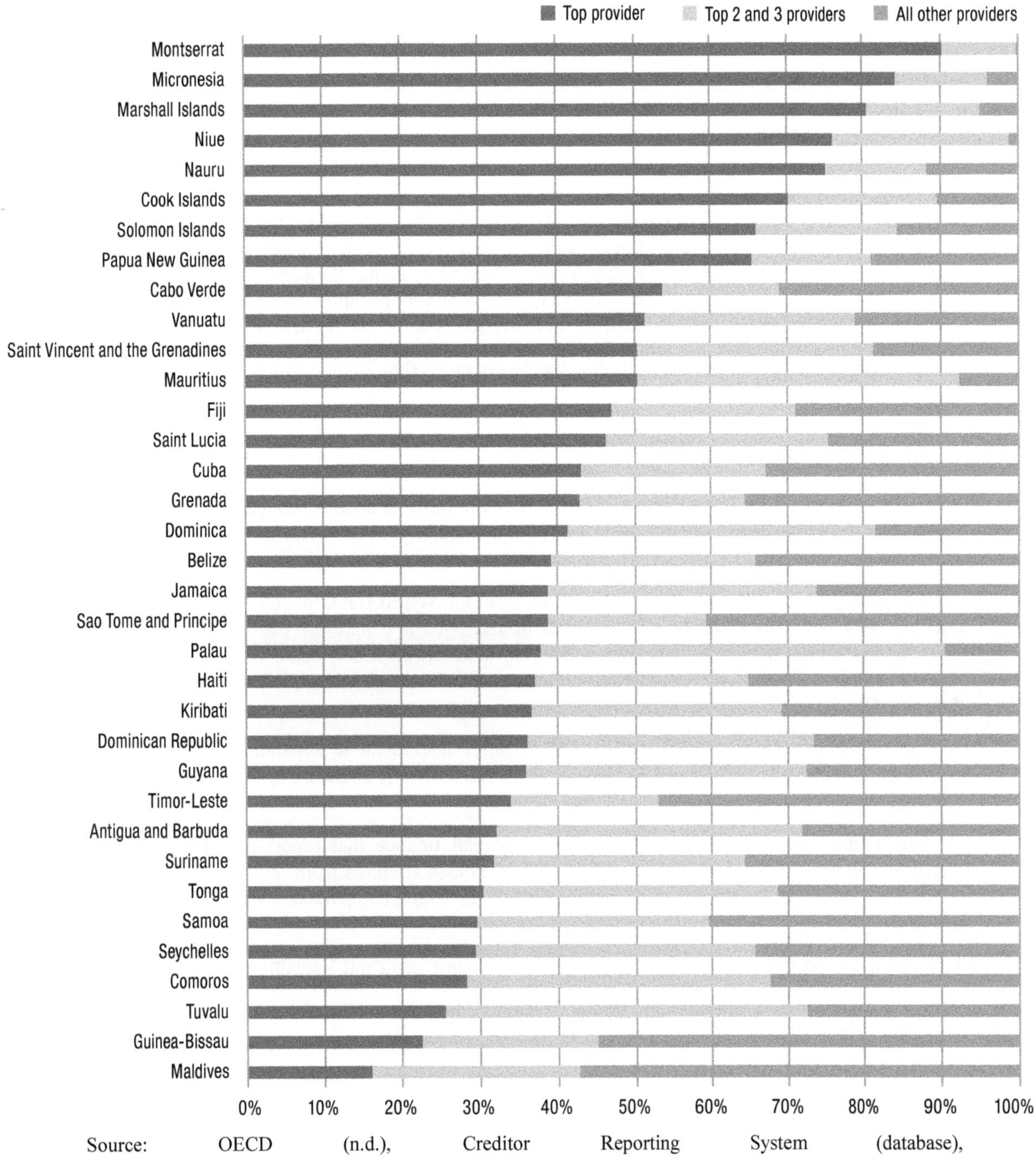

Source: OECD (n.d.), Creditor Reporting System (database), https://stats.oecd.org/Index.aspx?DataSetCode=CRS1.

StatLink http://dx.doi.org/10.1787/888933646105

On aggregate, half of the providers extending concessional finance to SIDS collectively accounted for about 1% of total concessional finance to these countries in 2012-15, and 80% of providers accounted for 10% of the total. The figures also point to a proliferation of small activities. In 2012-15, the total volume of concessional finance reaching SIDS was committed[26] through 21 212 transactions, and each SIDS managed 151 transactions[27] per year on average. About 70% of transactions were fairly small (averaging USD 24 700) and accounted for only 2% of the total concessional finance, while the largest transactions, of USD 7.5 million on average, (the top 10%, or 10th decile) made up 87% of total concessional finance. Bilateral and multilateral providers display a similar pattern, with an aggregated average transaction amount of USD 1.0 million for multilateral providers and USD 0.9 million for bilateral providers.

Notes

1. Papua New Guinea is assessed at a "low" risk of debt distress; Comoros, Guinea-Bissau, Guyana, Solomon Islands, Saint Lucia, Timor-Leste, Tonga and Vanuatu are assessed at a "moderate" risk of debt distress; Cabo Verde, Dominica, Haiti, Kiribati, Maldives, Marshall Islands, Micronesia, Samoa, Sao Tome and Principe, Saint Vincent and the Grenadines and Tuvalu are assessed at a "high" risk of debt distress and Grenada is currently "in debt distress".

2. These are non-concessional flows to developing countries that include export credits and have a primarily commercial motive.

3. To date, the survey includes more than 110 private philanthropic foundations. www.oecd.org/dac/stats/beyond-oda-foundations.htm.

4. In line with OECD Development Assistance Committee statistics, concessional finance is defined as grants and concessional loans from both bilateral providers and multilateral providers that meet the ODA definition.

5. This is calculated using the 2015 GNI figures from the World Bank for the 32 SIDS for which data are available. The Cook Islands, Montserrat and Niue are therefore excluded. Where 2015 GNI figures are not available, the most recent year is substituted. 2011 data were used for Cuba, and 2014 data were used for Papua New Guinea and Vanuatu. Concessional finance figures are from the Credit Reporting System in 2015 prices.

6. "All developing countries" refers to all official development assistance (ODA)-eligible countries, as per the DAC List of ODA Recipients (OECD DAC, 2014b). For more details, please refer to: www.oecd.org/dac/stats/daclist.htm.

7. This figure only includes providers of concessional finance that report data to the OECD Creditor Reporting System (OECD, no date a). It excludes amounts from important providers to SIDS, such as China, Venezuela and Chinese Taipei, for which comparable statistical data are not available.

8. Timor-Leste provided financing to Cabo Verde, Guinea-Bissau and Vanuatu in this period.

9. For more information, please refer to the Small States Roadmap: http://pubdocs.worldbank.org/en/982421496935264348/Small-States-Roadmap.pdf#zoom=70.

10. The following eight global funds are considered here: the Adaptation Fund, the Climate Investment Funds, the Global Alliance for Vaccines and Immunization, the Global Environment Facility, the Global Fund, the Global Green Growth Institute, the Green Climate Fund and the UN Peacebuilding Fund.

11. While these providers are referred to as 'emerging', many of them have a long tradition providing support to other countries.

12. Please note that the comparability of these figures with ODA figures has not been verified. Therefore, the level of concessionality and the developmental nature of this financing may be different than those required to meet the ODA definition.

13. Azerbaijan, Estonia, Israel, Kazakhstan, Kuwait, Lithuania, Romania, Russia, Thailand, Timor-Leste, Turkey and United Arab Emirates.

14. In other words, 10 out of the 16 DAC members that replied to the Survey questionnaire regarding OECD DAC members' policies and practices supporting SIDS conducted in 2016.

15. Concessional finance includes three main types of finance: grants and equity, loans, or debt relief.

16. General budget support is excluded from the analysis in this section, which only considers sector-specific support.

17. Another indication of this comes from more evenly distributed support across activities in the Caribbean SIDS (1.86% median share to each sector) and AIMS SIDS (1.87% to each sector), compared to 0.74% in the Pacific SIDS.

18. When providers report their activities in the Creditor Reporting System database, they use gender markers, indicating whether an activity had a primary or significant gender component, or no gender component at all. For the methodology, please refer to: www.oecd.org/dac/gender-development/dac-gender-equality-marker.htm.

19. This comprises concessional finance allocated to regional projects in the Caribbean and the Pacific only.

20. These two projects were approved in 2017 and do not appear in the OECD Creditor Reporting System database yet.

21. 2013 OECD DAC Survey on Multilateral Allocations. For a broader discussion on the opportunities and costs of earmarked funding, please refer to OECD (2015).

22. For reference, the top five providers of concessional finance for climate and disaster resilience accounted for a similar, yet slightly larger share: 61% (OECD-World Bank, 2016).

23. Monserrat is a British Overseas Territory.

24. These are Maldives and Guinea-Bissau, where the top three providers accounted for 43% and 45% of total 2012-15 financing.

25. Fiji, Kiribati, Nauru, Papua New Guinea, Samoa, Solomon Islands, Timor-Leste, Tonga, Tuvalu and Vanuatu.

26. The analysis throughout this report is based on disbursed amounts. This section on fragmentation, however, uses amounts committed based on the consideration that committing funds is more transaction-heavy than disbursements, which often do not require further negotiation and transactions. The concessional finance committed to SIDS in 2012-15 was slightly higher (USD 19.8 billion) than disbursements.

27. There are some differences in the way providers structure their aid commitments and in the number of transactions they report to the OECD Creditor Reporting System. Therefore, for most providers the number of transactions was identified through the "project identification number". For other donors it was identified through the long or short "project description" (i.e. Caribbean Development Bank, Global Green Growth Institute, OPEC Fund, UNAIDS, UNFPA, UNHCR and WHO). The transactions considered here exclude all donor costs ("imputed student costs", "refugee in donor countries", "administrative costs" and "development awareness"), "debt relief" and "scholarships".

References

Dornan, M. and P. Brant (2014), "Chinese Assistance in the Pacific: Agency, Effectiveness and the Role of Pacific Island Governments", *Asia & the Pacific Policy Studies*, vol. 1, no. 2, pp. 349–363, Wiley Publishing Asia Pty Ltd and Crawford School of Public Policy at The Australian National University, http://onlinelibrary.wiley.com/doi/10.1002/app5.35/pdf.

Horscroft, V. (2014), "Public Sectors in the Pacific Islands: Are They 'Too Big' and Do They 'Crowd Out' the Private Sector?" *World Bank Policy Research Working Paper* 7102, World Bank Group, Washington D.C., http://documents.worldbank.org/curated/en/986481468098052675/pdf/WPS7102.pdf.

IMF (2017), *List of Low Income Countries' Debt Sustainability Analysis for Poverty Reduction and Growth Trust-Eligible Countries*, International Monetary Fund, Washington D.C., https://www.imf.org/external/Pubs/ft/dsa/DSAlist.pdf (accessed in July 2017).

IFAD (2014), *IFAD's approach in Small Island Developing States: A global response to island voices for food security*, United Nations International Fund for Agricultural Development, Rome, www.ifad.org/documents/10180/127f9ca4-420f-41c9-a21d-5f511d6d01d0.

OECD (2016), *Global Private Philanthropy for Development*, OECD, Paris, www.oecd.org/dac/financing-sustainable-development/development-finance-standards/beyond-oda.htm.

OECD (2015), *Multilateral Aid 2015: Better Partnerships for a Post-2015 World*, OECD Publishing, Paris, http://dx.doi.org/10.1787/9789264235212-en.

OECD (2013), *Identification and Monitoring of Potentially Under-Aided Countries,* OECD, Paris, www.oecd.org/dac/financing-sustainable-development/Identification%20and%20Monitoring%20of%20Potentially%20Under-Aided%20Countries.pdf.

OECD (no date a), *Creditor Reporting System* (database), OECD, Paris, https://stats.oecd.org/Index.aspx?DataSetCode=CRS1.

OECD (no date b), *International Development Statistics* (database), OECD Paris, www.oecd.org/dac/financing-sustainable-development/development-finance-data.

OECD DAC (2014a), *DAC High Level Meeting Communiqué* from the DAC High Level Meeting, 16 December 2014, OECD, Paris, www.oecd.org/dac/OECD%20DAC%20HLM%20Communique.PDF.

OECD DAC (2014b), *DAC List of ODA Recipients*, OECD, Paris www.oecd.org/dac/financing-sustainable-development/development-finance-standards/daclist.htm.

OECD-World Bank (2016), *Climate and Disaster Resilience Financing in Small Island Developing States*, OECD Publishing, Paris, http://dx.doi.org/10.1787/9789264266919-en.

UN (2015), *Addis Ababa Action Agenda,* from the Third International Conference on Financing for Development, 27 July 2015, United Nations, New York, http://undocs.org/A/RES/69/313.

UNDP (2017a), *China's South-South Cooperation with Pacific Island Countries in the Context of the 2030 Agenda for Sustainable Development*, United Nations Development Programme, New York, www.cn.undp.org/content/china/en/home/library/south-south-cooperation/1--china_s-south-south-cooperation-with-pacific-island-countries.html.

UNDP (2017b), *Financing the SDGs in the Pacific Islands: Opportunities, Challenges and Ways Forward*, United Nations Development Programme, New York, www.undp.org/content/undp/en/home/librarypage/poverty-reduction/financing-the-sdgs-in-the-pacific-islands--opportunities--challe.html.

UNDP and UNOHRLLS (2015), "Financing for Development and Small Island Developing States: A Snapshot and Ways Forward" *UNDP & UN-OHRLLS Discussion Paper,* June 2015, United Nations Development Programme, New York, https://sustainabledevelopment.un.org/content/documents/2181(UNDP%20&%20OHRLLS%202015)

%20Financing%20for%20development%20and%20SIDS%20A%20snapshot%20and%20ways%20forward.pdf.

World Bank (2017), *International Debt Statistics* (database), World Bank Group, Washington D.C., https://data.worldbank.org/data-catalog/international-debt-statistics.

World Bank (2016a), *Engagement with Small States: Taking Stock,* World Bank, Washington D.C. www.worldbank.org/en/country/smallstates/publication/engagement-with-small-states-taking-stock.

World Bank (2016b), *Migration and Remittances Factbook*, World Bank Group, Washington, D.C., https://openknowledge.worldbank.org/bitstream/handle/10986/23743/9781464803192.pdf?sequence=3.

World Bank (2015), *Grenada: A Nation Rebuilding. An assessment of reconstruction and economic recovery one year after Hurricane Ivan*, World Bank Group, Washington, D.C., http://siteresources.worldbank.org/INTDISMGMT/Resources/grenanda_rebuilding.pdf.

World Bank (n.d.), *World Development Indicators* (database), World Bank Group, Washington D.C., https://data.worldbank.org/data-catalog/world-development-indicators.

Further reading

IMF (2013), *Caribbean Small States: Challenges of High Debt and Low Growth*, International Monetary Fund, Washington D.C., https://www.imf.org/external/np/pp/eng/2013/022013b.pdf.

Khor, H., R. Kronenberg, & P. Tumbarello (2016), *Resilience and Growth in the Small States of the Pacific, USA*, International Monetary Fund, Washington D.C., http://dx.doi.org/10.5089/9781513507521.071.

Laframboise, N., and B. Loko (2012), "Natural Disasters: Mitigating Impact, Managing Risks" *IMF Western Hemisphere Department Working Paper*, Washington D.C., https://www.imf.org/external/pubs/ft/wp/2012/wp12245.pdf.

PIFS (2016), *Developing a "Regional Finance Facility" for the Pacific: From Concept to Design*, Pacific Islands Forum Secretariat, Suva, www.forumsec.org/resources/uploads/attachments/documents/Developing_a_Regional_Finance_Facility_for_the_Pacific_(Report)_webCopy.pdf.

PIFS (2015), *Five Years of Improving Development Effectiveness,* Pacific Islands Forum Secretariat, Suva, www.forumsec.org/resources/uploads/memberdocs/Final_2015_tracking.pdf.

PIFS (2009), *The Cairns Compact*, Pacific Islands Forum Secretariat, Suva, www.forumsec.org/pages.cfm/strategic-partnerships-coordination/pacific-principles-on-aid-effectiveness/forum-compact/cairns-compact-1.html?printerfriendly=true.

World Bank (2017), *Small States: A Roadmap for World Bank Group Engagement*, World Bank Group, Washington, D.C., http://pubdocs.worldbank.org/en/982421496935264348/Small-States-Roadmap.pdf#zoom=70.

Chapter 3. Innovations and good practices for a new way to respond to the complexity of development co-operation in small island developing states

Small island developing states (SIDS) face a set of specific development challenges and vulnerabilities that make achieving sustainable development particularly difficult. To help SIDS tackle those challenges and embark on a path of sustainable development, development co-operation needs to work better for SIDS. To this end, this chapter presents a set of recommendations that build on examples of innovative solutions and good practices of development co-operation with SIDS in relation to: (i) enhancing access, modalities and partnerships; (ii) using concessional resources innovatively to leverage more resources for development, including through support to unlock greater domestic resources, to create more fiscal space and to incentivise private investments; (iii) channelling resources to priority areas that could foster growth and development and move, at least some SIDS, closer to self-sufficiency: low-carbon investments and climate resilience, the blue economy, and stronger private and trade sectors.

As discussed in Chapter 2, concessional finance remains a vital source of financing for many SIDS but it is strongly concentrated on a few providers and few recipients, scattered across small projects, and insufficiently used to address some of the major vulnerabilities that hinder further development in SIDS, such as climate vulnerabilities, lack of fiscal space, and limited private sector development. In addition, while SIDS could see increases in climate-related finance in the near future (mainly because of resources from the Green Climate Fund), additional increases in concessional finance remain more uncertain, including because of the current absorption capacity constraints. Therefore, to maximise the effectiveness of these resources it will be essential to: (i) enhance access, modalities and partnerships; (ii) use concessional resources innovatively to leverage more resources for development, including through support to unlock greater domestic resources, to create more fiscal space and to incentivise private investments; (iii) channel resources to priority areas that could foster growth and development and move, at least some SIDS, closer to self-sufficiency: low-carbon investments and climate resilience, the blue economy, and stronger private and trade sectors.

By focusing on these three areas, this chapter recalls some of the key challenges identified in Chapters 1 and 2 and illustrates positive examples of actions and initiatives undertaken by the international community to tackle them. While these measures are often country specific and their applicability may be more challenging in some SIDS than in others, there is a need to invest more to replicate and scale them up. Building on these positive examples, the chapter provides a matrix of recommendations to the international communities for a more tailored and more effective approach to development co-operation in SIDS, to break a negative cycle of low growth and high vulnerability and to chart the course to prosperity for their people and their environments (Figure 3.1).

Figure 3.1. Recommendations for better financing to small island developing states

Enhancing access, modalities and partnerships for concessional finance

- Building capacity and technical assistance
- Encouraging partnerships with a larger range of actors, including through triangular co-operation
- Expanding the evidence base and policy dialogue around the complexity of development in SIDS

Using concessional finance innovatively to leverage additional resources

- Improving access to new and existing financing, including climate finance and private sector investments
- Fostering domestic resource mobilisation
- Preserving debt sustainability

Channelling resources to priority areas

- Transitioning to low-carbon, climate-resilient economies
- Fostering new growth opportunities such as the blue economy
- Supporting private sector development, enhancing trade and attracting private finance

3.1. Enhancing access, modalities and partnerships for concessional finance

Providers can do much to improve the ways and modalities in which they extend concessional finance so as to maximise impact. Here three specific areas were selected where good practices and innovative approaches were found that could be replicated or further expanded: (i) building capacity and increasing absorptive capacity, (ii) using modalities that foster mutual learning and crowd-in additional resources, such as triangular co-operation; and (iii) fostering a reflection on the global architecture of concessional finance for SIDS.

For SIDS it will be essential to release capacity constraints and enhance the ability to mobilise, manage and spend financial resources from a wider array of sources to decrease dependence on a single provider. This could be done through long-term approaches to capacity development, innovative uses of technology, and a careful assessment of which functions could be performed at a regional level, which will need to remain at the national level, and which could be outsourced privately. Using pooled mechanisms to reduce transaction costs and modalities could also help to strengthen national capacities.

Partnerships with a larger set of stakeholders will bring a wider set of perspectives and approaches to the complexity of development in SIDS and could provide an alternative source of financing as SIDS move to higher levels of national per capita income. Collaboration between "traditional" and "emerging" donors could also be instrumental to in reducing transaction costs and enhancing policy dialogue in SIDS. Positive examples of multi-donor trust funds used to channel resources, such as the one established in Nauru with contributions from Australia and Chinese Taipei, could be replicated in other SIDS.

While several SIDS have flagged the negative consequences of losing access to concessional finance after graduating from bilateral or multilateral financing, no exhaustive analysis has been conducted on the real impacts of losing access to these sources. More evidence and policy dialogue needs to be fostered to understand the impacts of different graduation processes on financing landscapes and growth opportunities in order to maintain development gains as countries transition through different income levels and development phases, i.e. the "development continuum".

3.1.1. Building capacity and increasing absorptive capacity

Recommendations - Finding long-term solutions to critical capacity constraints:

- Managing external resources more effectively and tapping into a larger array of resources will require investing in strengthening internal capacities and releasing absorption-capacity constraints. A more systematic approach to national capacities – including through assessing which functions could be performed at a regional level which could be outsourced privately, and which will need to remain at the national level – could be beneficial. Innovative approaches and technologies could help tailor more sustainable capacity building approaches to the specific context of SIDS.
- Because of the acute capacity constraints in SIDS, using pooled mechanisms to reduce transaction costs and modalities to strengthen national capacities is even more urgent than in other developing countries. The revival of budget support in some SIDS, especially in the Pacific, is welcome and could be further expanded to other countries – especially in other SIDS where the use of budget support is currently limited. Attention should be paid to the new 'conditionalities' attached to budget support, to ensure that SIDS governments preserve ownership.

Domestic capacity is inherently limited in SIDS, affecting all areas and the full spectrum of institutional needs. Low numbers of qualified staff working in key capacities – especially procurement, financial management and project management – particularly constrain the ability of SIDS to access and manage different sources of concessional finance, and limit their absorption and implementation capacity. SIDS often record significant undisbursed balances and limited capacities also constrain access to the full range of available sources, including to some large global funds. Therefore, actions to effectively enhance SIDS' ability to absorb currently available resources, as well as new flows, will be critical.

Box 3.1. Lessons from New Zealand's support for public financial management reform in the Pacific

The New Zealand Aid Programme has for many years worked closely with partner governments and other development partners to strengthen public financial management (PFM) systems in the Pacific. PFM systems in the Pacific function very differently from the comprehensive systems that larger developing countries use. For example, evidence suggests that limited human resource pools, driven by competition from employers outside the public service, create severe constraints for Pacific countries to achieve higher PEFA scores, which are an internationally established tool for assessing the status of public financial management[1]. These differences mean that an effective reform programme requires considerable discipline to:

- *Prioritise* a few key reforms that can be effectively implemented and sustained in a capacity constrained environment.
- *Look* beyond capacity building to substitute or regionally supplement key technical skills that are hard to recruit and retain in the region.
- *Accept* that some reforms that could drive higher PEFA scores in the short-run are not sustainable or necessary in the Pacific context.

A recent study of PFM reform experiences in Kiribati and Tonga found that reforms that were well targeted, consistent with capacity, and enjoyed political support were more likely to achieve their objectives (Bontjer et al, 2016). Where reforms were not prioritised or contextualised, they were either not successfully achieved or were enacted and not implemented. A key recommendation in the study was to ensure that implementation approaches reflected Pacific realities. The study suggested the following approaches to working within the Pacific SIDS context:

- Altering the technical assistance model to focus on implementation and outcomes (e.g. better public services) rather than the policy or legislative process.
- Ensuring that technical assistance plans account for the longer implementation timeframes that are required in the Pacific.
- Allowing consultants greater leeway to change approaches and outputs when contracted to support a particular reform.
- Greater use of financing linked to direct service delivery outcomes as a way of complementing financing linked to regulatory and legislative policy reform.
- Considering regional capacity sharing for certain PFM functions that are hard to maintain in an individual country context.

The challenges that the Pacific faces in reforming its public financial management systems are not uncommon to those of other SIDS. Greater discipline in tailoring global reform best practices to the context of SIDS could significantly increase the effectiveness of PFM reforms in delivering better public services and development outcomes in small island developing states.

Source: Adapted from Government of New Zealand data

Concessional finance providers sometimes put in place temporary solutions to fill human resource gaps with a view to increasing the speed of delivery and achieving results in the short term. While in some of the smallest SIDS technical assistance could be expected in perpetuity, innovative, longer term solutions for supporting national capacities and expertise have also been tested and implemented. The section below presents three selected examples of development co-operation initiatives aimed at enhancing capacities in SIDS. They relate to: (i) improving public financial management (Box 3.1); (ii) facilitating direct access to finance from the Green Climate Fund; and (iii) strengthening statistical capacity through regional approaches.

Readiness support to enhance access to Green Climate Fund resources

The many existing global climate funds are likely to contribute to an increasing share of financing for SIDS. However, at present, these resources are not delivering at full scale, with only relatively small volumes reaching SIDS. Access to these resources is limited by the complex array of accreditation procedures, application processes and fiduciary requirements which generally exceed SIDS' limited administrative and technical capacities.

The lack of domestic capacity to directly access these global funds leads to reliance on intermediary accredited agencies, including the World Bank, United Nations agencies and other multilateral development banks. These intermediary agencies are often the main channels through which SIDS can obtain financing from vertical funds, and generally also provide the technical and co-ordination support needed to implement the related projects. However, the large transaction costs involved in the small scale of SIDS project proposals can weaken prioritisation by multilateral intermediaries and thus result in fewer opportunities for funding. Because of the implementation charges applied, intermediation comes at a cost (up to 8% of the project value as a fee) reducing the overall resources reaching the beneficiary country.

Therefore, more than for other developing countries, a trade-off exists for SIDS between investing in national capacities to gain direct access versus relying on an intermediary agency. Direct access confers greater ownership of the activities, builds domestic capacity and systems, and ensures that the maximum amount flows to the beneficiary government. However, for SIDS with acute capacity constraints, the resources required to engage with the fund directly can be prohibitive and make partnering with an accredited entity faster and more cost effective.

To facilitate greater access to financing from these global funds, priority should be given to adopting streamlined application procedures that are proportionate to the domestic capacities of SIDS. At the same time, the international community could also do more to help SIDS meet the application standards. In this respect, the actions taken by the Green Climate Fund to scale up its funding for readiness programmes and support enhanced direct access modalities represent positive steps.

The Green Climate Fund is currently the largest existing global fund. It aims to constitute a major source of financing for SIDS and other developing countries, with a target to disburse at least 50% of its adaptation resources to least developed countries, SIDS and African countries. Technical capacity, fiduciary compliance and the resources required to become an accredited entity to the Green Climate Fund, however, are often beyond the scope of many developing countries, especially those with such small civil services and limited expertise as SIDS.

The Green Climate Fund provides "readiness support" to help countries engage with the fund and meet its requirements to access finance. These resources, provided as grants up to USD 300 000, aim to address specific gaps in National Designated Authority[2] programming to comply with the application requirements to access the Green Climate Fund. To date, the Green Climate Fund has disbursed readiness finance totalling USD 10.3 million to 59 countries, of which two thirds was allocated to SIDS, least developed countries and African states. At present 14 SIDS have drawn on these resources; the experiences of Vanuatu and Antigua and Barbuda and described in Box 3.2.

In addition, the Commonwealth Secretariat has developed the Climate Finance Access Hub, a capacity building initiative to build long-term capacity within National Designated Authorities. Long-term technical advisers embedded within National Designated Authorities provide both strategic and hands-on support to address capacity gaps limiting access to climate finance. In many SIDS, this support focuses on drawing down readiness support, and addressing financial management and compliance gaps. The first technical adviser was deployed in Jamaica in April 2017. New Zealand is supporting Pacific island countries to access Green Climate Fund funding in several ways. In 2016, it initiated the Green Climate Fund "Technical Assistance for Pacific Access" programme which supports the development of successful Green Climate Fund proposals. New Zealand has also partnered with the Green Climate Fund Secretariat to deliver a series of national awareness raising workshops in Kiribati, Niue, Tonga, and Tuvalu; and is providing USD 1.1 million over three years to the Secretariat of the Pacific Regional Environment Programme to support it in its role as an accredited entity to the Green Climate Fund.

Box 3.2. Lessons from Green Climate Fund readiness funding: the experience of Vanuatu and Antigua and Barbuda

The Government of Vanuatu is working with Secretariat of the Pacific Regional Environment Programme (SPREP) as an implementing entity to develop a project around Climate Information Services for Resilient Development. As part of this, the Green Climate Fund allocated USD 157 000 over nine months up until April 2017. The activity gathered data in order to better understand the island's Climate Information Service needs and will now be used to inform the development of a proposal to the Green Climate Fund. This process included several workshops and consultations to hear from a range of national and sub-national stakeholders, government officials, planners and policy developers to better understand needs. This programme is now a leading example of a project that has gone through the entire project cycle. The subsequent project Climate Information Services for Resilient Development Planning in Vanuatu was approved at the fifteenth board meeting with a value of USD 27 million including a USD 23 million grant from the Green Climate Fund.

The Government of Antigua and Barbuda accessed readiness support directly. This support totalled USD 300 000 and lasted 12 months. It was used to strengthen the NDA and develop a country programme in order to submit a full funding proposal. Specifically, the money funded two inter-ministerial consultations, a policy adviser, a financial expert, a consultant specialised in Knowledge Information Management System development, a web developer to establish an online knowledge portal and three internal policy guides on operations. The NDA is well advanced in preparations to submit an application and to co-ordinate with other countries in the eastern Caribbean on a project proposal for enhanced direct access.

The value of regional approaches for statistical development in SIDS

For most SIDS maintaining a fully functional national statistical system can be challenging. Yet, such systems are crucial to delivering the data required to assess the effectiveness of government programmes and policies, and monitor progress against development goals. A number of initiatives have been launched in both the Caribbean and Pacific regions to foster both stronger regional statistics and the development of national statistical systems. These initiatives aim to address the key constraints inhibiting progress in developing better statistical capacities in SIDS, including:

- Human resource shortfalls regarding professional and/or technical competence across key thematic statistical areas, insufficient numbers of statisticians in national statistics offices to work on a broad spectrum of statistics and lack of statistical staff in other government agencies
- lack of sustainable investment by governments and donors in the continuous development of statistical systems
- institutional weaknesses arising from outdated statistical legislation, weak statistical leadership, ineffective co-ordination across the system and absence of a strong statistical culture promoting the use of statistics in decision making
- lack of political recognition and support for statistics as a tool for policy making, development management and governance.

Strong regional statistical co-operation is valuable for both regions and countries. It is helping diminish the cost of a comprehensive national statistical system, expand the range of regionally – and, to some extent, globally – comparable statistical measures, and improve the quality of the data generated by national statistical systems as countries adhere to regional statistical standards and methods. It has also facilitated access to technical assistance on a range and mix of skills essential in a national statistical system; made available predictable and sustained funding from development partners for major statistical operations (e.g. surveys and censuses); and provided opportunities for establishing relevant statistical infrastructures in countries with limited resources. Finally, it complements statistical operations in countries with limited capacity.

These achievements were possible through the following actions and steps:

- Establishment of regional statistical centres and/or programmes in the respective regional bodies: the Caribbean Community (CARICOM) for the Caribbean and the Pacific Community for the Pacific provide technical support to countries, and facilitate pan-regional co-ordination of statistical programmes and activities. These centres and programmes have helped strengthen national statistical systems and contributed to the compilation and harmonisation of regional statistics. The CARICOM Secretariat has a Regional Statistics Programme, while the Pacific Community Secretariat has a Statistics Development Division, both provide statistical capacity building support to national statistical systems; an enabling environment for statistical development; and technical support on thematic concerns for their member states.
- Adoption of strategic frameworks to improve statistics in the medium and long term: the CARICOM Action Plan on Statistics and the Ten Year Pacific Statistics Strategy 2011-2020 contain short and long-term programmes in key statistical areas, which governments and donors use as a basis for resource allocation. This strategic approach to region-wide statistical development promotes a co-ordinated and harmonised approach to statistical financing.

- Institutionalisation of regional statistical governance and co-ordination mechanisms: regular convening of the Standing Committee of Caribbean Statisticians and the Pacific Statistics Steering Committee, comprising chief statisticians, provides statistical leadership, and sets direction and guidance on statistical development in the region.
- Development of regional standards, classifications and common methodologies: in line with international recommendations, allowing for more harmonised and comparable statistics in the region (e.g. Pacific Household Income and Expenditure Survey Questionnaire; Caribbean Common Census Framework and Pacific core Population and Housing Census modules; Pacific core statistical indicators and Caricominfo; CARICOM Model Bill; Pacific statistical classifications and standards on industrial, occupational, individual consumption according to purpose; etc.).

Similar approaches could be replicated for the benefit of SIDS in the Africa, Indian Ocean, Mediterranean and South China Sea (AIMS) region, under the leadership of an individual SIDS or of a regional institution, such as the African Union. In addition, innovative approaches and the use of new technologies could help further tailor capacity building approaches to the specific context of SIDS. Support could also be provided to make greater use of open data networks and observatories, which can increase efficiency and overcome capacity constraints.

3.1.2. Using modalities that foster mutual learning and crowd-in additional resources – stepping up triangular co-operation

Recommendations - encouraging partnerships with a larger range of actors, including through triangular co-operation:

- Triangular-co-operation initiatives can combine expertise and resources from a broad range of actors and encourage mutual learning. Partnerships with a larger set of stakeholders will bring a wider set of perspectives and approaches to the complexity of development in SIDS and could provide an alternative source of financing as SIDS transition through the development continuum. Collaboration between "traditional" and "emerging" donors could also be instrumental to reducing transaction costs and enhancing policy dialogue in SIDS. Positive examples of multi-donor trust funds used to channel resources, such as the one established in Nauru with contributions from Australia and Chinese Taipei, could be replicated in other SIDS contexts.
- Triangular co-operation can also be a means to foster greater policy dialogue. As development finance from China, Chinese Taipei, Russia, Venezuela and other non-DAC providers exceeds that from "traditional" providers in several individual SIDS, policy dialogue will need to be inclusive and look beyond traditional boundaries. China, India and other countries own the largest shares of the public debt of several SIDS. Given the increasing risk of debt distress, an inclusive reflection on possible measures to alleviate debt burdens should underpin development co-operation with SIDS.

As illustrated in Chapter 2, a broader set of sovereign states are establishing co-operation and partnerships with SIDS. Strengthening mutual learning and collaboration among a larger set of stakeholders will be fundamental for SIDS going forward, especially as access concessional finance decreases in line with higher national income and "graduation" in SIDS.

Triangular co-operation brings together expertise and resources from a diverse range of actors, creating opportunities to explore new ways of working together (Box 3.3). It provides SIDS with a relevant modality to tackle their development challenges (OECD, 2017a), by bringing together SIDS governments, Development Assistance Committee (DAC) members, other providers, such as China, and other middle-income countries (such as Mexico and Malaysia) to address shared development objectives. Triangular co-operation features in the 2030 Agenda for Sustainable Development as a powerful means of implementation.

Box 3.3. What is triangular co-operation?

Triangular co-operation is a dynamic partnership modality involving:

- a pivotal partner who shares its development solutions, knowledge, expertise, technology and other resources.
- a beneficiary partner who is the target of a development intervention, in line with its national development priorities and needs.
- a facilitating partner who helps connect countries and organisations in the form of a triangular partnership, and provides financial and/or technical support to the collaboration.
- These roles can evolve over time or projects. In some cases involving SIDS, the same country can play different roles. For instance, the Dominican Republic benefits from the experience of Chile and the United States in youth employment with support from the private sector. At the same time, the Dominican Republic is a pivotal partner in training Haitian agriculture and forestry professionals together with Japan.

According to responses to the OECD-DAC Survey on Triangular Co-operation (OECD, 2017a), in 2012-15, 92 triangular co-operation projects were implemented in SIDS. This represents one fifth of the over 450 reported triangular co-operation projects implemented worldwide in the same period (Table 3.1).[3]

Table 3.1. Small island developing states involved in triangular co-operation

SIDS involved in triangular co-operation projects	No. of Projects
Dominican Republic	37
Haiti	18
Cuba	14
Timor-Leste	13
Belize	9
Guyana, Jamaica, Kiribati, Samoa, Suriname	7
Fiji	6
Guinea-Bissau	5
Cabo Verde, Papua New Guinea, Sao Tome and Principe, Solomon Islands, Tonga	4
Cook Islands, Federated States of Micronesia, Marshall Islands, Seychelles, Vanuatu	3
Nauru, Palau, Tuvalu	2
Antigua and Barbuda, Dominica, Grenada, Mauritius, Montserrat, Niue, Saint Lucia	1
Total	**92**

Source: Responses to the OECD Survey on Triangular Co-operation (OECD, 2017a), http://dx.doi.org/10.1787/a8b14341-en.

The majority of the reported triangular co-operation projects with SIDS were implemented in the Caribbean (66%), followed by the Pacific (26%). Only 8% of the projects involved more than one region, unlike the prevailing global trends, where a larger share (18%) of reported triangular co-operation projects worldwide are implemented across different regions. Thus, there seems to be scope for a greater exchange of experiences between regions through triangular co-operation. Table 3.2 provides an example of a project between a country in Asia and one in the Caribbean.

Table 3.2. Triangular co-operation among Suriname, Malaysia and the Islamic Development Bank: joining forces to work on rice production

Project name:	Rice production
Countries/IOs:	Suriname, Malaysia, Islamic Development Bank
Objective:	To enable Suriname to achieve and maintain self-sufficiency in rice production and increase its high-quality rice exports.
Budget:	USD 6 million
Project period:	2016-19

Source: Responses to the OECD Survey on Triangular Co-operation (OECD, 2017a), http://dx.doi.org/10.1787/a8b14341-en.

The sectoral focus of triangular co-operation in SIDS mirrors the overall allocation of concessional finance (see Chapter 2), with the largest share of finance supporting the government and civil society sector (29%). Among the other top sectors, triangular co-operation in SIDS has the strongest focus on health (17%, compared to 13% in other developing countries) and food security (11%, compared to 5% in other contexts), followed by agriculture (8%) and business (7%). Despite the strong vulnerabilities of SIDS to climate events and natural disasters, only small shares are directed towards climate change mitigation and adaptation (3%) or disaster risk management (2%) (Figure 3.2).

Figure 3.2. Triangular co-operation with SIDS by sector

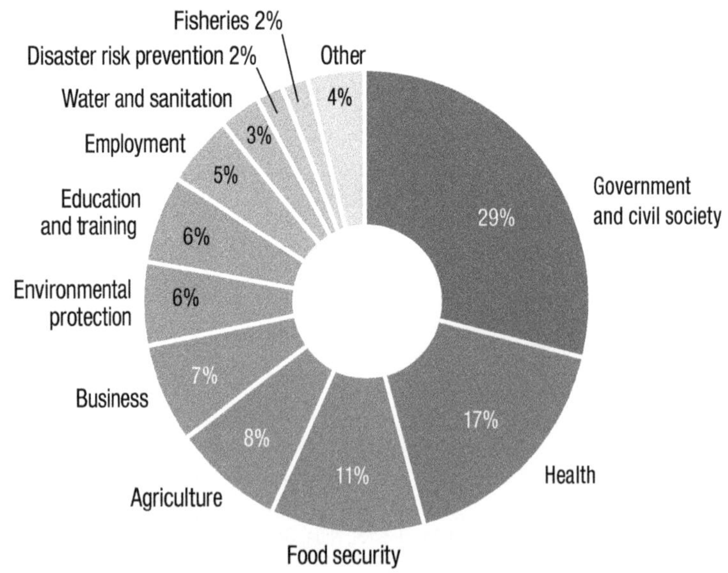

Source: Responses to the OECD Survey on Triangular Co-operation (OECD, 2017b) http://dx.doi.org/10.1787/a8b14341-en.

StatLink http://dx.doi.org/10.1787/888933646124

Respondents from SIDS reported engaging in triangular co-operation mainly through project-type interventions, such as the Te Mato Vai project between the Cook Islands, China and New Zealand[4] or the triangular co-operation between Cuba, Mexico and Germany[5] on renewable energies and energy efficiency. Governments or international organisations are the main actors involved in triangular co-operation with SIDS (73% of the reported projects). However, one quarter of the projects also involved academia, research institutions, civil society organisations, the private sector and other non-governmental organisations.

The most typical triangular co-operation project with SIDS (61% of the cases) involved two or more middle-income countries and one or more high-income countries or international organisations. The second most typical arrangement involved one or more high-income countries or international organisations, middle-income countries and least developed countries. In 16% of the projects involving SIDS, four types of actors were involved with high-income countries, international organisations jointly engaged in triangular co-operation projects with middle-income countries and least developed countries.

Recognising the growing prominence of this approach in the Pacific, as well as the importance of developing and sharing best practice, the Pacific Islands Forum Secretariat has established a trilateral peer review mechanism. Along with its development partners, Australia and New Zealand, the Secretariat will evaluate progress and identify bottlenecks in this type of development co-operation. The objective of the peer reviews is to assess: 1) the political directives and policies shaping co-operation among the Pacific Islands Forum members and their main development partners; 2) the alignment of development co-operation with national and sectoral development plans; 3) the monitoring and evaluation procedures, and the role of the Forum Island Compact in this process; and 4) sector-specific targets and indicators for the regular monitoring of behaviour changes in development partners.

All SIDS respondents to the Survey (OECD, 2017a) replied that receiving support to carry out South-South co-operation was their main motivation for engaging in triangular co-operation, followed by building capacity to engage and manage development co-operation, and learn and share experience with partners in South-South co-operation. Samoa also stated that Pacific countries are eager to learn from their peers through triangular co-operation.

Survey respondents reported that triangular co-operation allows them to combine different assets – e.g. specific expertise, and technology and cultural proximity – to maximise the benefits for all actors, especially developing countries facing similar challenges. For instance, "by combining the comparative advantages in terms of financing, technical expertise and local knowledge, China and other development partners could assist Pacific Island Countries in strengthening their capacities to minimize the negative impact of climate change" (UNDP China, 2017). Respondents also called for a more strategic use of triangular co-operation by pooling different actors' expertise and resources. In the long run, this evolution can lead to greater ownership by the actors involved, as well as involvement by other actors, and the scaling and joint implementation of activities designed to achieve both the Sustainable Development Goals and the actions agreed at the Third International Conference on Small Island Developing States, held in Samoa in 2014[6].

3.1.3. Better understanding the global architecture of concessional finance for SIDS

Recommendations - expanding the evidence base and policy dialogue around the complexity of development in SIDS

- Development partners could foster policy dialogue with SIDS at different steps of the income ladder to help identify development solutions that respond to the specific circumstances of SIDS.
- Some SIDS – especially microstates, which face more limited economic prospects – may present a structural need for sustained support from the international community. Some will soon see their free association status with larger economies terminated (as with the Marshall Islands and the Federated States of Micronesia ["Micronesia"] in 2023), and due consideration will need to be given to maintaining the development gains after this transition.
- SIDS that have recently graduated from least developed country status, such as Cabo Verde and Samoa, have quickly moved from a moderate to a high risk of debt distress. While several SIDS have flagged the negative consequences of losing access to concessional finance after graduating from bilateral or multilateral financing, no exhaustive analysis has been conducted on the real impacts of losing access to these sources. More evidence is needed to understand the impacts of different graduation processes on financing landscapes and growth opportunities in order to maintain development gains and ensure that co-operation instruments and approaches meet countries' needs as they transition through the "development continuum".

SIDS are confronted with a complex web of classifications and eligibilities

Globally, a wide array of sources of concessional finance exists, comprising OECD DAC members, non-DAC sovereign states and a multitude of multilateral sources. Especially for climate finance, which SIDS are highly in need of to build resilience to their high exposure to climate risks, a myriad funds exist, some more recent and some decades old, including the Adaptation Fund, the Green Climate Fund, the Global Environment Facility, the Least Developed Countries Fund, the Special Climate Change Fund and the Climate Investment Funds.

However, SIDS are confronted with an intricate web of eligibilities and requirements to access concessional finance, limiting their actual ability to tap into these resources. In fact, while in aggregate, SIDS received concessional finance from 72 providers in 2012-15 (see Chapter 2), the financing landscape for individual SIDS can be fairly different. Eligibility for concessional finance from most sources is primarily linked to the World Bank's income classifications, which identify low, middle or high-income countries based on gross national income (GNI) thresholds. However, actual eligibility rules vary depending on the institution, with different providers applying different income thresholds and exceptions, resulting in different financing landscapes for different SIDS and sometimes inconsistent treatment across SIDS (Table 3.3).

Table 3.3. The landscape of concessional financing to SIDS: a complex system of eligibilities

Small island developing states	ODA-eligible	Green Climate Fund	Global Fund	International Bank for Reconstruction and Development	IDA-eligible	IDA - small island economy exception	IDA - blend countries	Poverty Reduction Growth Trust-eligible	Poverty Reduction Growth Trust - small country exception	Poverty reduction Growth Trust - short term vulnerabilities exception	Poverty Reduction Growth Trust micro-state exception	Asian Development Bank	African Development Bank	Caribbean Development Bank	Inter-American Development Bank
Antigua and Barbuda	■	■		■										■	
Belize	■	■	■	■										■	
Cabo Verde	■	■	■			■	■		■				■		
Comoros	■	■	■		■								■		
Cook Islands	■	■													
Cuba	■	■	■												
Dominica	■	■	■			■	■				■			■	
Dominican Republic	■	■	■	■											
Fiji	■	■		■											
Grenada	■	■	■			■	■		■					■	
Guinea-Bissau	■	■	■		■			■					■		
Guyana	■	■	■				■		■					■	■
Haiti	■	■	■		■			■						■	■
Jamaica	■	■	■	■										■	
Kiribati	■	■	■			■		■				■			
Maldives	■	■	■			■				■					
Marshall Islands	■	■	■			■					■	■			
Mauritius	■	■	■	■											
Micronesia	■	■	■			■					■	■			
Montserrat	■	■												■	
Nauru	■	■	■	■								■			
Niue	■	■													
Palau	■	■	■	■								■			
Papua New Guinea	■	■	■				■	■				■			
Samoa	■	■	■			■					■	■			
Sao Tome and Principe	■	■	■			■		■					■		
Seychelles	■	■		■											
Solomon Islands	■	■	■		■			■				■			
Saint Lucia	■	■	■			■	■				■			■	
Saint Vincent and the Grenadines	■	■	■			■	■	■						■	
Suriname	■	■	■	■											
Timor-Leste	■	■	■				■		■			■			
Tonga	■	■	■			■					■	■			
Tuvalu	■	■	■			■					■	■			
Vanuatu	■	■	■			■			■			■			

Source: Authors

Low-income status – i.e. per capita income below USD 1 025 as of July 2016 – is the main eligibility criterion for financing from the International Development Association (IDA, the soft window of the World Bank Group), and four SIDS are eligible for IDA financing based on this criterion. However, recognising the limitations of income classifications, the World Bank has introduced a number of "exceptions" that allow countries exceeding the low income threshold to remain eligible for IDA financing. In total, 17 SIDS[7] are eligible for IDA financing through its Small Economy Exception or IDA blend terms. However, some SIDS – e.g. Nauru and Palau – do fall in some sort of "limbo", being assessed as too rich for accessing IDA financing and yet lacking the creditworthiness necessary for accessing the International Bank for Reconstruction and Development. Low-income status is also the main eligibility criterion to access concessional finance from most other international institutions; but these organisations also apply additional criteria or exceptions. The Asian Development Bank, for example, considers Nauru as fragile/vulnerable owing to its weak institutional and economic capacity, and thus eligible for its concessional financing.

Eligibility for ODA can play a role in determining bilateral donors' allocations to SIDS, but is not binding: some bilateral providers continue to allocate concessional finance to SIDS that have graduated from ODA.[8] Besides low-income countries, all middle-income countries (i.e. countries with a per capita GNI up to USD 12 745 in 2016) are eligible to receive ODA.[9] Only high-income countries are excluded.[10] However, the DAC List of ODA Recipients (OECD DAC, 2014) rules out exceptions, and one in four SIDS is expected to graduate out of ODA by 2025.

Several SIDS have lost access to multilateral concessional funding because they exceeded income thresholds, and some have moved in and out of eligibility over time. Among all developing countries, 44 have transitioned from low to middle-income states, and out of eligibility for concessional finance, since the 1960s. Several countries have transitioned in and out of the same income class, and 11 countries transitioned back from middle-income to low-income status. Many of these countries had graduated to middle-income status in the 1980s and then reverted to low-income status because of trends in global commodity prices or political instability. Fifteen countries also reverted from high-income to middle-income status between 1990 and 2015, three of them transitioning in and out at least twice. The SIDS in this group include: Antigua and Barbuda, Aruba, Barbados, American Samoa and Guam. Some oil-rich economies and other countries that experienced large external shocks also fall in this group (e.g. Bahrain, Equatorial Guinea, Saudi Arabia, Venezuela, Hungary, Korea and the Russian Federation).

The examples of "reverse graduation" illustrate that development is not linear, and that setbacks and shocks are often part of the process. More importantly for SIDS, their exposure to economic and climate vulnerabilities linked to some of their geophysical features do not diminish, even as per capita GNI levels rise. In SIDS where national income per capita chiefly increased because of growth in a tourism sector largely owned by foreign investors or due to financial services, with little positive impact on the living standards of large swaths of the population, governments will need to implement more inclusive growth policies. Yet the global systems of international financial regulations, international taxation and multinational corporate governance also need to be geared to supporting more inclusive growth policies in these countries. Moreover, most SIDS are in a different position than larger countries when it comes to finding alternative drivers for the economy, and many may continue to remain structurally dependent on transfers from other countries and the international community.

The assumption underlying the current global system of concessional finance that higher per capita income levels allow countries to mobilise domestic and international capital may hold for larger economies, but does not generally apply to SIDS (World Bank, 2017a). Strong vulnerabilities, stemming from their geophysical and economic features (see Chapter 1), often lead to narrow tax bases, limited cash surpluses, low levels of international reserves, inadequate capital formation and insufficient levels of domestic credit. Combined, these factors constrain the ability of SIDS to mobilise greater public and private domestic resources, and international private finance.

Opportunities and challenges of including vulnerability criteria to expand eligibility

Because of their special development case and their challenges in accessing concessional financing owing to their relatively high national income levels, SIDS have voiced on countless occasions – and at the highest levels of representation – the need for a co-ordinated effort by development partners to review the rules governing access to concessional finance and include vulnerability aspects in the criteria for eligibility to concessional funding. Already in 1994, through the Barbados Programme of Action (BPOA, 1994), SIDS had called for metrics integrating ecological fragility and economic vulnerability to supplement eligibility criteria and ensure access to additional resources. More recently, they renewed the call in the SIDS Accelerated Modalities of Action (SAMOA) Pathway (UN, 2014) adopted at the United Nations Third International Conference on Small Island Developing States in 2014, and again at the Small States Forum in 2015 and 2016.

Several technical and political challenges exist to supplementing eligibility criteria with a vulnerability metrics. Vulnerability is determined by a multitude of factors, including location, income, assets, access to resources, and institutional and legal systems. For several of these indicators, data pertaining to SIDS may be limited. Moreover, the choice of sub-indicators, as well as their weighting and aggregation, could yield different results, affecting country rankings and classifications. Several vulnerability indexes already exist; [11] whether they converge significantly is not clear. In addition, both DAC members and financing institutions have expressed concerns revising eligibility criteria could divert resources from the poorest countries. Any reforms of the eligibility criteria for concessional finance would need to be accompanied by a careful analysis of the incremental resources that would be reaching SIDS, as well as of the global winners and losers, and the potential need for additional accompanying measures. An important concern remains that revising eligibility criteria may result in insufficient resource allocations to SIDS, highlighting the need to explore other options to ensure that SIDS can access adequate levels of development finance. Ultimately, given a global context of limited concessional finance, it will be fundamental to focus on using existing resources more catalytically to attract additional flows from public and private sources. This is the focus of the next part of this chapter.

Box 3.4. Lessons from the World Bank-UNDP Inter-agency Task Force on the link between vulnerability and access to concessional finance

The OECD Development Co-operation Directorate is part of the Inter-Agency Task Force on the link between vulnerability and access to concessional finance established in 2016 by the World Bank's Small States Forum Secretariat and the United Nations Development Programme and also comprising the United Nations Office of the High Representative for Least Developed Countries, the United Nations Department of Economic and Social Affairs, the Commonwealth Secretariat, International Monetary Fund, Asian Development Bank, and Caribbean Development Bank.

The Task Force aims to review existing vulnerability measures, exploring how they could be implemented and examining whether their adoption would result in sufficient levels of concessional finance for upper middle and middle-income small states that are currently excluded from IDA eligibility. The Task Force will also explore innovative financing instruments and mechanisms to help SIDS gain access to development finance, including through innovative financing instruments such as insurance schemes (e.g. similar to the Caribbean Catastrophe Risk Insurance Facility, and the Pacific Catastrophe Risk Assessment and Financing Initiative), debt reduction instruments and approaches to leveraging climate finance (e.g. from the Green Climate Fund and the Global Environment Facility). Given a global context of limited concessional finance, it will be fundamental to focus on using existing resources more catalytically to attract additional flows from public and private sources.

3.2. Using concessional finance innovatively to leverage additional resources

Innovative uses of concessional finance have been tested in recent years, which have the potential to unlock more domestic resources, creating fiscal space, and crowd-in private investments. This section describes some of these approaches and suggests how the international community could enhance them and bring them to scale.

Domestic resource mobilisation could be enhanced through diaspora investment schemes; internationally co-ordinated fiscal reforms to expand tax coverage (especially to include high revenue-generating segments of the economy); and policies to reduce "leakages" from key sectors – especially tourism – and support linkages with other domestic sectors to effectively expand the taxable production base.

Debt relief opportunities, such as debt for nature swaps, and innovative countercyclical instruments, such as loans that automatically postpone debt servicing in the event of a major shock (e.g. through "hurricane" clauses) could help address debt sustainability and free resources for sustainable development including for the blue and green economy.

Innovative financial instruments, such as green and blue bonds, and blending arrangements to bring climate finance to scale, are promising sources of development finance for SIDS. However, none of these have been rolled out at scale in a SIDS context. Development partners can do much to support the design and implementation of these instruments, and back these new products with guarantees and co-financing schemes to encourage economic diversification and invest in building long-term resilience.

3.2.1. Mobilising greater domestic resources through stronger systems and tax reforms

Recommendations - Generating more domestic revenues for development:

- Enhanced tax collection systems can yield greater domestic revenues. To this end, providers could consider channelling greater support towards international initiatives, such as the Addis Tax Initiative and Tax Inspectors without Borders[12].
- Development partners could support fiscal reforms in SIDS aimed at expanding tax coverage, especially to include high revenue-generating segments of the economy and favour progressive taxation systems. Support could also be provided to assess the consequences of changes in the mix of tax policies, such as increases in already low corporate taxes or the removal of tax exemptions. Crucially, these country-specific interventions will need to be part of a wider global reform and co-ordinated across SIDS to avoid any race to the bottom.
- Tangible opportunities exist in many SIDS to expand the mobilisation of domestic resources through enhanced management of key sectors, including fisheries, tourism and natural resource extraction. Policies to reduce "leakages" from key sectors – especially tourism – and support linkages with other domestic sectors (e.g. food and agriculture, consumer goods and construction) could effectively expand the taxable production base. Support from the international community could also target curbing illicit, unreported and unregulated fishing, as a way to enhance domestic resources available for development.

As discussed in Chapter 1 and 2, SIDS tend to have small and erratic domestic revenues and the challenges associated with domestic resource mobilisation in developing countries are compounded in SIDS. SIDS with only a few major economic sectors have a narrower tax base; consequently, their revenue can be more vulnerable to external shocks, such as changes in international commodity prices or natural disasters. SIDS with a large informal sector also have more difficulty raising internal revenue. For instance, the agricultural sector is often more difficult to tax, owing to the large number of small businesses and prevailing informality in the sector.

Improving the efficiency of revenue collection and enlarging the tax base are essential efforts needed to increase the resources required to sustain progress towards the United Nations' Sustainable Development Goals. International providers allocated USD 19 million to this end in 2014-15,[13] reaching 16 SIDS. This support built the capacity of tax authorities, with a view to increasing domestic revenues. In 2015, the United States provided USD 3 million to the Treasury of Haiti to build the tax function. Similarly, New Zealand provided USD 4 million in 2014-15 to strengthen the Inland Revenue Department of the Solomon Islands, with a specific focus on compliance. These amounts represent only 0.19% of the total official development assistance to SIDS in this period, hinting at room for expanding investments in this area. Providers might increasingly look to support initiatives like the OECD-United Nations Development Programme's "Tax Inspectors without Borders", launched at the Financing for Development summit Conference in Addis Ababa in 2015, which provides tax audit support and builds capacity to help mobilise resources. Successful pilots have been carried out in larger developing countries, such as Colombia, which saw an increase in tax revenues from USD 3.3 million in 2011 to USD 33.2 million in 2014. While outreach has been carried out to several SIDS, to date, Jamaica is the only SIDS to have benefitted from this programme. Further support in this area might help more SIDS pass the 20% of GDP target for tax collection, which could grow revenues and fiscal space.

Some providers have been particularly active in supporting SIDS in the area of domestic resource mobilisation. For instance, Australia has provided technical assistance to the Kiribati Taxation Office to support the implementation of the value added tax (VAT) and automated tax system. Australia also helped the Vanuatu government identify potential new sources of revenue and improve its revenue administration. This support led to an estimated AUD 12.5 million increase in VAT receipts in 2014 and to improvements in the customs administration. In the Solomon Islands, Australia has provided support for revenue forecasts, as well as assistance to the national Customs and Excise Division to increase revenue and create a level playing field for the private sector, including through the introduction of an automated customs system.[14]

In addition, much can be done by the international community to enhance the management of industries that are key for revenue generation in SIDS. For instance, improving the management of fisheries, and curbing illicit, unreported and unregulated (IUU) fishing activities, could significantly enhance domestic revenues in many SIDS. With their vast economic exclusion zones (EEZs), considerable revenues accrue to SIDS both through direct fishing and, often more importantly, fishing licences. Therefore, IUU fishing activities not only negatively impact biodiversity and natural resource sustainability in SIDS, but also reduce domestic revenues, and challenge economic and social sustainability. At the same time, the cost of enhancing the monitoring, control and surveillance of the vast coastal and sea areas of SIDS EEZs can far exceed the capacities and resources of SIDS. The OECD is currently working to expand its database on policy frameworks and initiatives to combat IUU fishing and the related economic crimes, as a contribution to the follow-up and implementation of Sustainable Development Goal 14.4.[15] The aim is to provide policy makers with a better understanding of the remaining policy gaps and regulatory loopholes and help identify the tools that some countries could strengthen or introduce to bridge these gaps. Although, there is no "one size fits all" solution to IUU fishing, promoting greater transparency on existing procedures and legal systems as well as awareness of the tools at hand should help governments adopt better approaches. Improving the management of natural resources and mining resources would also help SIDS augment their domestic revenues. In this regards, a positive example is offered by Australia and other donors supporting the introduction of a mining tax framework in the Solomon Islands to improve tax generation.

In general, SIDS face important choices in developing an appropriate tax policy that can generate adequate government revenues and promote greater equity in the population's living standards, while at the same time entice investment, support competitive markets and economic growth. Several SIDS, recently adhered to the OECD-led tax information exchange system, recognising that a better way to attract foreign direct investment is to improve infrastructure, education, and health standards. Some SIDS do not collect income taxes, and the largest share of their tax revenues often accrues from non-progressive tax instruments, such as VAT. Corporate taxes are fairly low in many SIDS, and in some cases existing tax caps prevent governments from raising them. For example, the Cook Islands has a 25% tax-to-GDP cap imposed by the Manila Agreement, which set conditions for the debt restructuring undergone by the country in 1998.[16] Vanuatu's 2016 Revenue Reform and Modernisation Review, which builds on co-operation with Australia, provides a recent example of an attempt to address some of these trade-offs (Box 3.5).

Box 3.5. Lessons from the Vanuatu Revenue Reform and Modernisation Review

Vanuatu's 2016 Revenue Reform and Modernisation Review (Government of Vanuatu, 2017) highlighted that insufficient tax revenue is generated from VAT and import duties, and that the government misses out on a large source of potential revenue through low collection of, and compliance with, business taxes and fees. The review also noted that allocating tax revenues to public services, such as health and education, would stimulate economic growth and, in turn, help attract foreign direct investments. The review concluded by suggesting that Vanuatu raise corporate tax to 17% and introduce a personal income tax in a bid to move away from taxing consumption, which overly burdens the poor. While the approach presents potential challenges in terms of short-term slowdowns in economic activity, the reforms are a progressive attempt to address the domestic resource gap and donors could support similar projects.

3.2.2. Improving debt sustainability in SIDS, including through upstream actions

Recommendations - Implementing upstream and downstream measures to improve debt sustainability

- Counter-cyclical products include loans that automatically postpone debt servicing in the event of a major shock, as well as loans featuring "hurricane" clauses. They can help SIDS manage the risks of exogenous shocks and can limit their impacts on debt sustainability and economic health. Development partners could do more to further test and roll out these products, which can make SIDS' borrowing more climate-resilient and sustainable.
- Debt-for-nature swaps and other buy-back instruments could help alleviate severe debt burdens but their application remains limited to only one SIDS (Seychelles). Development partners can do much to support the use of these instruments, including by absorbing design and implementation costs.

As discussed in Chapter 2, debt remains a critical issue for many SIDS, compounded by their structural and environmental vulnerabilities, which can trigger crises. While debt-to-GNI ratios considerably decreased for the five SIDS that benefitted from the Heavily Indebted Poor Countries Initiative, many SIDS have seen their debt levels increase. This has been the case especially for upper middle-income SIDS, but also for SIDS that recently from least developed country status, such as Cabo Verde and Samoa. In 2012-15, the total ODA allocated to action relating to debt was USD 856 million – although nearly 97% of this went to just three SIDS, including 78% to Cuba.

Given the acute nature of the debt issues facing SIDS, and the fact that concessional finance only sporadically addresses them, alternatives approaches are required. Providers have little appetite for debt forgiveness to SIDS – especially those with higher incomes – in part because this does not address the underlying drivers of debt distress (Haque T. et al., 2016) and might create perverse incentives and induce moral hazard. However, providers have proactively sought to address debt sustainability with innovative financing instruments, including climate-related debt swaps. The international community should prioritise making greater use of these instruments and developing additional tools to address the drivers of debt distress. Development co-operation that does not address debt sustainability will not break the cycle of low growth and high vulnerability. Debt relief innovations, including Seychelles debt for nature swap, are presented in Box 3.6.

In the aftermath of major exogenous shocks SIDS often struggle to meet debt servicing costs. State-contingent debt instruments can help governments at a time like this. The main idea behind these instruments is to help sovereign states preserve policy space and mitigate the negative impact of shocks by indexing a product with a state variable like GDP – which is a proxy for a country's capacity to pay out or repay the product. State-contingent debt instruments can reduce the likelihood of debt distress and limit the impact of a shock on its capacity to finance public spending.

Counter-cyclical loans are also an ex ante instrument that can help SIDS in the aftermath of a disaster, by delaying repayments. As part of a broader risk management approach, counter-cyclical loans featuring a moratorium period following the triggering of an index linked to a disaster can provide a far more valuable injection of liquidity than ex post contributions. Well-designed products providing enhanced capacity to weather shocks will also help raise the creditworthiness of SIDS and foster investor confidence.

Box 3.6. Lessons from the debt for nature swap adopted by the Government of Seychelles and other debt swaps proposals

The debt for nature swap adopted in 2015 by the Government of Seychelles and its Paris Club[17] creditors could be replicated in other SIDS. This was the first debt-swap aimed specifically at ocean conservation and climate adaptation. As such, it allowed the Government of Seychelles to reduce immediate debt burdens while also increasing resources targeted toward climate action. Under this mechanism, providers used concessional finance to gradually write down the debt stock of Seychelles under the condition that funds otherwise used for debt service payments would be used for climate investments.

Several variations of debt swaps are presently under discussion, including through the joint Commonwealth Secretariat-World Bank "Multilateral Debt Swap for Climate Action" World Bank. (Commonwealth Secretariat, 2015). In this case, bilateral climate finance pledges would be used to buy back multilateral debt and to redirect debt payments to fund climate adaptation and mitigation. A pilot was initially planned in Jamaica, where high levels of external debt (103% of GDP) and debt-servicing costs (equating to 94% of the value of exports) combined with strict fiscal austerity measures imposed by the International Monetary Fund, effectively rule out any new borrowing, placing a major strain on public services. Given that less than half of Jamaica's public debt is multilateral privately owned, additional measures to those envisaged to write off multilateral debt could be required to effectively address debt sustainability. The Economic Commission for Latin America and the Caribbean also proposed a similar model, where resources from the Green Climate Fund would be used (ECLAC, 2017).

3.2.3. Making remittances work for development

Recommendations - Making remittances work for development:

- The international community could co-ordinate measures to reduce the cost of remittances, including through appropriate regulations and a development-focused forum where regulators could come together to share the perspectives of sending and receiving countries.
- Labour mobility programmes in the Pacific led to an increase in remittance flows, developed new skills for migrant workers and met a capacity gap for companies in the country. Providers could explore the scope for further expanding such schemes in the Pacific as well as in other SIDS regions.
- Diaspora investment schemes could be promising sources of development finance for SIDS, and yet have been rolled out at scale in a SIDS context. Development partners can do much to support the design and implementation of these instruments, and back these new products with guarantees and co-financing schemes.

As discussed in Chapter 2, remittances represented the largest flow of external finance to SIDS in 2012-15 (54%). While they are relatively stable – especially compared to the volatility of foreign direct investment – donors can do more to facilitate their flow as well as create more opportunities for migrant labour. The anti-money laundering and counter-terrorist financing (AML-CFT) regulations implemented in 2009 seek to strengthen the health of the global economy, but the ensuing loss of correspondent banking relationships has resulted in higher transaction costs for transferring remittances. There is a need for greater policy coherence in this area if the international community is to increase the flow of remittances and maximise their benefits to development.

Labour mobility schemes in the Pacific have proven beneficial for SIDS and larger partner countries

New Zealand operates a successful labour-mobility programme in the Pacific that has led to an increase in remittance flows, developed new skills for migrant workers and met a capacity gap for companies in the country.[18] The programme operates at a volume that makes a tangible contribution to receiving countries, but the success of the initiative depends upon adequate facilitation by the source country, and its efficacy decreases with distance from New Zealand. A recent analysis (Berkelmans and Pryke, 2016) concluded that expanding access to Australia's labour market could deliver significant development gains for SIDS. More specifically, permitting 1% of the Pacific region's population – an average intake of fewer than 3 000 people – to work permanently in Australia would result in greater benefit to the Pacific peoples by 2040 than Australia's current aid programme.

Experimenting with diaspora bonds to pool and channel remittances to larger development projects

Remittances are mainly used to smooth consumption expenditure and contribute to poverty alleviation. However, diaspora bond products might channel migrant savings towards businesses and development projects in SIDS. Diaspora bonds are not new – examples of countries where they have been issued successfully include Israel and India – but they have often been unsuccessful. Hence, some lessons should be considered before applying them in a SIDS context. In the Caribbean, a relatively large, educated diaspora that generally left to seek employment should be predisposed to invest in diaspora bonds, which essentially draw on patriotic sentiment. However, Caribbean SIDS might struggle to issue diaspora bonds because of their low or non-existent credit ratings, and prevailing perceptions of corruption and weak government effectiveness. Diaspora bonds also require good marketing; they should be flexible, and designed with the customers in mind. Poor credit ratings and a poor track record with debt would likely be a barrier to many migrants buying such products in the Caribbean, but the product could first be tested in a high-income small state, such as the Bahamas, or Trinidad and Tobago, and then replicated if successful. Donors can support SIDS in this effort by helping them improve their credit ratings, by bearing some of the costs of developing such products, and by issuing guarantees.

3.2.4. Financial innovations and approaches to mobilise private financing

Recommendations - Increasing resources for development through blending arrangements and other financial innovations:

- Official finance can be used more catalytically to de-risk investments or structure returns in a way to mobilise finance from the private sector through new and emerging blended finance arrangements.[19] Grants, guarantees, syndicated loans and other instruments can crowd in the private sector, especially in sectors with potential for positive returns. Providers can also contribute technical assistance, can absorb the costs of project preparation and help with the identification of a pipeline of bankable projects. Care should be taken, however, to avoid over-subsidising individual private sector players and privatising gains. Adherence to the OECD DAC (2017) 'Principles on Blended Finance' will be important[20] in this regard.
- Under the leadership of the Government of Grenada, a "fund-of-funds" is currently being developed as a means to pool concessional finance, catalyse public and private finance sources, and create a pipeline of bankable projects aggregating smaller country projects. This initiative could sensibly reduce transaction costs, alleviate capacity constraints and help address the financing gap SIDS face with respect to their intended nationally determined contributions and the 2030 Agenda for Sustainable Development.
- The country coverage of risk-transfer mechanisms, such as pooled insurance schemes, could be expanded to cover SIDS in all regions and innovative mechanisms could be developed to further reduce the cost of premiums and facilitate access to these products. Further use of contingency funds or contingent credit lines could also be encouraged.

Providers are increasingly using grants and other instruments, such as guarantees and syndicated loans, to deepen private sector involvement and leverage additional financing sources. The European Union has established specific blending mechanisms benefiting SIDS countries, such as the Caribbean Investment Facility and the Investment Facility for the Pacific. Through these facilities, grant finance from the European Development Fund envelope leveraged public and private resources, including from regional development banks and other organisations, contributing to several infrastructure projects in SIDS. A similar partnership exists in African SIDS, notably between the European Investment Bank and the African Development Bank. In the Pacific, the European Union supplemented blending through the Investment Facility for the Pacific for very small, debt-stressed SIDS that are unable to take investment loans. The Caribbean Investment Facility is open to 11 of the 13 Caribbean SIDS considered in this report,[21] as well as to 4 high-income (non-ODA eligible) Caribbean island states. The instrument financed nine projects between 2012 and 2015, with a grant allocation of EUR 68.6 million and a total investment cost of EUR 541 million, thus leveraging finance at an estimated 1:8 ratio (Latin America Investment Facility, 2015). While EUR 40 million of this amount is a direct allocation from the Facility, Guyana was able to include EUR 30.2 million from the overall country allocation received from the European Union. Two of these projects were at the regional level; there were two projects each in the Dominican Republic and Guyana, and one project each in Belize, Dominica and Suriname.

A new OECD survey provides new evidence on private amounts mobilised through official interventions

Overall, based on data collected through the 2016 OECD-DAC Survey on Amounts Mobilised from the Private Sector, (Benn et al, 2017), official development finance interventions mobilised USD 701 million of private resources for SIDS (USD 175 million on average per year) in 2013-15. The main leveraging instruments used were guarantees (44%, or USD 306 million), followed by syndicated loans (40%, or USD 285 million). Private finance was mostly mobilised by the International Finance Corporation's (IFC) interventions (43%), the United States (31%), and the Inter-American Development Bank (13%), followed by the European Union (6%), France (4%), the International Development Association (3%), Denmark (0.17%) and the African Development Bank (0.07%).

Figure 3.3. Official development finance mainly mobilised private financing in small island developing states with relatively larger and more developed markets

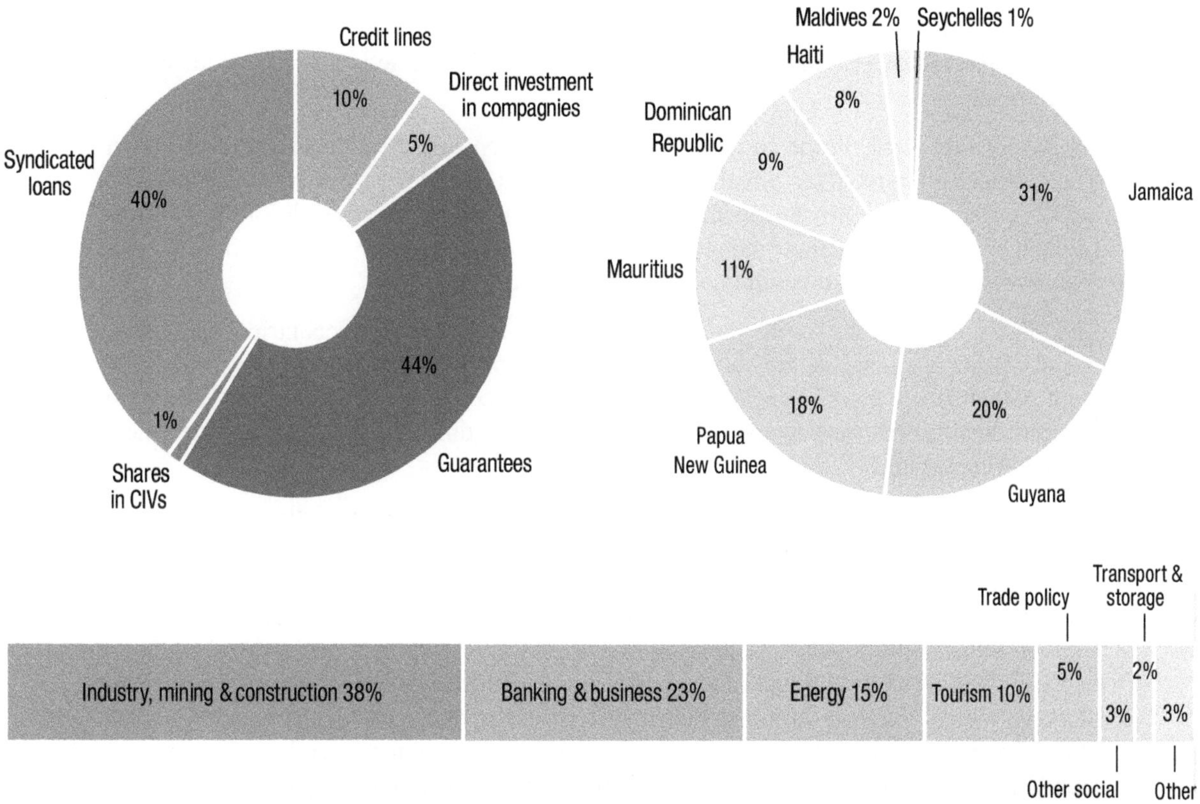

Note: Sectoral allocations of amounts mobilised by official development-finance interventions to SIDS, 2013-15.
Source: Data received for the OECD DAC Survey on Private Finance Mobilised through Official Development Assistance, (Benn et al. 2017) http://dx.doi.org/10.1787/8135abde-en.

StatLink http://dx.doi.org/10.1787/888933646143

As illustrated in Figure 3.3, official development finance leveraged private resources in only nine SIDS in 2013-15. SIDS with relatively larger domestic markets and fairly good private sector potential, such as Jamaica and Guyana, were the main beneficiaries of these funds, accounting together for 51% (USD 358 million) of the total in 2013-15. Private finance mobilised in Jamaica mainly targeted the energy sector (42%) and tourism (31%), while in Guyana the entire amount targeted the industry, mining and construction sector. Overall, main sectors where official development finance was used to mobilise private financing were: the industry, mining and construction (38%), banking and private business (23%), energy (15%) and tourism (10%), with the social sector receiving fairly limited support (3%).

With the exception of Papua New Guinea, no SIDS in the Pacific region benefitted from the use of official development finance instruments to mobilise private financing. As expressed by the key providers in the region (OECD, 2016), this reflects the difficulty of mobilising the private sector in this region through credit guarantees and other instruments, unless other more structural impediments to private investing are addressed.

Box 3.7. Lessons from Grenada's proposal on fast track fund-of-funds for small states

At the International Monetary Fund/World Bank Spring Meetings in April 2017, Grenada's Prime Minister Mitchell set out his vision for Grenada's chairing of the Small States Forum until October 2018 (the Forum includes all members of the World Bank with a population below 1.5 million). Prime Minister Mitchell highlighted Grenada's plans to work with partners to enable ambitious and innovative finance solutions for small states. This includes opportunities to advance national-scale transformative climate action, both for adaptation and mitigation.

As part of this work, Prime Minister Mitchell has proposed the establishment of a Fast Track "Fund of Funds" for Small States. This would seek to use some public funds to mobilise far greater private sector investment, and to overcome the long-standing challenges posed by fiscal constraints; market invisibility; perceived absence of sufficient scale investment opportunities; and perceived uncertainty and risk.

The Fast Track Fund will target catalytic investments for countries that seek transformational climate action, rather than project-by-project incremental change. In doing so, it will collaborate with development partners, and seek to boost small states' ability to harness existing financing channels, while at the same time opening up significant new financing opportunities.

With support from the World Bank's Small State Secretariat and other development partners, work has already started to advance the identification and development of commercially viable, climate-friendly, at-scale public and private investments. This work was first discussed during the Annual Meetings of the International Monetary Fund/World Bank in October 2017. After the Annual Meetings, efforts will continue to build business cases, as well as to market and facilitate transformative investments in the private capital markets. Work will also continue with development partners to (i) identify and access affordable public finance channels such as new IDA resources for several small states; (ii) identify, and where possible expand, existing international fiscal space initiatives to develop more ambitious climate action investment programmes; (iii) identify risk management and mitigation opportunities, in conjunction with development partners, through the use of insurance products.

The work builds from Grenada and other small states' participation in other collaborative efforts to advance ambitious climate action and broader sustainable development. Notably, in the run-up to COP22, Grenada participated in a high-level meeting with other development partners hosted at the OECD DAC in Paris to contribute to the efforts led by HE Mary Robinson, then the United Nations Secretary-General's Special Envoy on Climate Change and Mr Erik Solheim, then the Chair of the OECD DAC. These efforts enabled a dialogue on international climate finance between senior officials from OECD DAC members, least developed countries, SIDS and the V20 group of vulnerable countries. A report summarising issues raised by least developed countries, SIDS and the V20 – entitled "Escaping the Triple Trap" identified how least developed countries and SIDS might escape the "triple trap" of climate change, fossil fuel dependence and fiscal constraints through innovative financing. Importantly, the report identified specific finance building blocks to advance climate action. Grenada has pointed out that these building blocks have the potential to fast-forward many of the measures set out in the Small States Strategic Roadmap, and advance the Prime Minister's priorities before October 2018.

Source: Interview with the Government of Grenada.

Devising and adopting adequate risk transfer mechanisms

Risk transfer mechanisms are risk-management tools that involve the transfer of financial responsibility for some or all of the risk and any costs associated with the materialisation of that risk (OECD, 2017b). These mechanisms include insurance and reinsurance contracts, catastrophe bonds, contingent credit facilities and reserve funds as part of risk transfer from governments to financial markets.

The use of such market-based financing mechanisms is increasing globally. SIDS, however, struggle to access these because of their high-risk profiles (which drive up costs), and in some cases, their weak technical capacities to manage them. Despite these challenges, progress has been made in this area, and should continue through the development of risk transfer mechanisms and insurance markets that meet the needs and circumstances of SIDS.

Through regional sovereign insurance facilities, such as the Caribbean Catastrophe Risk Insurance Facility (CCRIF) and the Pacific Catastrophe Risk Assessment and Financing Initiative (PCRAFI), some SIDS created regional risk pools, resulting in reduced premiums for individual member countries. These initiatives also include a donor-subsidisation component. The PCRAFI provided Vanuatu with USD 1.9 million following Cyclone Pam in 2015 and extended about USD 1.2 million to Tonga following Tropical Cyclone Ian in 2014. So far, five Pacific SIDS[22] have received a combined USD 43 million in insurance payments against tropical cyclones, earthquakes and tsunamis.

Building on the CCRIF, the World Bank, the U.S. Department of State, the Food and Agriculture Organization, the Nature Conservancy are currently developing the Caribbean Oceans and Aquaculture Sustainability Facility, a climate-risk insurance product for vulnerable fishing communities in the Caribbean. This project aims to establish a platform for innovative insurance financing that could support SIDS governments in addressing the intertwined set of challenges relating to food insecurity, climate resilience and livelihoods. Through the Caribbean Oceans and Aquaculture Sustainability Facility, countries that incorporate measures to foster climate resilience and marine protection would benefit from lower, co-financed insurance premiums. So far,

Belize, Grenada and Jamaica have expressed interest in participating in the Facility, and the World Bank is also considering its global application.[23]

To explore how to deploy climate risk insurances more broadly, providers could also leverage efforts under InsuResilience, a Group of Seven (G7) Initiative on Climate Risk Insurance established under Germany's G7 presidency in 2017. InsuResilience aims to increase access to direct or indirect insurance coverage against the impacts of climate change for up to 400 million of the most vulnerable people in developing countries by 2020.

Box 3.8. Lessons on enhancing access to finance from international capital markets

Compared to larger developing countries with similar per capita incomes, SIDS struggle to access international financial markets. Most Pacific SIDS are not sufficiently creditworthy to raise funds in capital markets; only Fiji, Papua New Guinea and the Solomon Islands have a sovereign credit rating from one or more of the main international credit rating agencies. As for Caribbean SIDS, they have seen a rapid deterioration in international capital-market ratings by key credit-rating agencies, with a consequent rise in risk premiums. Obstacles to accessing private international capital market are connected to issues relating to challenges in government budgets planning and control, public financial management and, sometimes, critical debt situations. International support for fiscal reforms, public sector management and public sector investments are thus critical to help SIDS enhance their capacity to mobilise international private capital.

Australia's technical advice and support helped the Government of Solomon Islands to obtain a Moody's credit rating (B3 in November 2015) in order to gain access to international credit markets. In March 2017, the Solomon Islands' government signed for the first time a Domestic Development Bond Agreement worth USD 150 million with the Solomon Island National Provident Fund.

3.3. Channelling resources to priority areas

To break the cycle of low growth and vulnerability facing SIDS, public international finance will need to continually seek innovative ways to strengthen the role of the private sector and its contribution to sustainable development in these varied contexts. This will include the promotion of adequate policy and regulatory frameworks as well as support to increase the economic and financial viability of income-generating activities and to promote trade integration and global value chains participation.

Specific opportunities could arise from the development of the blue economy, which could boost economic growth and help address unemployment, poverty and food insecurity. In this area, the international community could provide advisory services and legal and regulatory support to address cross-border policy challenges relating to the development of the blue economy. Development partners should also support the development of appropriate financing instruments, including blue bonds.

Lastly, long-term development gains need to be "climate-proof" in SIDS. Development partners will need to maintain a focus on fostering climate-resilient economies in SIDS and on facilitating a transition to low-carbon economies. This will require helping SIDS integrate climate and disaster risks into national policies and planning, and project design; support them in accessing climate financing by using their influence to encourage the adoption of proportionate, streamlined approaches for accessing finance from the global funds; removing the barriers to investments for renewable energy sources would significantly reduce import costs for SIDS, improve debt sustainability and create more fiscal space for development investments.

3.3.1. Fostering private sector development and trade

Recommendations - Supporting private sector development and enhancing trade:

- Opportunities for developing stronger domestic private sectors and enhancing international trade may differ significantly across SIDS. To break the cycle of low growth and vulnerability facing SIDS, public international finance will need to continually seek innovative ways to strengthen the role of the private sector and its contribution to sustainable development in these varied contexts, including through the promotion of policy and regulatory frameworks, support to increase the economic and financial viability of income-generating activities and trade integration.

Chapter 1 highlighted that domestic private sectors are often shallow, especially in the Pacific, while Chapter 2 pointed to the small contribution of private finance to the external financial flows reaching SIDS. Opportunities for developing stronger domestic private sectors and enhancing international trade may differ significantly across SIDS. The smallest and most remote SIDS face the greatest challenges to developing a competitive private sector and finding a niche in global markets.

For many SIDS, the main challenge remains the economic and financial viability of income-generating activities in the context of structural constraints such as a higher cost of inputs, higher transportation costs, and frequent extreme-weather events and natural disasters. In the case of English-speaking SIDS in the Caribbean, the proximity of the North American labour market makes it very hard to find highly qualified human resources to work in managerial positions on the islands. A lack of adequate policy and regulatory frameworks also prevents greater development of the private sector and of investments.

A large share of financing to SIDS aims to foster an enabling environment for private sector development

The good news is that concessional finance to support private sector development is increasing. According to the framework developed by the OECD to measure official finance for private sector development (Miyamoto and Chiofalo, 2017),[24] the international community deployed an estimated USD 3.3 billion in 2012-15 to improve policies and regulations, as well as governance, for the private sector in SIDS – a little less than 20% of the total concessional finance provided over the period. An additional USD 3 billion was allocated by the international community to "support market functioning" in SIDS, including through activities – such as enhancing physical infrastructure through road extensions and electrical efficiency gains – aiming to reduce costs and barriers to economic activity. A smaller amount (USD 1 billion) was allocated to increasing enterprise resources across SIDS, including through activities aiming to heighten small farmers' productivity, enhance community-based fisheries and aquaculture, and implement education programmes and scholarships.

Across geographical regions, support to private sector development mainly targeted SIDS in the Pacific (46%) and Caribbean (41%), followed by SIDS in the AIMS region. However, these regional trends hide important differences. The largest shares of support were directed to: Haiti, some natural resource-rich SIDS (e.g. Papua New Guinea, Solomon Islands and

Timor-Leste) and the Dominican Republic. Support mainly targeted enhancing the policy environment and governance in least developed and fragile SIDS, in natural resource-rich SIDS and in some of the smallest SIDS in the Pacific, as the shallow domestic markets in these countries call for some important preconditions to be met, and structural barriers to be lifted, before more support can be given directly to private actors. SIDS with relatively larger and more developed private sectors received most of private sector development support as financing aimed to strengthen market functioning (Figure 3.4).

Figure 3.4. A large share of financing to small island developing states aims to foster an enabling environment for private sector development

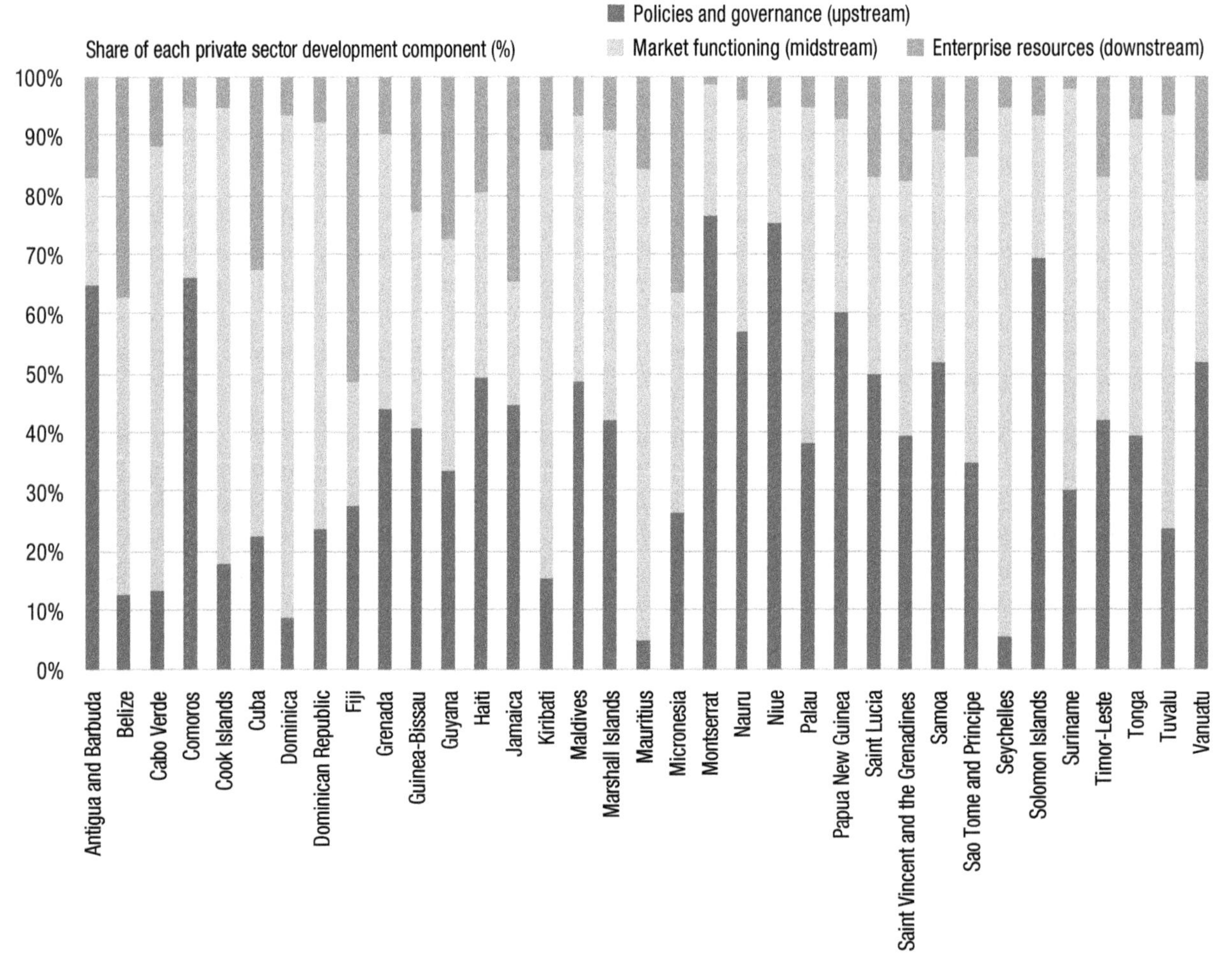

Source: OECD (n.d.), Creditor Reporting System (database), https://stats.oecd.org/Index.aspx?DataSetCode=CRS1.

StatLink http://dx.doi.org/10.1787/888933646162

Several development partners are developing new approaches to private-sector development. The World Bank has developed the "Cascade" approach (Box 3.10.) aiming at crowding in private finance for infrastructure in developing countries. The World Bank sees this approach as potentially meeting shortages in development finance and infrastructure gaps in SIDS (World Bank, 2017a), but the approach will need to be adequately tailored to the context of SIDS. In addition, the World Bank Private Sector Window will use IDA18 concessional funds for market creation and private sector engagement in the riskiest of markets, with IFC as main implementer. It targets fragile and low-income states and SIDS account for 26% of eligible countries but represent a tiny portion if calculated in terms of market size/population. The Asian

Development Bank has carried out a Private Sector Development Initiative, including in SIDS. The main achievements are briefly described below.

Box 3.9. The cascade principles for infrastructure finance

In its Forward Look: A vision for the World Bank Group in 2030 – progress and challenges (World Bank, 2017b), the World Bank Group presented its long-term vision and approach to crowding in private-sector investment and "creating markets". By introducing "cascade" principles for infrastructure finance, this report attempts to operationalise the call to scale up private finance outlined by the World Bank, the IMF and five other multilateral development banks in the 2015 From Billions to Trillions (World Bank, 2015).

Forward Look explains that "to maximise the impact of scarce public resources, the cascade first seeks to mobilise commercial finance, enabled by upstream reforms where necessary to address market failures and other constraints to private sector investment at the country and sector level. Where risks remain high, the priority will be to apply guarantees and risk-sharing instruments. Only where market solutions are not possible through sector reform and risk mitigation would official and public resources be applied". While currently focused on infrastructure, the document highlights that the cascade approach will be expanded to other areas, including finance, education, health and agribusiness.

The World Bank includes this approach in the "package" of initiatives and measures it makes available to small states (which include the SIDS eligible for concessional finance from the International Development Association) in Small States: A Roadmap for World Bank Group Engagement (World Bank, 2017a). The "judicious" use of scarce public finance, including of international concessional finance, and the need for upstream reforms and for addressing market failures suggested by the cascade approach, seem to be in line with providers' approach to private sector development in SIDS. Extending this approach to the social sectors and private sector provision of social sectors, however, could raise concerns along the lines of those expressed by the civil society (Brettonwoods Observer, 2016), and may be more challenging to implement in a SIDS context.

Source: Adapted from World Bank (2017b) and World Bank (2015).

Enhancing access to international trade

In 2012-15, the international community also channelled USD 1.1 billion in concessional finance to activities supporting better integration in the international trading system (i.e. "aid for trade"). While this support targets enhancements along the same three dimensions as in the private sector development framework (i.e. policy and regulations, economic infrastructure and productive capacity), some overlap exists between support to private-sector development and aid for trade.[25] In 2012-15, examples of aid for trade in SIDS in these three areas include: (i) support from the European Union under the 10th European Development Fund for the CARICOM Single Market and Economy and for the Economic Integration Programme; (ii) support from Japan to Kiribati to develop the Betio Port, including finance to improve berthing facilities as well as cargo-handling equipment; and (iii) funding by the Inter-American Development Bank for a market-access and agricultural diversification programme in Guyana. To promote greater regional trade linkages, much of aid for trade provided at the regional level (i.e. 20% to the Pacific and 28% to the Caribbean) supports policy and regulatory measures.

Box 3.10. Lessons from the Asian Development Bank's Private Sector Development Initiative

According to the Asian Development Bank's independent evaluation of private sector operations (ADB, 2016), Pacific countries showed varying degrees of success under regional private equity funds and trade finance programmes. Nevertheless, the Asian Development Bank's Pacific Private Sector Development Initiative, now in its seventh year of operation, has demonstrated a strong track record of achievement in the private sector. Achievements include:

- Improved access to finance in the Marshall Islands, Micronesia, Palau, Solomon Islands, Tonga and Vanuatu, through secured transaction reform: as a result of the new secured transaction laws and registries, financial institutions in these Pacific countries have extended approximately 28 000 new formal sector loans.
- Assistance to microfinance institutions in Papua New Guinea, Timor-Leste and Vanuatu resulted in a significant growth in savings accounts, particularly in remote areas, with women being the major beneficiaries: over 50 000 new savings accounts have been opened since 2010. The Pacific Private Sector Development Initiative is also assisting financial institutions in improving rural outreach through branchless mobile phone banking systems.
- In business-law reforms, the Pacific Private Sector Development Initiative has helped Samoa and the Solomon Islands establish online business registries, leveraging the digital revolution to make it easier to start a formal business. The Initiative facilitated a new business registry and an innovative Companies Act support local communities and women's groups start businesses.
- The Company House online registry installed by the Solomon Islands in 2010 reduced the necessary time to license a business from 45 days to 1.5 days, thereby doubling the rate of business formation. Similarly, the rate of business registrations doubled after Samoa launched its online company registry in 2013.
- The Initiatives' large, ongoing programme to help Pacific governments improve their outdated commercial laws is bringing more businesses into the formal sector, with corresponding improvements in productivity and wages.
- The Initiative has also helped a number of countries improve the governance and efficiency of state-owned enterprises, and the state owners' capacity to hold them accountable for commercial results. The Finding Balance series of publications highlights the very substantial drag on growth state-owned enterprises create throughout the region. The Initiative has assisted with a number of privatisations, with resulting efficiency improvements and job creations. It has also assisted Papua New Guinea and Timor-Leste in establishing policy and legal frameworks for public-private partnerships, as well as identifying opportunities for public-private partnerships in infrastructure, several of which are undergoing further development.

Finally, the Pacific Private Sector Development Initiative has initiated pilots to increase women's private sector activity, e.g. by training them in technical and business development skills, facilitating their access to finance and markets, and mentoring them in entrepreneurship skills.

Source: ADB, 2016

3.3.2. Prioritising the climate and resilience

Recommendations - Supporting transitions to low-carbon, climate-resilient economies:

- Development partners need to continue to help SIDS integrate climate and disaster risks into national policies and planning, and project design. This will include supporting the adoption of policies and regulations – such as building codes, incentives for efficient water use and prevention of new assets in exposed areas – that promote climate resilience by influencing the choices of private actors.
- Complex application processes and fiduciary standards exceeding the capacities of SIDS constrain access to financing from the global climate funds. Development partners could use their influence to encourage the global climate funds to adopt proportionate, streamlined approaches promoting greater access and project implementation.
- Providers need to do more to remove the barriers to investments for renewable energy sources. The status of renewable technologies and the large extra- resource allocation potentially available for climate action make this the perfect moment to increase the renewable capacity in SIDS. The international community should drive this agenda, which could also reduce import costs, improve debt sustainability and create more fiscal space.
- Financial innovations will be central in mobilising climate finance at scale. Already, the Green Climate Fund is using grants to promote investments in adaptation activities; concessional loans to absorb high market rate costs of debt; and guarantees and equity to de-risk investments and increase the commercial viability of investments projects. This financing is likely to be used for higher return investment projects, and in SIDS could contribute, for example, to climate-resilient infrastructure, maritime-infrastructure investments and renewable energy projects.

As discussed in Chapter 2, the sectoral focus of concessional finance in SIDS reflects in part the specialisation of providers and it may fail to adequately target sectors and areas that are critical for advancing development in this context. A clear example stems from providers' investments in climate and disaster resilience, and more broadly for climate adaptation and mitigation. Globally, SIDS bear the brunt of climate change impacts. Rising sea levels and ocean acidification pose existential challenges to SIDS. While hurricanes and cyclones have been a feature of life on islands for centuries, the effects of climate change are exacerbating their intensity and making extreme weather events more likely to happen. These circumstances will increase the cost of achieving sustainable development in SIDS.

In addition, as discussed in Chapter 1, transitioning to a low-carbon economy will be an important step for SIDS to move towards more sustainable development, abating the costs of an economy that relies on expensive imported fossil fuels. While most SIDS have ideal situations to exploit renewable energy, many struggle to bear the large initial costs of investments for renewable energy sources, in part owing to limited borrowing capacity.

National policies as well as donor interventions in SIDS take into account the current and future impacts of climate change, in the interest of both the viability of the investment as well as SIDS' debt sustainability. Development partners need to continue to support SIDS integrate climate and disaster risks into national policies and planning, and project design, including through policies and regulations – such as building codes, incentives for efficient water use and prevention of new assets in exposed areas – that can promote climate resilience by influencing the choices of private actors.

Box 3.11. Lessons from an innovative use of Green Climate Fund resources

The Green Climate Fund will be an important source of finance for SIDS, as well as a vehicle for innovation in development finance. Having received to date USD 10.3 billion in pledges, it is now the largest vertical fund operating at a global level; the first formal replenishment will be triggered once 60% of the initial resource mobilisation has been spent.[26] The co-chairs commissioned further consultations at the 16th meeting of the Green Climate Fund board in April 2017, with a view to triggering the replenishment process in the near future. The Green Climate Fund has been operational since 2015 and now has 45 approved projects.[27]

To date, eight of the projects are in SIDS and two regional initiatives include SIDS as beneficiaries. Of the direct projects, six are in the Pacific and two in the AIMS region; three are least developed countries, one is a lower middle-income country and four are upper middle-income countries. Both regional initiatives are in the Caribbean. In SIDS, the Green Climate Fund is using both grant financing and more complex financing arrangements that blend sources with varying degrees of concessionality. These projects generally include government co-financing.

One of the first projects the Green Climate Fund approved in 2015 was a regional initiative comprising four countries, including two SIDS. The project will be piloted in Mexico and will then include Columbia, Dominican Republic and Jamaica. The project aims to enhance energy efficiency in Latin America and the Caribbean, and will aggregate resources to mobilise institutional funds to finance SMEs involved in servicing this sector.[28] It is being implemented by the Inter-American Development Bank, with additional financing from the Clean Technology Fund and the private sector.

The project provides loans for energy efficiency projects. It will bundle multiple projects to underpin the issuance of partly guaranteed green bonds. The pilot in Mexico will cost USD 2 million in grants for programme development and a further USD 20 million in credit guarantees. For the following phase a further USD 195 million has been allocated. The programme targets a minimum emission reduction of 13.2 million carbon dioxide tons equivalents (tCO2e) (2.5 million tCO2e in Phase 1) and USD 780 million (150 million USD in Phase 1) of private sector bond issuances, with potential for further up-scaling and replication in other developing countries. This could provide a valuable financing modality: not only are concessional resources being used catalytically to leverage capital, but collaboration with larger developing countries will effectively leverage growth in the private sectors of SIDS. There is scope to apply such a model to the AIMS region, which is less well defined, and where most SIDS have strong ties with continental African states.

Source: Adapted from the Green Climate Fund website www.greenclimate.fund/home

Climate finance will need to be scaled up. This will require the adoption, to the extent possible of streamlined application processes that are proportionate to SIDS constrained capacities. It will also require innovation from a broad range of actors and will provide an opportunity to trial new instruments. The Green Climate Fund will be an important source of financing and of innovation (Box 3.11). The Global Innovation Lab for Climate Finance - a multi-partner platform led by the United Kingdom, Germany, Denmark, France, Japan, United States, Netherlands and Norway - could also be an important actor in this regard. Along with private sector partners, it seeks to catalyse new approaches, by bringing together experience and expertise to identify, design and pilot the next generation of climate- finance instruments. These will provide concrete solutions to the financing challenges facing real projects, as well as build new markets, attract new investors and help to unlock resources for new climate-friendly investment in SIDS.

3.3.3. Navigating new frontiers – supporting the development of the "blue economy"

Recommendations - Exploring new opportunities for growth, including through the "blue economy":

- The international community could provide advisory services and legal and regulatory support to address cross-border policy challenges relating to the development of the blue economy. Development partners should also support the development of appropriate financing instruments, including blue bonds.
- Specific attention could be dedicated to developing instruments that finance the conservation of marine protected areas, linked to national blue economy strategies. Valuation of marine resources and ecosystems – and especially the full value of ocean resources – must inform policy.

As discussed in Chapter 1, SIDS' economic vulnerabilities largely stem from their reliance on few economic sectors and trading partners, which exposes them to fluctuations in the global markets. If they fail to expand their narrow productive and export bases, SIDS will continue to experience precarious cycles of vulnerability.

Increasingly, the greatest scope for diversification and expansion lies within the vast oceans surrounding many SIDS. The sustainable development of marine resources (i.e. "blue economy") could open new opportunities to develop new competitive sectors and diversify the economy. Maritime resources, which are already closely linked to key income generating sectors such as the tourism and fisheries, could lead to greater economic diversification and more rapid growth through innovative investments that integrate and develop a broader range of land-based, coastal and ocean-based sectors in a sustainable fashion. The development of the blue economy could boost food, energy, transport and other sectors, and foster sustainable and inclusive development in SIDS.

To effectively help SIDS develop the blue economy and make the best of it for their economies and their people, the international community will need to support SIDS in the development of adequate policies and regulations, expertise and technical capacities, as well as be responsive in helping them to have sufficient fiscal space and adequate resources to invest in this endeavour. Therefore, there is scope for the innovations and good practices described so far in this chapter to catalyse achievements for the blue economy. The remainder of this section explores current support for the blue economy and highlights how these efforts could be brought to scale going forward.

Current financing will need to be scaled up, and be part of an integrated and strategic approach

Of the USD 18.8 billion in concessional finance channelled to SIDS in 2012-15, approximately USD 1.15 billion (6.11%) went to sectors relating to the ocean economy.[29] Bilateral and multilateral providers of concessional finance have steadily increased their support (from USD 264 million in 2012 to USD 329 million in 2015, an average increase of 8% per year). The bulk of this financing has targeted transport policy and administration management (41%), and water transport (30%). Over the same period, concessional finance for the ocean economy also targeted the fisheries (13%) and tourism (7%) sectors.

The SIDS that received the largest share of this investment are Papua New Guinea (23%), Haiti (17%) and Cabo Verde (7%). The biggest donors are: Australia (21%), the Inter-American Development Bank Special Fund (18%) and Japan (14%).

Examples of donor support to the ocean economy emerge from responses to a survey on DAC members' development co-operation policies and practices vis-à-vis SIDS conducted for this report. These include:

- Australia supported Timor-Leste in the tendering programme for the Tibar Bay Port construction, and provided an AUD 5 million (Australian dollars) grant to the Pacific Island Forum Fisheries Agency.
- Italy supported SIDS in the Caribbean region to strengthen supply chains around key economic sectors, including tourism and agribusiness, and promotes public-private partnerships to this end.
- Japan provided technical assistance and grants to SIDS in the Eastern Caribbean to develop the fisheries sector and promote sustainable development.
- New Zealand supported the Pacific SIDS at a regional level to develop the fisheries sector, including through scientific, management, regulatory and technical support.
- The United States has been working with Haiti to develop the Cap Haïtien Port, supporting the development of critical infrastructure and regulatory reform in order to modernise the facilities and grow trade. The United States has also supported the growth of aquaculture programmes in Guyana.

While these are positive examples to build on, achieving a sustainable ocean economy calls for an integrated and strategic approach to better align policies across multiple sectors. It entails integrating the value provided by ecosystems into our economic decision-making frameworks, scaling up finance in innovative ways, and investing these resources more efficiently and strategically. Consequently, fostering the blue economy will require a combination of enabling factors: a concerted national strategy supported by adequate international support; expertise from various fields to come together and establish synergies; partnerships between national and international actors, the private sector and civil society; and adequate financing approaches and instruments. An important component of the blue economy will be marine protected areas (Box 3.12).

Box 3.12. Italy's leadership in promoting marine protected areas: the 10X20 Initiative

Oceans are facing unprecedented pressures from human activity. Protecting them is essential, not only to spearhead future economic growth, but to preserve the very existence of humankind. This is why promoting marine protected areas is a critical element of the global blue economy.

Together with the Ocean Sanctuary Alliance, the Government of Italy has launched the 10X20 Initiative, a plan of action to support the achievement of Target 5 of the U.N Sustainable Development Goal 14: *conserving at least 10% of coastal and marine areas by 2020*. This initiative aims to assist countries in achieving this globally agreed commitment through a scientifically based framework. It aims to create a co-ordinated global network of marine protected areas, to achieve the 10% target to conserve biodiversity. The network will foster an exchange of knowledge, information and best practices, and will pursue advocacy.

Investing in marine protected areas can help promote food and nutritional security, as well as economic security. It provides recreational value, and preserves cultural and spiritual values. It contributes to well-functioning ecosystems and helps regulate the earth's climate. It is estimated that the economic benefits from establishing new marine protected areas can offset the costs in as few as five years (Sala et al., 2016). In Hawaii, a review of six marine managed areas showed that they generated cost-benefit ratios ranging from 3.8 to 41.5 (van Beukering and Cesar, 2004). In Vanuatu, a mean return on investment of 1.8 was achieved for five marine protected areas only five years after the initial investment (Pascal, 2011).

Marine protected areas require adequate financing for the transition period, as well as for enforcement and management. The international community can do much to support this by helping establish conservation funds, dedicated national budget allocations, user fees and fines.

Financial innovation will be needed to help boost the blue economy

Blue bonds, which have been implemented successfully in Indonesia, are a prospective source of revenue for SIDS. The Seychelles is a precursor among SIDS in this respect, issuing a USD 15 million, ten-year blue bond, including guarantees from the World Bank and grant finance from the Global Environment Facility. The new initiative was awarded the 2017 Ocean Innovation Challenge at the World Ocean Summit 2017 in Bali. The blue economy strategy in the Seychelles focuses on economic diversification, food security, and the protection and sustainable use of marine resources. The proceeds of the bond are aligned with this strategy: they will specifically finance fisheries management and planning activities, and will be loaned out to encourage public and private investment that adds value and job opportunities in areas that protect ocean resources. The funds will be disbursed by the Seychelles Conservation and Climate Adaptation Trust, and the Development Bank of Seychelles. These activities will proceed in tandem with the implementation of the Seychelles Marine Spatial Plan for its economic exclusion zone, which is one of the commitments included in the country's debt swap for conservation and climate adaptation.

3.4. Conclusions and recommendations

Small island developing states stand at a critical juncture on their paths towards sustainable development. As discussed in Chapter 1, economic growth, human development and vulnerability indicators point to specific challenges facing SIDS, suggesting that new development solutions and approaches are needed to chart the course to prosperity for their people and their environments.

New global trends could open up promising opportunities for SIDS, giving them access to new markets, boosting economic growth and helping some of them achieve economic self-sufficiency. By developing old and new sectors linked to the abundant marine resources of SIDS, the blue economy could fuel economic growth and help address food insecurity, high unemployment and poverty. Innovations in technology and world digitalisation could lift connectivity barriers to global markets, provide opportunities for participating in "virtual" labour markets through remote access and the use of holograms, reduce brain drain and stir the development of new economic niches. Sun, wind and ocean waves – all abundant in SIDS – are potentially powerful and exploitable energy sources that could be used to help break dependence on fossil fuels and create fiscal space to address critical development needs. These needs include enhancing resilience to the severe climate events and devastating natural disasters to which SIDS are highly exposed.

The international community has a critical role to play in helping SIDS seize these opportunities and embark on sustainable development pathways. The international community can invest in generating innovative thinking and creative solutions to lay out new, effective development options and paradigms for SIDS. This chapter presented some innovative solutions that providers could make greater use of or further develop. It suggested priority areas where the international community could take action for making development co-operation work better for SIDS and thus support them more effectively in achieving sustainable development. Building on this information, the international community, including SIDS governments, can move forward to take urgent action to pave the way for new development paradigms and sustainable development in SIDS. The recommendations presented in this chapter are summarised below.

- Enhancing access, modalities and partnerships for concessional finance:
  - **Building capacity and technical assistance:** Providers can do more to improve the absorption capacity of SIDS, and the ability to mobilise, manage and spend financial resources from a wider array of sources to decrease dependence on a single provider: through long-term approaches to capacity development, innovative uses of technology, and a careful assessment of which functions could be performed at a regional level, which will need to remain at the national level, and which could be outsourced privately. Using pooled mechanisms to reduce transaction costs and modalities could also help to strengthen national capacities.
  - **Encouraging partnerships with a larger range of actors, including through triangular co-operation:** Partnerships with a larger set of stakeholders will bring a wider set of perspectives and approaches to the complexity of development in SIDS and could provide an alternative source of financing as SIDS move to higher levels of national per capita income. Collaboration between "traditional" and "emerging" donors could also be instrumental to reducing transaction costs and enhancing policy dialogue in SIDS. Positive examples of multi-donor trust funds used to channel resources,

such as the one established in Nauru with contributions from Australia and Chinese Taipei, could replicated in other SIDS contexts.

   - **Expanding the evidence base and policy dialogue around the complexity of development in SIDS:** SIDS that have recently graduated from least developed country status, such as Cabo Verde and Samoa, have quickly moved from a moderate to a high risk of debt distress, signalling that development partners could do more to support and advise countries during transitions. While several SIDS have flagged the negative consequences of losing access to concessional finance after graduating from bilateral or multilateral financing, no exhaustive analysis has been conducted on the real impacts of losing access to these sources. More evidence and policy dialogue needs to be fostered to understand the impacts of different graduation processes on financing landscapes and growth opportunities in order to maintain development gains as countries transition through different income levels and development phases, i.e. the "development continuum".

- Using concessional finance innovatively to leverage additional resources:
   - **Access to new and existing financing, including climate finance and private sector investments:** Innovative financial instruments, such as green and blue bonds, and blending arrangements to bring climate finance to scale, are promising sources of development finance for SIDS. However, none of these have been rolled out at scale in a SIDS context. Development partners can do much to support the design and implementation of these instruments, and back these new products with guarantees and co-financing schemes to encourage economic diversification and invest in building long term resilience.
   - **Domestic resource mobilisation:** this could be enhanced through diaspora investment schemes; internationally co-ordinated fiscal reforms to expand tax coverage (especially to include high revenue-generating segments of the economy); and policies to reduce "leakages" from key sectors – especially tourism – and support linkages with other domestic sectors to effectively expand the taxable production base.
   - **Debt sustainability:** There is a need to work with partners to address debt sustainability and free resources for sustainable development including for the blue and green economies. Debt relief opportunities, such as debt for nature swaps, and innovative counter-cyclical instruments, such as loans that automatically postpone debt servicing in the event of a major shock (e.g. through "hurricane" clauses) could be further explored and expanded.

- Channelling resources to priority areas:
   - **Transitioning to low-carbon, climate-resilient economies:** Providers could do more to help SIDS integrate climate and disaster risks into national policies and planning, and project design and support them in accessing climate financing by using their influence to encourage the adoption of proportionate, streamlined approaches for accessing finance from the global funds. Removing the barriers to investments for renewable energy sources would significantly reduce import costs for SIDS, improve debt sustainability and create more fiscal space for development investments.
   - **Fostering new growth opportunities such as the blue economy:** The international community could provide advisory services and legal and

regulatory support to address cross-border policy challenges relating to the development of the blue economy. Development partners should also support the development of appropriate financing instruments, including blue bonds. Specific attention could be dedicated to developing instruments that finance the conservation of marine protected areas, linked to national blue economy strategies.

- **Supporting private sector development, enhancing trade and attracting private finance:** Opportunities to develop stronger domestic private sectors and enhancing international trade may differ significantly across SIDS. To break the cycle of low growth and vulnerability facing SIDS, public international finance will need to continually seek innovative ways to strengthen the role of the private sector and its contribution to sustainable development in these varied contexts, including through the promotion of policy and regulatory frameworks and support to increase the economic and financial viability of income-generating activities.

Notes

1. For further information please see https://pefa.org/.

2. To directly access funding, Green Climate Fund countries are required to designate national implementing agencies: i) national implementing entities are responsible for overseeing implementation of funded initiatives, and ensuring that finance received follows the Fund's objectives and meets its fiduciary standards and social safeguards; ii) National Designated Authorities are responsible for overseeing all resources coming into the country from the Fund. The authority is the point of communication with the Green Climate Fund and undertakes a wide range of functions, including aligning activities with national sustainable development objectives and frameworks; and iii) executing entities are responsible for the actual implementation of initiatives. These can be members of other government agencies, civil society, community organisations and the private sector. See: www.wri.org/sites/default/files/22DIRECT_ACCESS_TO_CLIMATE_FINANCE_LESSONS_LEARNED_BY_NATIONAL_INSTITUTIONS.pdf.

3. This survey involved responses by 60 stakeholders, namely: Argentina, Armenia, Australia, Austria, Benin, Brazil, Burkina Faso, Cameroon, Canada, Chile, Colombia, Cook Islands, Costa Rica, Dominican Republic, Ecuador, Fiji, France, Germany, Guatemala, Honduras, Indonesia, Israel, Italy, Jamaica, Japan, Kiribati, Korea, Madagascar, Mexico, Mozambique, New Zealand, Norway, Paraguay, Peru, Portugal, Russian Federation, Samoa, South Africa, Spain, Sudan, Sweden, Switzerland, Timor Leste, Tuvalu, United Kingdom and Uruguay; the African, Caribbean and Pacific Group of States, Asian Development Bank, Food and Agriculture Organization, Inter American Development Bank, International Labour Organization, Organisation Internationale de la Francophonie, Pacific Islands Forum, Pan American Health Organisation, United Nations Children's Fund (Mexico Office), United Nations Economic Commission for Europe, United Nations Volunteers, United Nations Industrial Development Organization, United Nations Office on South-South Co-operation and World Food Programme. The Islamic Development Bank and the United Nations Development Programme China contributed information on their triangular co-operation initiatives to the online project repository of the OECD..

4. This is a project over 2013-23 involving Cook Islands, China, New Zealand, and the World Health Organisation. This project, with a USD 42 million budget, aims at upgrading Rarotonga's water supply infrastructure to deliver a high-quality and reliable water supply, which is critical for growing tourism and safeguarding public health. The project will increase resilience to drought for the majority of the Cook Islands population who live on Rarotonga.

5. This project involves Cuba, Mexico and Germany over 2017-19. With a USD 500 000 budget, this project aims to strengthen the institutional capacities to implement renewable energy and energy efficiency measures in Cuba.

6. See https://sustainabledevelopment.un.org/sids2014.

7. Cabo Verde, Sao Tome and Principe, Maldives, Dominica, Grenada, Saint Lucia, Saint Vincent and the Grenadines, Guyana, Kiribati, Marshall Islands, Micronesia, Papua New Guinea, Samoa, Timor-Leste, Tonga, Tuvalu and Vanuatu.

8. This is the case, for example, of Japan, as indicated in Japan's response to a survey conducted to inform this report.

9. With the exception of G8 members and European Union members.

10. Countries above the high-income threshold for three consecutive years at the time of the review (which happens every three years) are removed from the List.

11. These include the United Nations Economic Commission for Latin America's structural-gap approach, the adapted Economic Vulnerability Index used by the United Nations Office of the High Representative for Least Developed Countries and the vulnerability metrics developed by the Commonwealth Secretariat.

12. See https://www.addistaxinitiative.net/ and http://www.tiwb.org/.

13. Aid-for-tax data is only available only from 2014.

14. Self-reported information provided by Australia through its response to an unpublished OECD DAC survey questionnaire regarding OECD DAC members' policies and practices supporting small island developing states conducted to inform this report.

15. SDG 14.4: by 2020, effectively regulate harvesting, and end overfishing, illegal, unreported and unregulated (IUU) fishing and destructive fishing practices and implement science-based management plans, to restore fish stocks in the shortest time feasible at least to levels that can produce maximum sustainable yield as determined by their biological characteristics.

16. The Manila Agreement was facilitated by the Asian Development Bank, and signed by the governments of Italy, Nauru and New Zealand.

17. The Paris Club is a group of officials from 22 major creditor countries which negotiate coordinated solutions to the payment difficulties experienced by debtor countries.

18. Responses to an unpublished OECD Survey on policies and practices in support of SIDS.

19. OECD definition of blended finance is "the strategic use of development finance (1) for the mobilisation of additional commercial (2) finance towards the SDGs in developing countries".

20. The Principles are intended to assist providers of development finance - DAC member governments, non-DAC donors, development co-operation agencies, philanthropies and any other interested stakeholders - in the design and implementation of blended finance policies and approaches. They aim to ensure that blended finance is deployed so as to mobilise additional capital effectively in order to deliver development outcomes and impact.

21. Neither Cuba nor Montserrat are members of the Africa, Caribbean and Pacific Group of States, through which much of the EDF's European Development Fund allocation to SIDS is channelled.

22. Cook Islands, Marshall Islands, Samoa, Tonga and Vanuatu.

23. For more information on the project, see World Bank (2016).

24. This framework comprises three main components: (i) polices and governance (ii) market functioning and (iii) enterprise resources. Budget support, which is included in original private sector development (PSD) framework, is excluded from the analysis presented here. The original framework includes budget support on the grounds that it contributes to macroeconomic stability, which is crucial for enabling investment. However, in a SIDS context where private markets are effectively very thin and budget support is often used to finance public services, counting general budget as a PSD component would likely over estimate its potential contribution to stimulating private investment.

25. This was estimated at USD 4.68 billion for SIDS in 2012-15.

26. www.greenclimate.fund/documents/20182/584114/GCF_B.16_Inf.11_-_Matters_related_to_the_replenishment_of_the_Green_Climate_Fund.pdf/4fba80f5-6c45-4134-85ea-26c8872fda28.

27. www.greenclimate.fund/projects/portfolio.

28. www.greenclimate.fund/documents/20182/87610/GCF_B.11_04_ADD.06_-_Funding_proposal_package_for_FP006.pdf/4be31e42-bda9-46a0-b200-bc2f78ed81d6.

29. The purpose codes considered to contribute to the blue economy are: water sector policy and administrative management; water resources conservation (including data collection); transport policy and administrative management; water transport, storage; marine energy; fishing policy and administrative management; fishery development; fishery education/training; fishery research; fishery services; transport equipment industry; tourism policy and administrative management; and flood prevention/control.

References

ADB (2016), “Comparative Institutional Review of ADB’s Private Sector Operations, August 2016”, *ADB Evaluation Occasional Papers,* Asian Development Bank, Manila, www.adb.org/documents/comparative-institutional-review-adb-private-sector-operations.

Benn, J., C. Sangaré and T. Hos (2017), "Amounts Mobilised from the Private Sector by Official Development Finance Interventions: Guarantees, syndicated loans, shares in collective investment vehicles, direct investment in companies, credit lines", *OECD Development Co-operation Working Papers*, No. 36, OECD Publishing, Paris, http://dx.doi.org/10.1787/8135abde-en.

Berkelmans, L., and J. Pryke (2016), *The development benefits of expanding Pacific access to Australia's labour market*, Lowy Institute for International Policy, Sydney, www.lowyinstitute.org/sites/default/files/documents/The%20development%20benefits%20of%20expanding%20Pacific%20access%20to%20Australia%27s%20labour%20market.pdf.

Bontjer, R., S. Hadley, T. Haque, P. Krause, and V. Nagaraj, (2016), ‘Strengthening Public Financial Management Reform in Pacific Island Countries’ *World Bank Policy Research Working Paper*, World Bank, Washington D.C., http://documents.worldbank.org/curated/en/303711471955858894/Final-output.

BPOA (1994), *Barbados Programme of Action*, United Nations, New York, https://sustainabledevelopment.un.org/conferences/bpoa1994.

Brettonwoods Observer (2016), *Development to the rescue of finance – the Bank's 'cascade' approach, July 2017*, www.brettonwoodsproject.org/2017/07/development-rescue-finance-banks-cascade-approach/.

Commonwealth Secretariat (2016), *Disconnecting from Global Finance: A Conversation on De-risking in the Commonwealth,* Commonwealth Secretariat, London, http://thecommonwealth.org/sites/default/files/inline/DisconnectingfromGlobalFinance2016.pdf.

Commonwealth Secretariat (2015), *Debt Swaps for Climate Change Adaptation and Mitigation: A Commonwealth Proposal*, Commonwealth Secretariat, London, http://thecommonwealth.org/sites/default/files/inline/Debt%20swaps%20for%20climate%20change%20adaptation%20and%20mitigation-%20A%20Commonwealth%20proposal%202015.pdf.

ECLAC (2017), *ECLAC's Proposal on Debt for Climate Adaptation Swaps: a strategy for growth and economic transformation of Caribbean Economies*. Presentation at the CARICOM-UN High Level Pledging Conference, November 2017, www.cepal.org/sites/default/files/news/files/nydbetreliefcaribbeannovember2017.pdf.

European Union (2016), *LAIF/CIF Operational Report*, Publications Office of the European Union, Luxembourg, https://ec.europa.eu/europeaid/sites/devco/files/operational-report-2015-laif-cif_en.pdf.

Government of Vanuatu (2017), *Vanuatu Revenue Review: Final report on the case for revenue reform and modernisation*, Revenue Review Committee, July 2017, Port Vila, https://revenuereview.gov.vu/images/Publications/RevenueReviewFINALReport_10072017.pdf.

Haque T., Z. Partow, S. Varma, L.E. Oliveira (2016), *Addressing Debt Vulnerabilities in Small States: The potential role of new financing instruments.* Discussion Paper 10, March 2016, http://lacer.lacea.org/handle/10986/24009.

Latin America Investment Facility (2015), 2015 Operational Report, European Union, Brussels, https://ec.europa.eu/europeaid/sites/devco/files/operational-report-2015-laif-cif_en.pdf.

Miyamoto, K. and E. Chiofalo (2017), "Development Co-operation for Private Sector Development: Analytical Framework and Measuring Official Development Finance", *OECD Development Co-operation Working Papers*, No. 32, OECD Publishing, Paris, http://dx.doi.org/10.1787/ded2028f-en.

OECD (2017a), "Dispelling the myths of triangular co-operation: Evidence from the 2015 OECD survey on triangular co-operation", *OECD Development Policy Papers*, No. 6, OECD Publishing, Paris, http://dx.doi.org/10.1787/a8b14341-en.

OECD (2017b), *OECD Recommendation on Disaster Risk Financing Strategies*, OECD, Paris, www.oecd.org/daf/fin/insurance/OECD-Recommendation-Disaster-Risk-Financing-Strategies.pdf.

OECD (2016), *The Ocean Economy in 2030,* OECD Publishing, Paris. http://dx.doi.org/10.1787/9789264251724-en.

OECD DAC (2017), *Principles on Blended Finance*, OECD, Paris, www.oecd.org/development/financing-sustainable-development/development-finance-topics/blended-finance.htm.

OECD DAC (2014), *DAC List of ODA Recipients*, OECD, Paris, www.oecd.org/dac/financing-sustainable-development/development-finance-standards/daclist.htm.

OECD (no date), *International development statistics* (database), OECD, Paris, www.oecd.org/dac/financing-sustainable-development/development-finance-data/.

OECD-World Bank (2016), *Climate and Disaster Resilience Financing in Small Island Developing States*, OECD Publishing, Paris, http://dx.doi.org/10.1787/9789264266919-en.

Pascal, N (2011), *Cost-Benefit analysis of community-based marine protected areas: 5 case studies in Vanuatu*, CRISP, SOC, New Caledonia, https://cmsdata.iucn.org/downloads/nicolas_pascal_2011_cba_mma_spc.pdf.

Sala, E., C. Costello, J.D.B. Parme, M., Fiorese, G. Heal, K. Kelleher, R. Moffitt, L. Morgan, J. Plunkett, K.D. Rechberger, and A.A. Rosenberg, (2016), "Fish banks: An economic model to scale marine conservation" Marine Policy, 73, pp.154-161. http://www.sciencedirect.com/science/article/pii/S0308597X16300586.

UN (2014), *SAMOA Pathway*, United Nations Conference on Small Island Developing States, Apia, Samoa, 1-4 September 2014, United Nations, New York, http://www.sids2014.org/index.php?menu=1537.

UNCTAD (2014), *Trade and Development Report*, United Nations Convention on Trade and Development, Geneva, http://unctad.org/en/PublicationsLibrary/tdr2014_en.pdf.

UNDP (2017), *Financing the SDGs in the Pacific islands: Opportunities, Challenges and Ways Forward.* http://www.undp.org/content/undp/en/home/librarypage/poverty-reduction/financing-the-sdgs-in-the-pacific-islands--opportunities--challe.html.

UNDP China (2017), "China's South-South Cooperation with Pacific Island Countries in the Context of the 2030 Agenda for Sustainable Development", *Series Report: Climate Change Adaptation* p. 34, United Nations Development Programme, Beijing, www.cn.undp.org/content/china/en/home/library/south-south-cooperation/1--china_s-south-south-cooperation-with-pacific-island-countries.html.

Van Beukering, P. and Cesar, H.S., (2004), "Ecological economic modeling of coral reefs: Evaluating tourist overuse at Hanauma Bay and algae blooms at the Kihei Coast, Hawai'I", *Pacific Science,* 58(2), pp.243-260.

Wenner, M. (2015), "Can Diaspora Bonds be Used in the Caribbean?" *Country Technical Note*, October 2015, Inter-American Development Bank, Creative Commons Attribution-CC-IGO BY-NC-ND 3.0 IGO http://www20.iadb.org/intal/catalogo/PE/2015/15820.pdf.

World Bank (2017a), *Small States: A Roadmap for World Bank Group Engagement,* World Bank Group, Washington D.C., http://pubdocs.worldbank.org/en/982421496935264348/Small-States-Roadmap.pdf#zoom=70.

World Bank (2017b), *Forward Look - a vision for the World Bank Group in 2030 progress and challenges,* World Bank Group, Washington D.C., http://siteresources.worldbank.org/DEVCOMMINT/Documentation/23745169/DC2017-0002.pdf.

World Bank, (2016), *World Bank Group Engagement with Small States: Taking Stock,* World Bank, Washington, D.C., License: Creative Commons Attribution CC BY 3.0 IGO http://pubdocs.worldbank.org/en/244361475521083722/Small-States-Stocktaking-2016.pdf.

World Bank (2015), *From billions to trillions: MDB contributions to financing for development*, World Bank Group, Washington, D.C., http://documents.worldbank.org/curated/en/602761467999349576/From-billions-to-trillions-MDB-contributions-to-financing-for-development.

Chapter 4. Small island developing states: Profiles

These profiles present key figures on concessional finance to individual small island developing states, as well as providing a snapshot of the weight of concessional finance to the overall external financing and a summary of key vulnerabilities and structural challenges. All figures refer to the 2012-15 period, unless otherwise specified.

Figure 4.1. Antigua and Barbuda

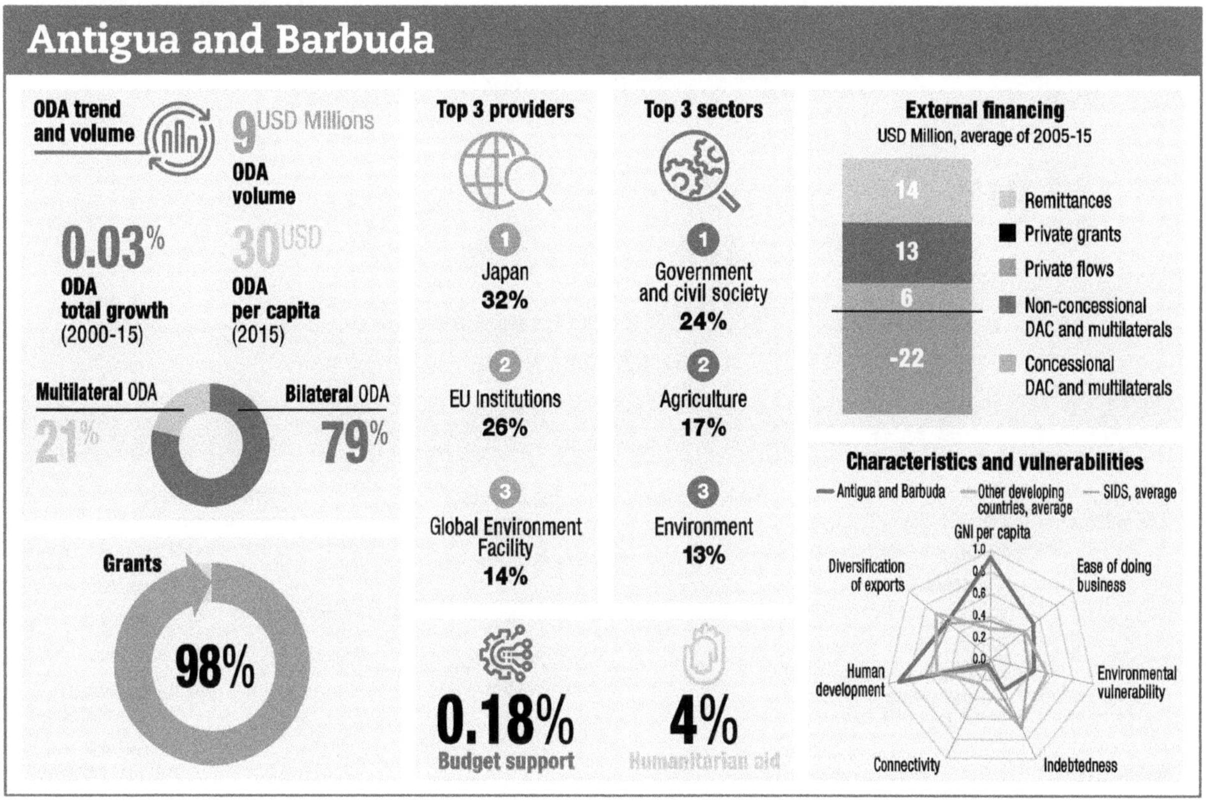

Figure 4.2. Belize

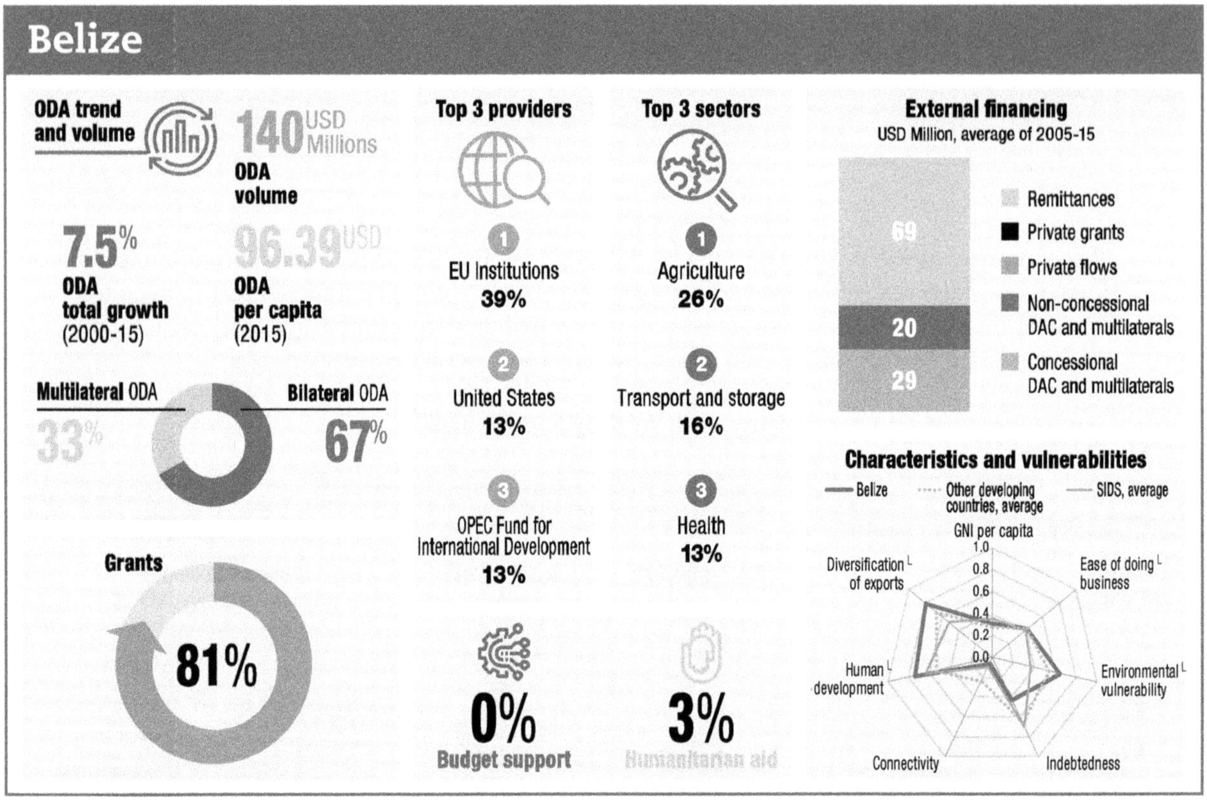

Figure 4.3. Cabo Verde

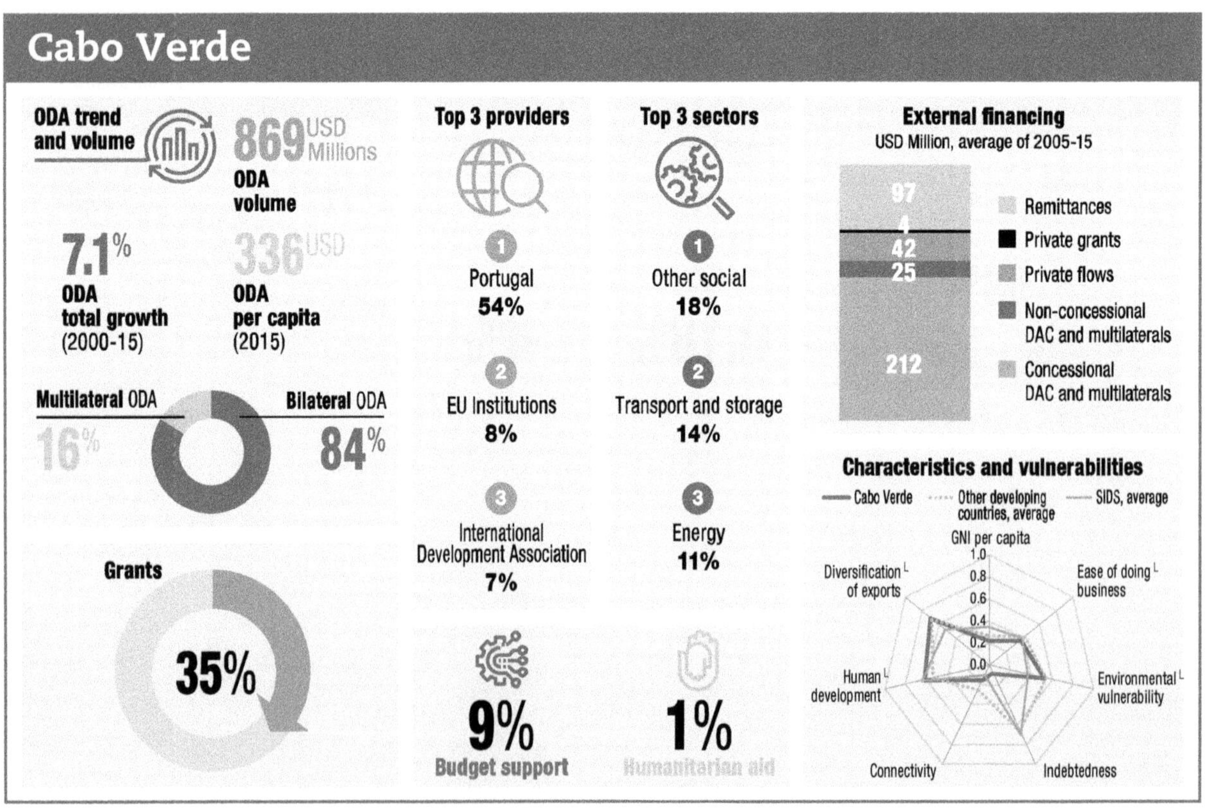

Figure 4.4. Comoros

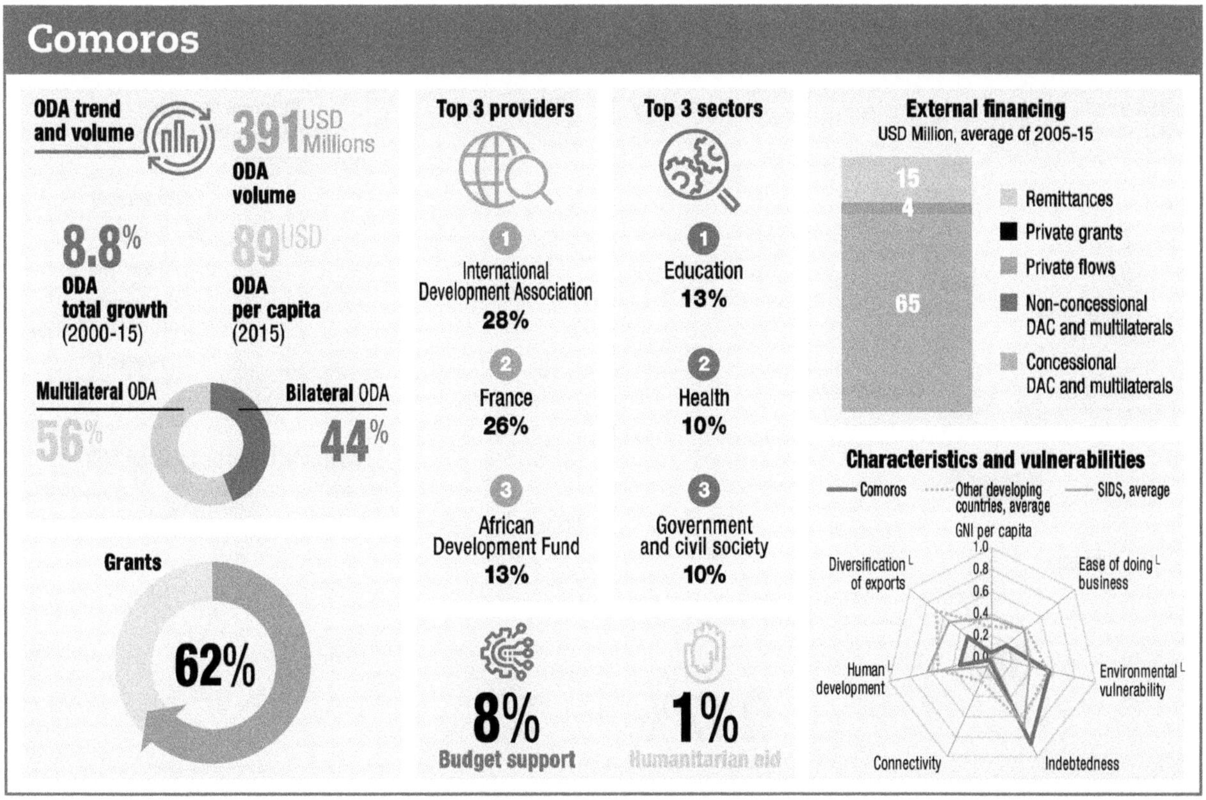

Figure 4.5. Cook Islands

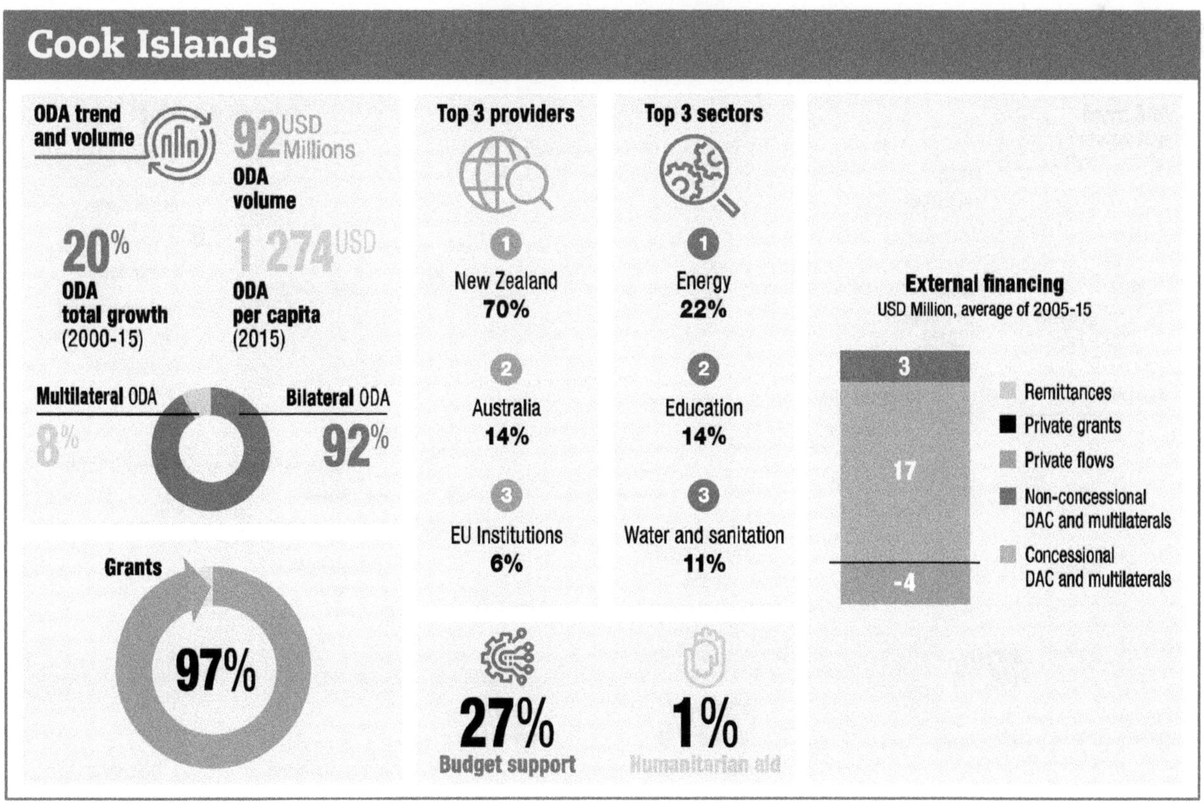

Figure 4.6. Cuba

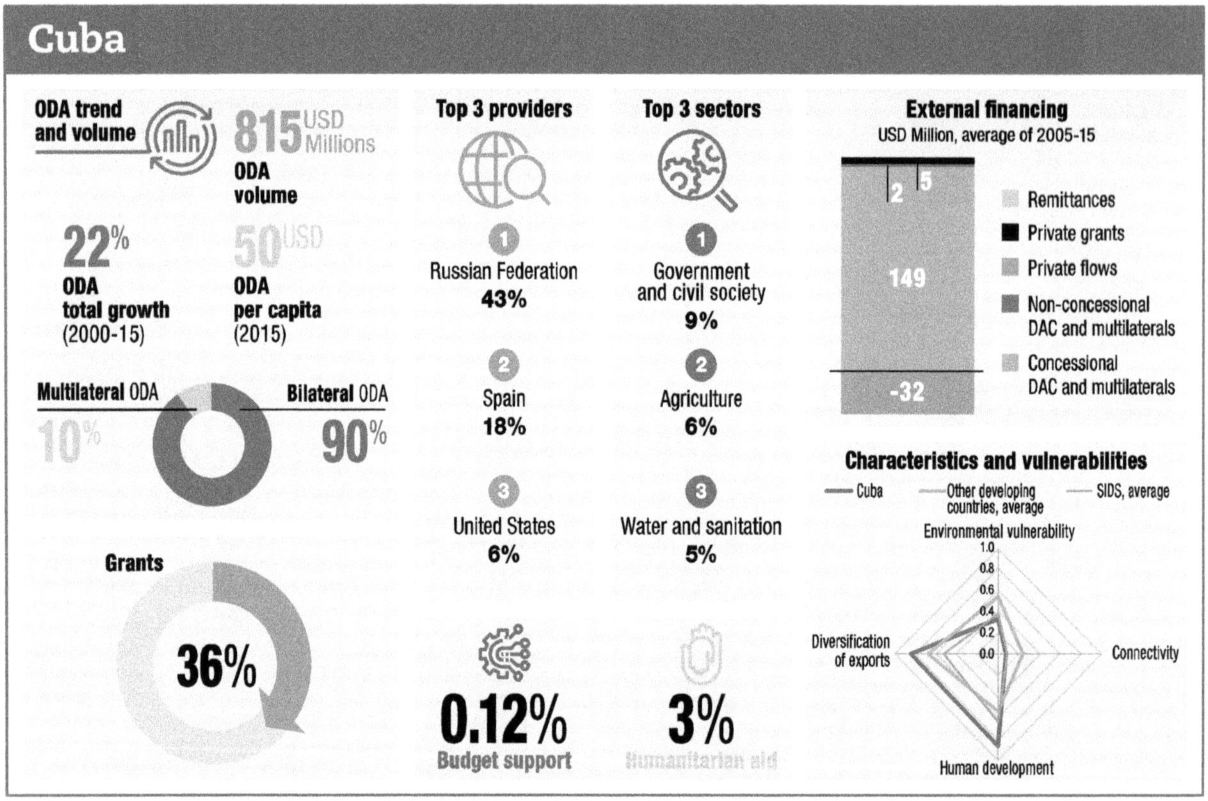

Figure 4.7. Dominica

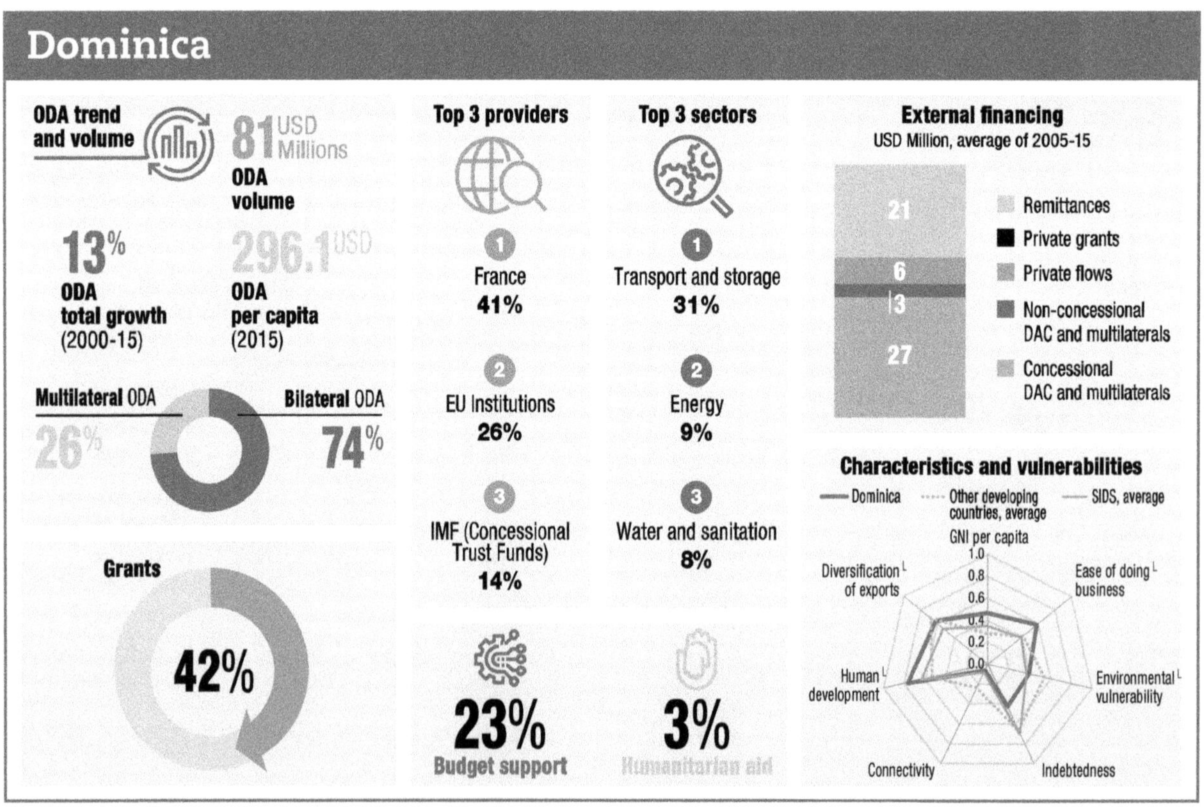

Figure 4.8. Dominican Republic

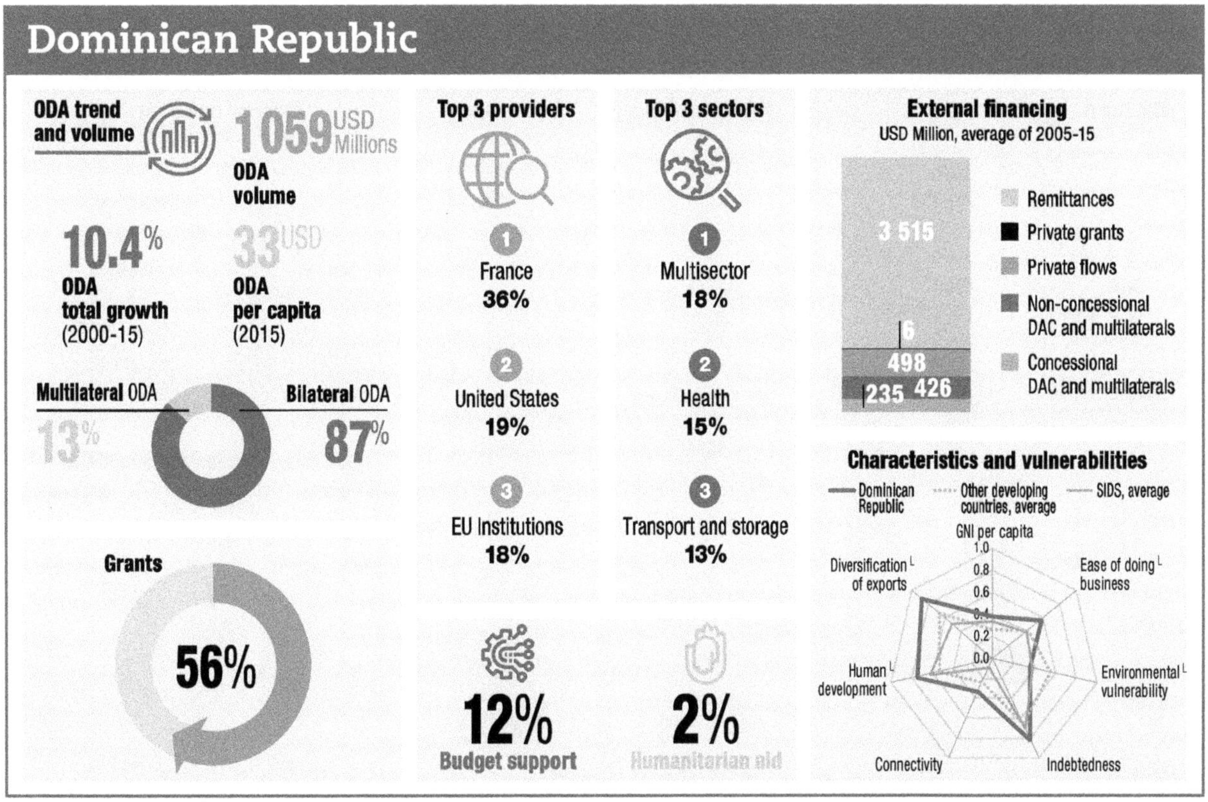

Figure 4.9. Fiji

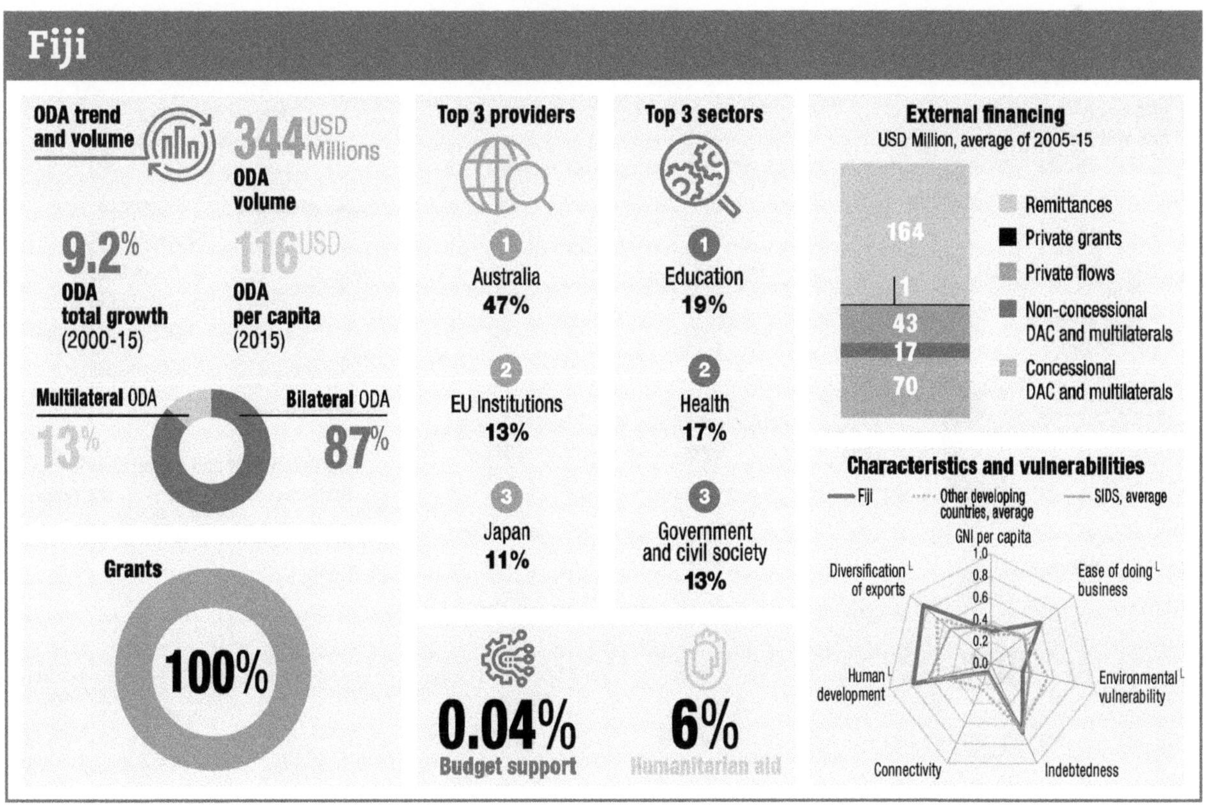

Figure 4.10. Grenada

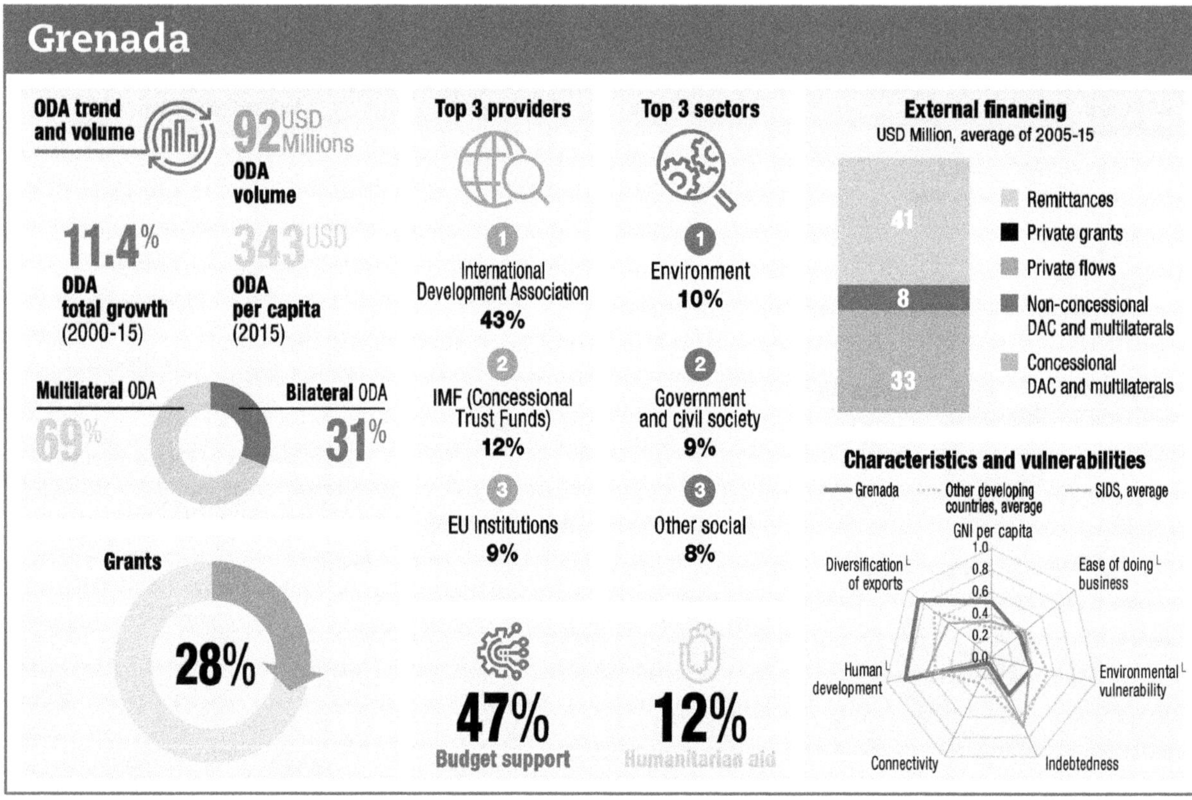

Figure 4.11. Guinea-Bissau

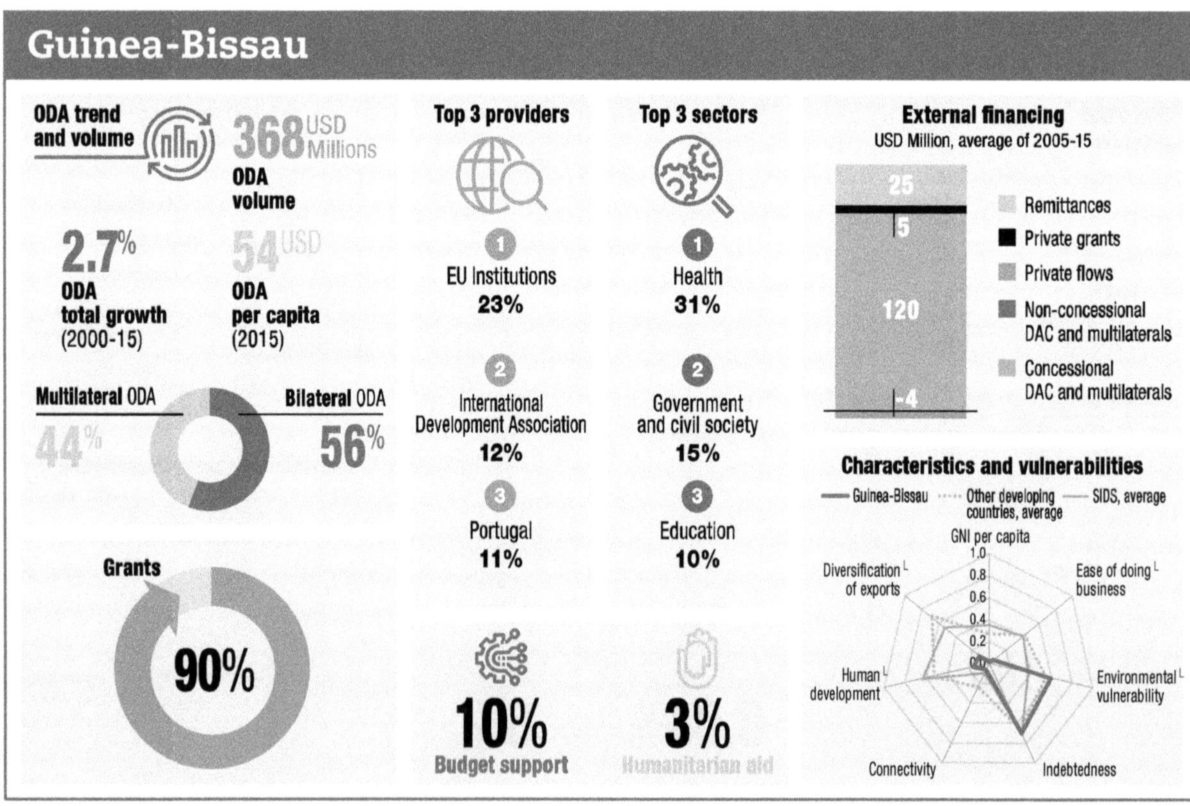

Figure 4.12. Guyana

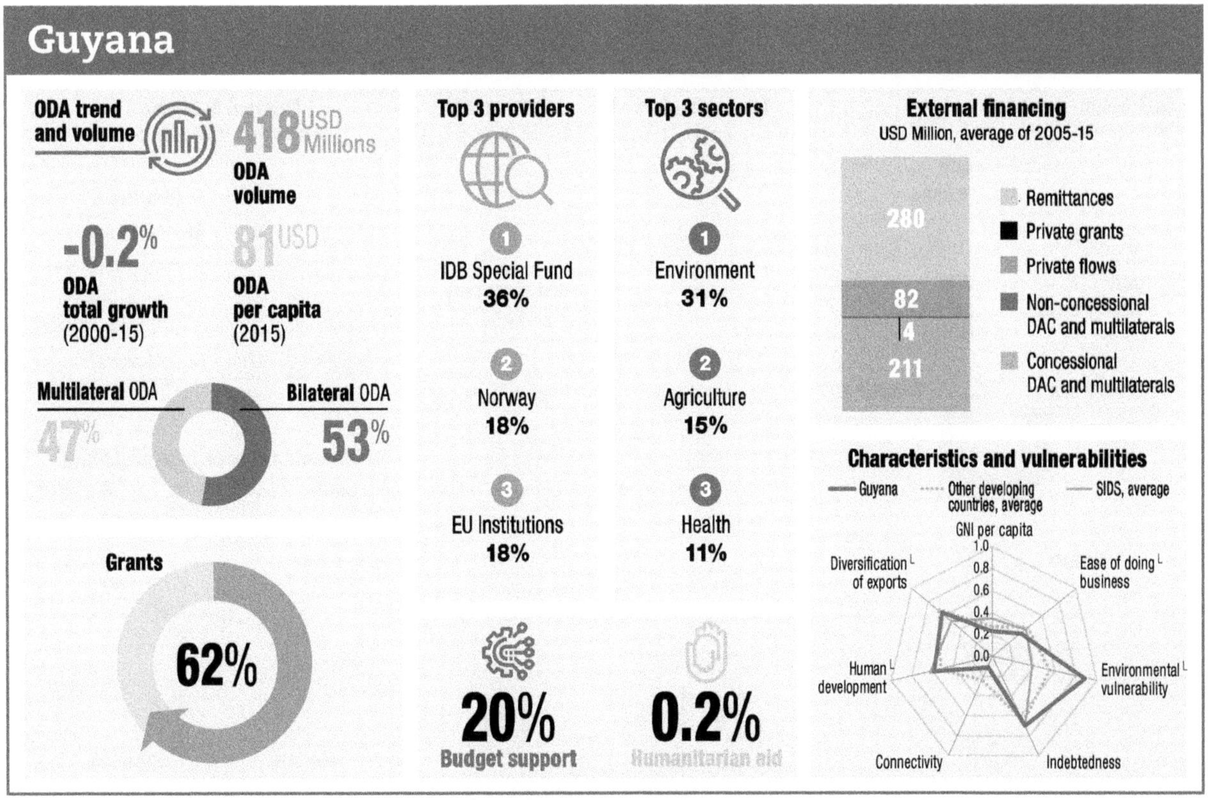

Figure 4.13. Haiti

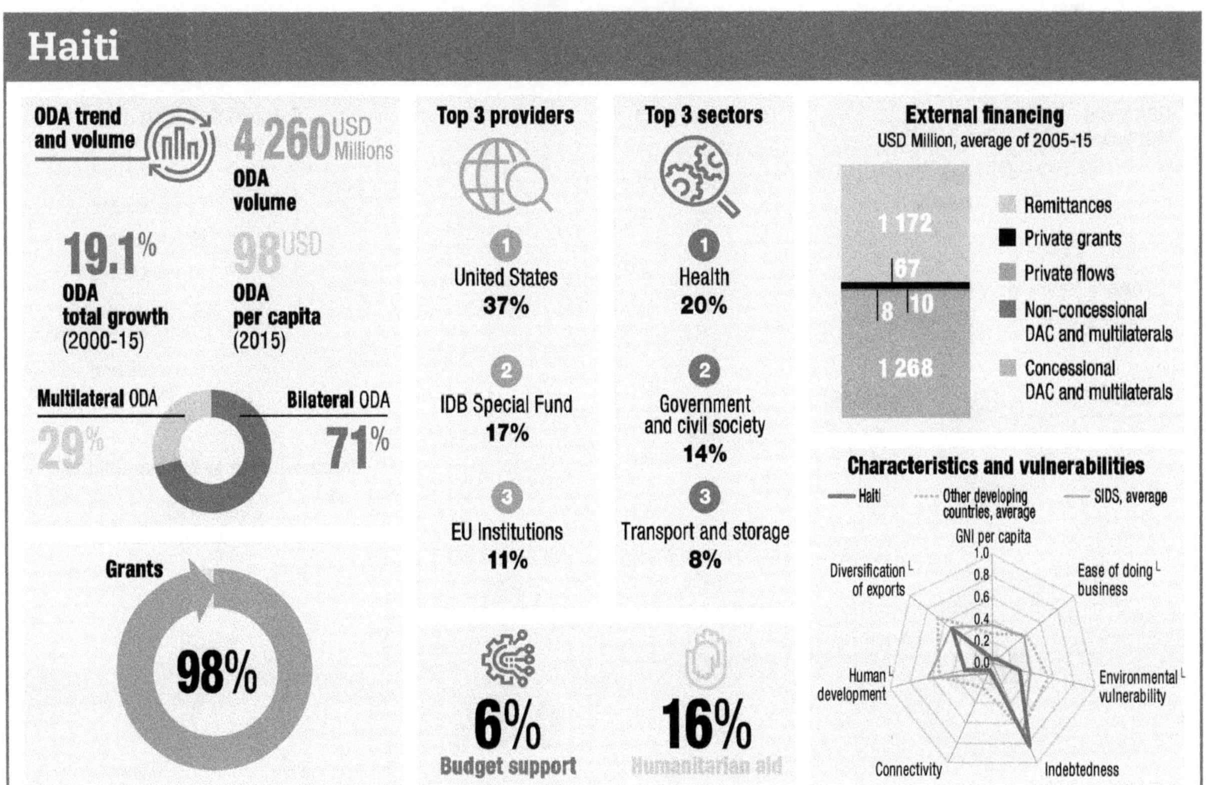

Figure 4.14. Jamaica

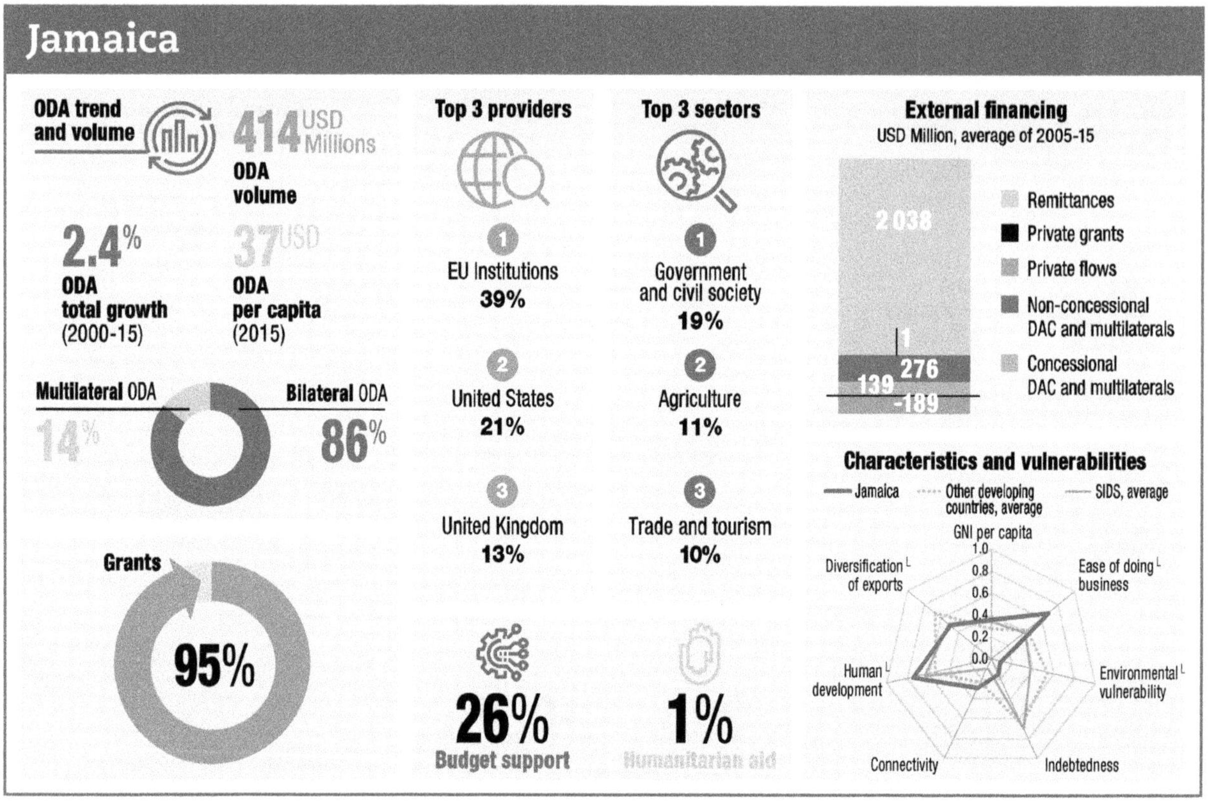

Figure 4.15. Kiribati

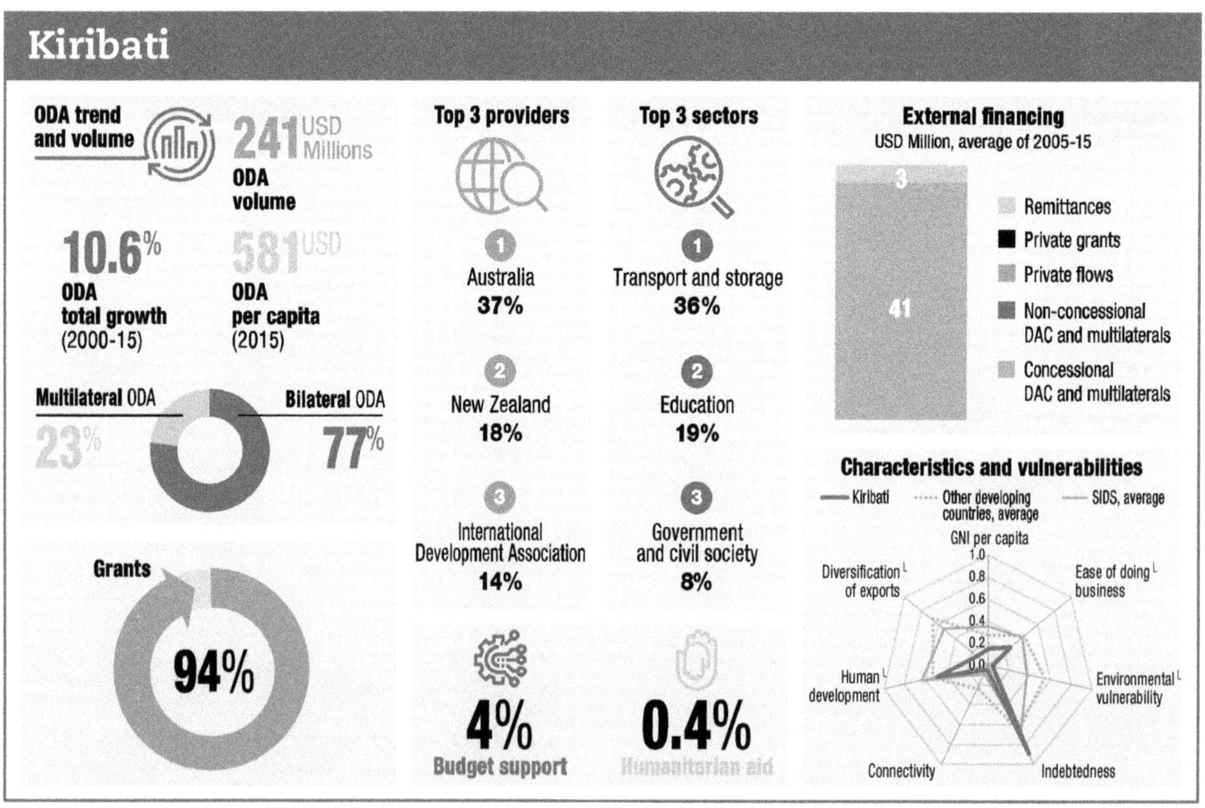

Figure 4.16. Maldives

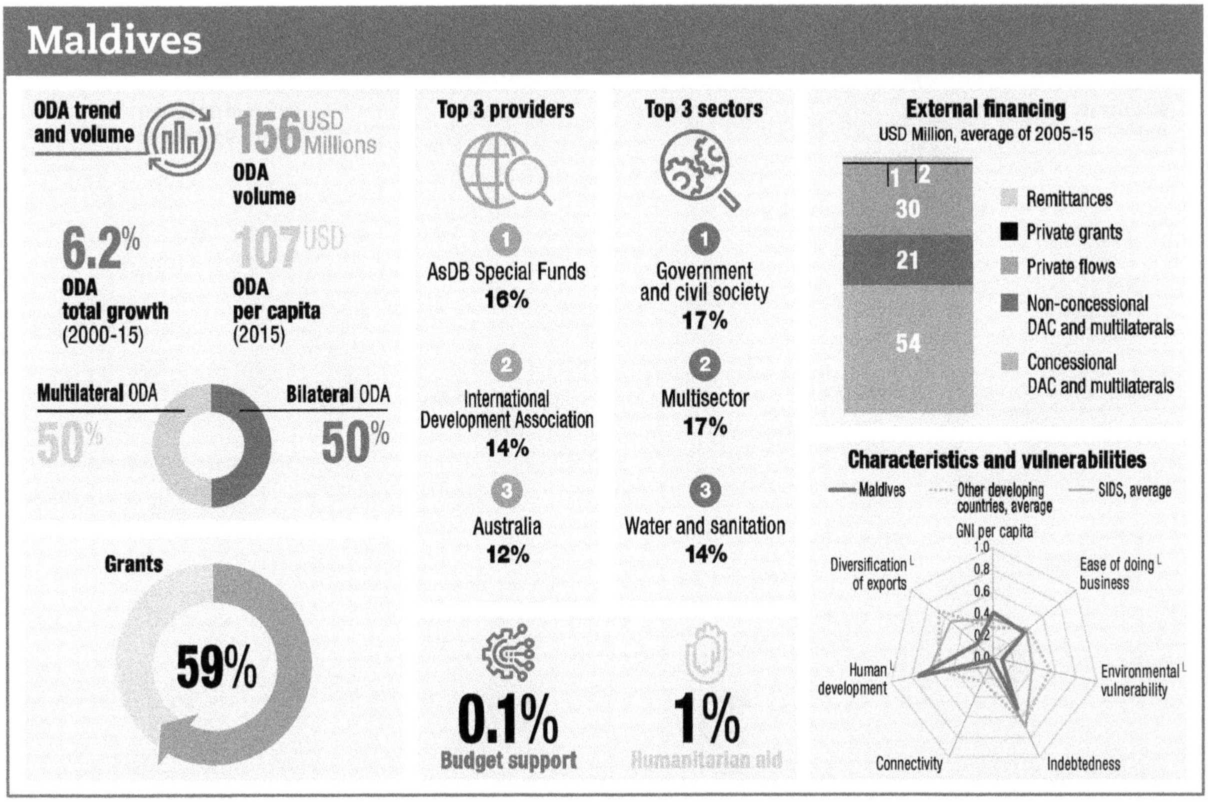

Figure 4.17. Marshall Islands

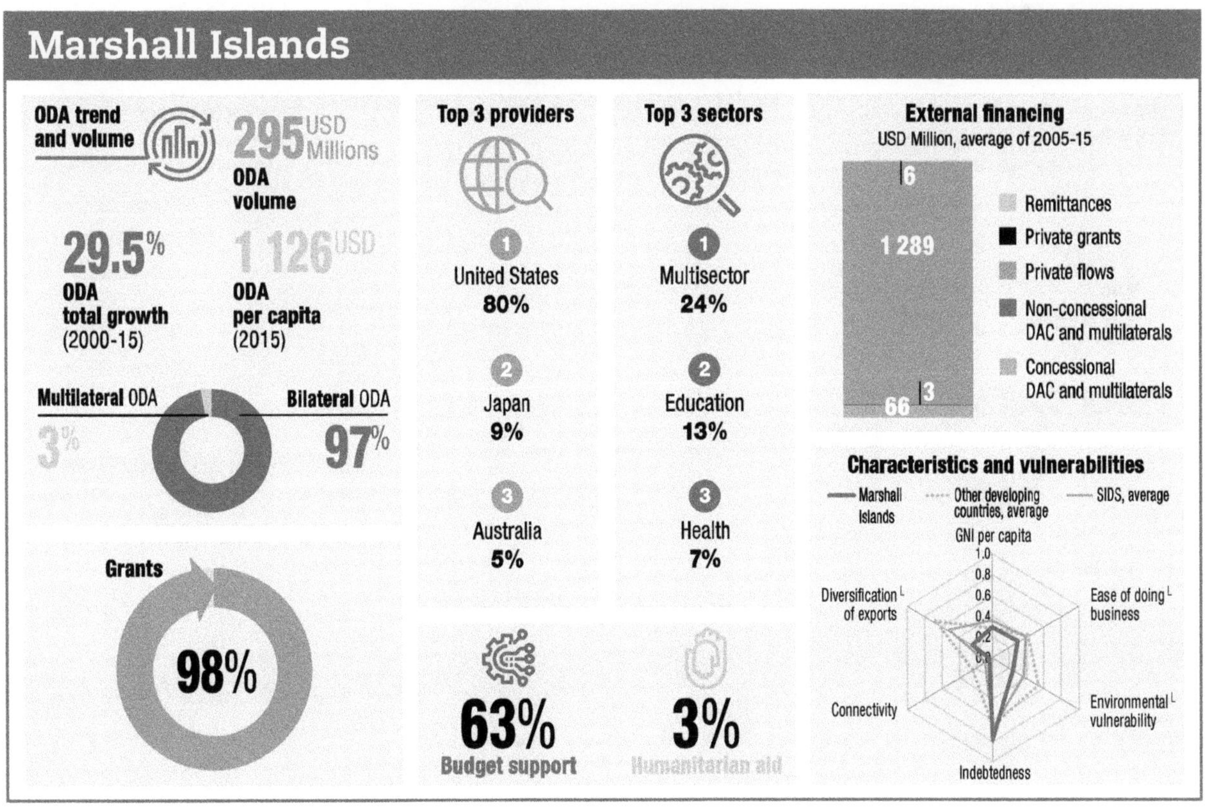

Figure 4.18. Mauritius

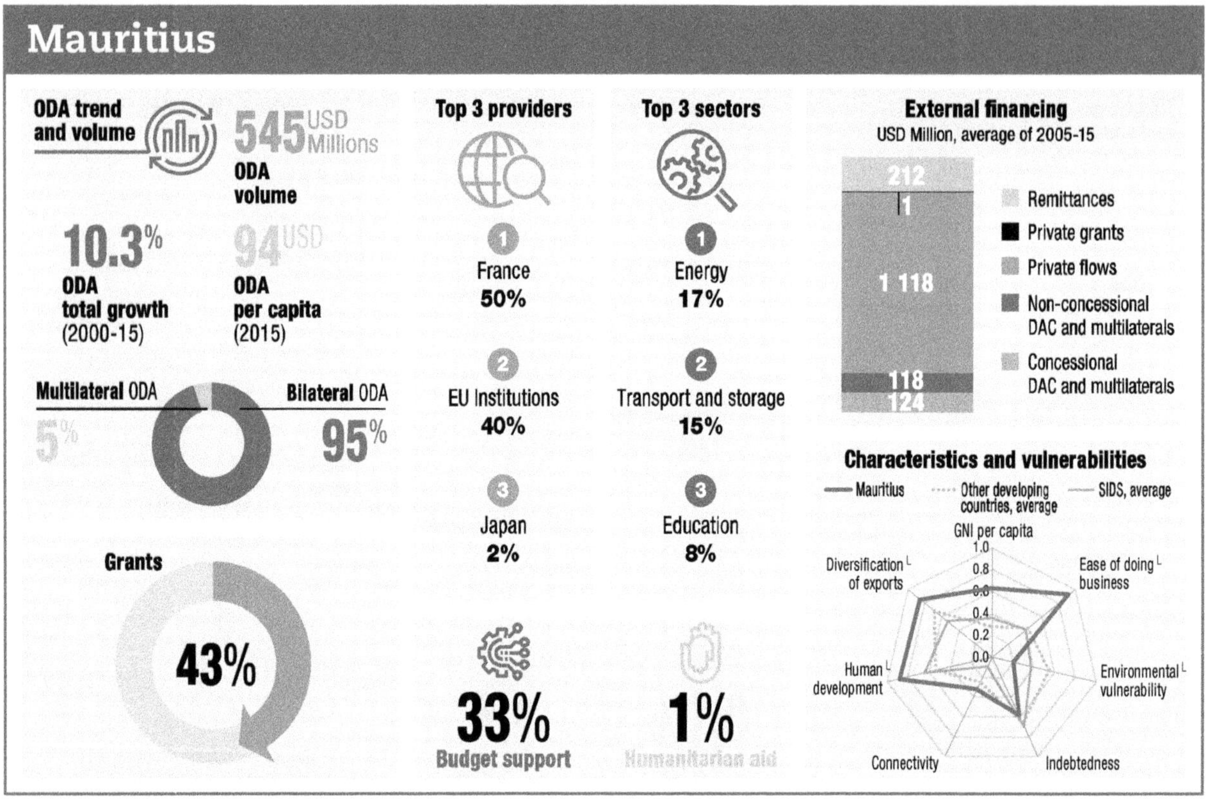

Figure 4.19. Micronesia

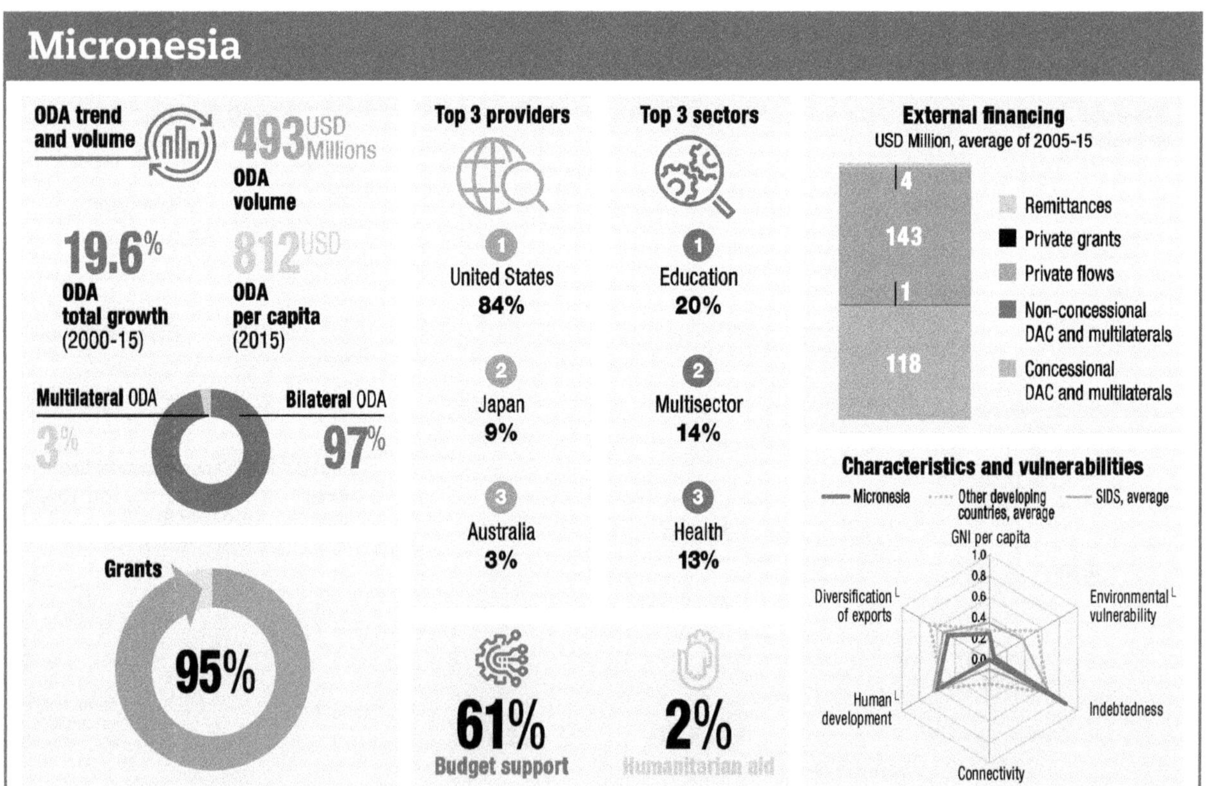

Figure 4.20. Montserrat

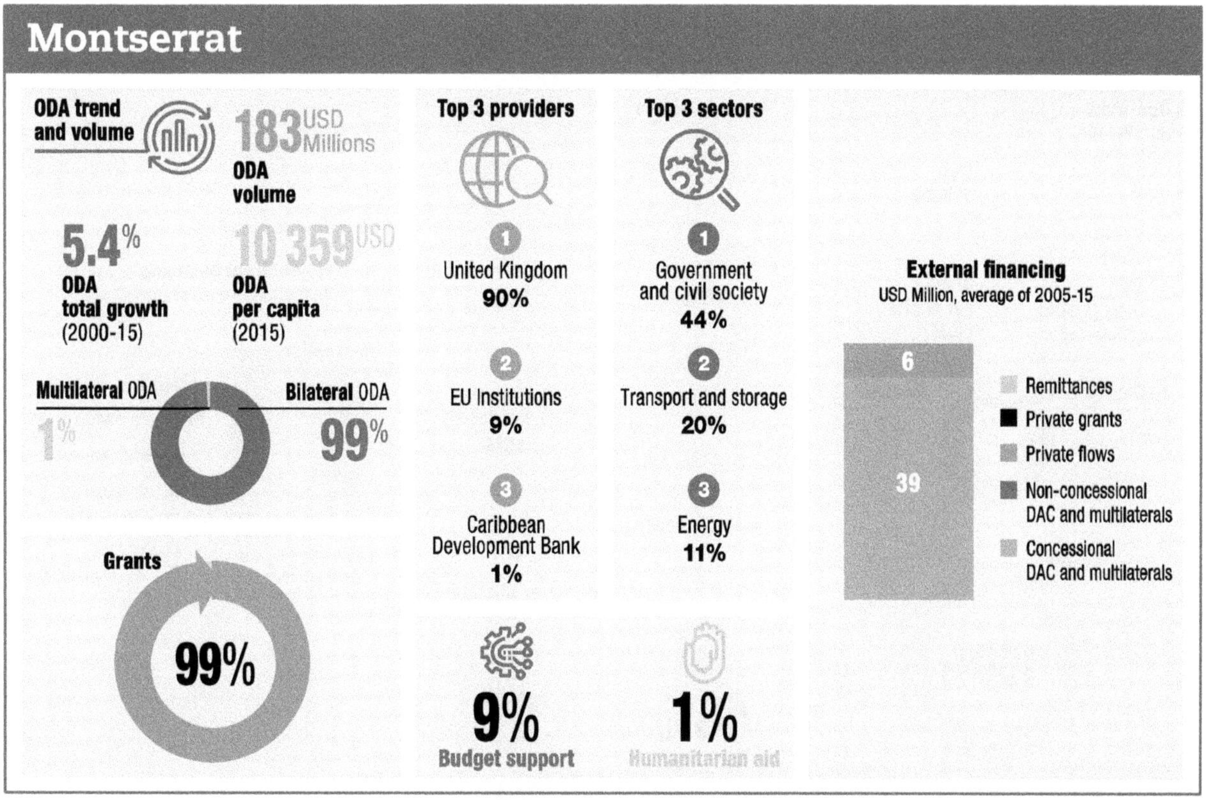

Figure 4.21. Nauru

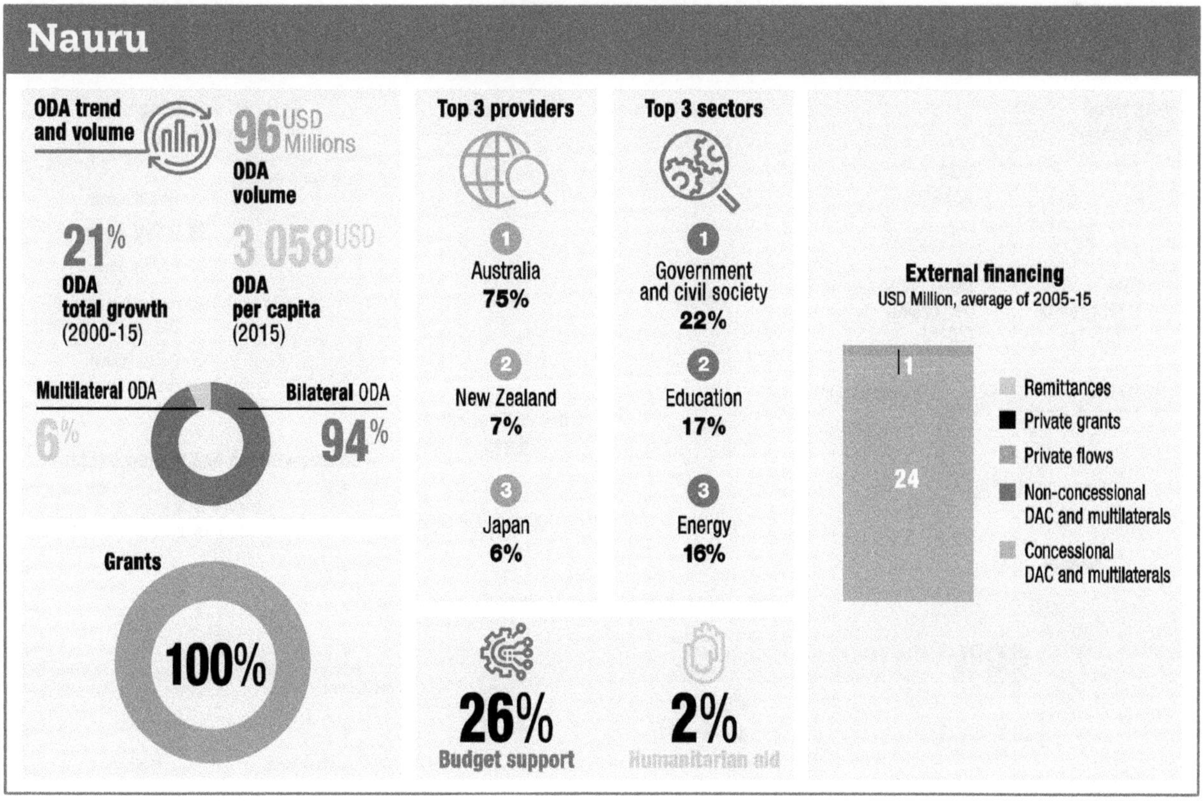

Figure 4.22. Niue

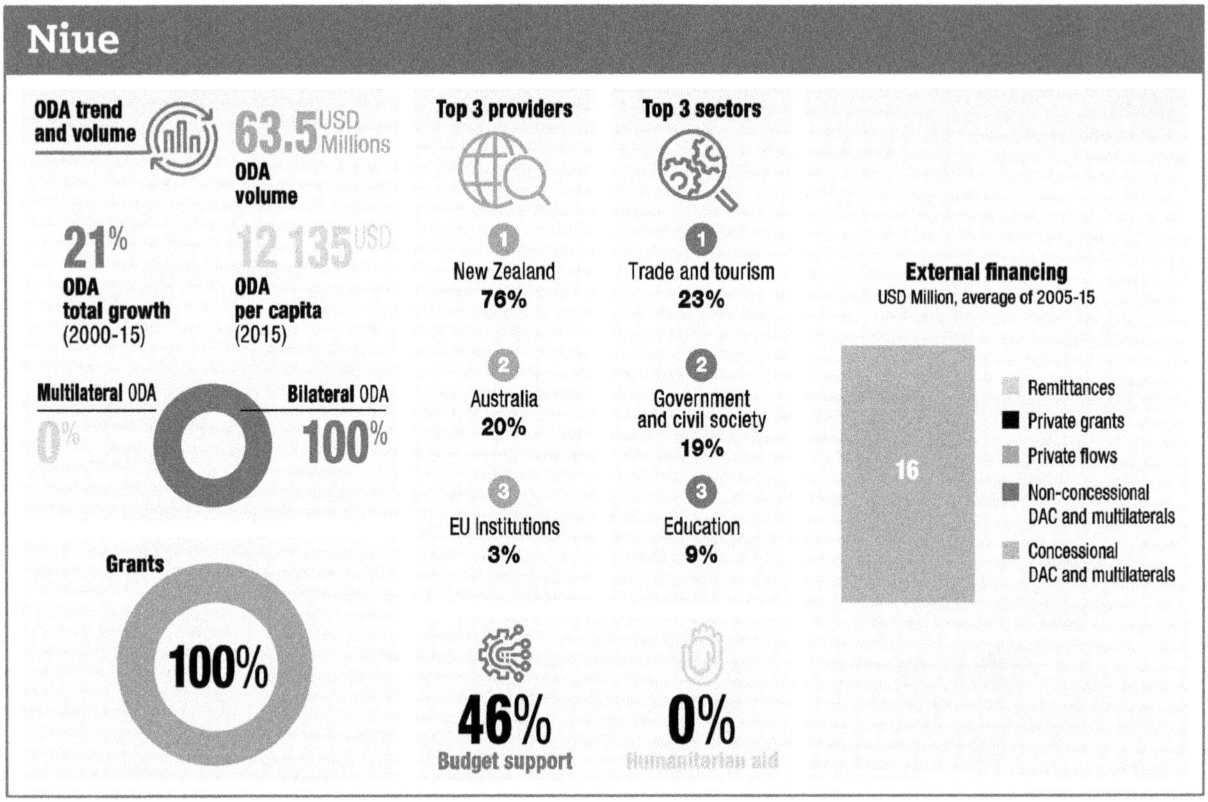

Figure 4.23. Palau

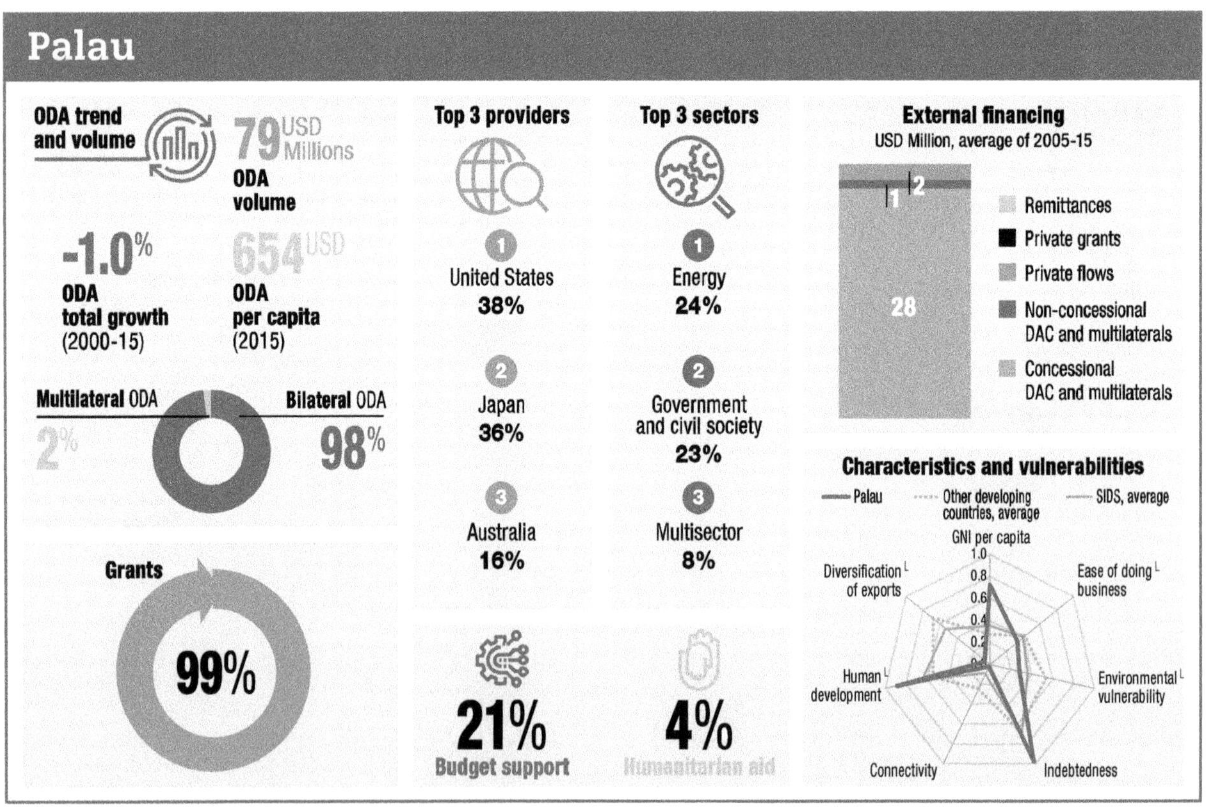

Figure 4.24. Papua New Guinea

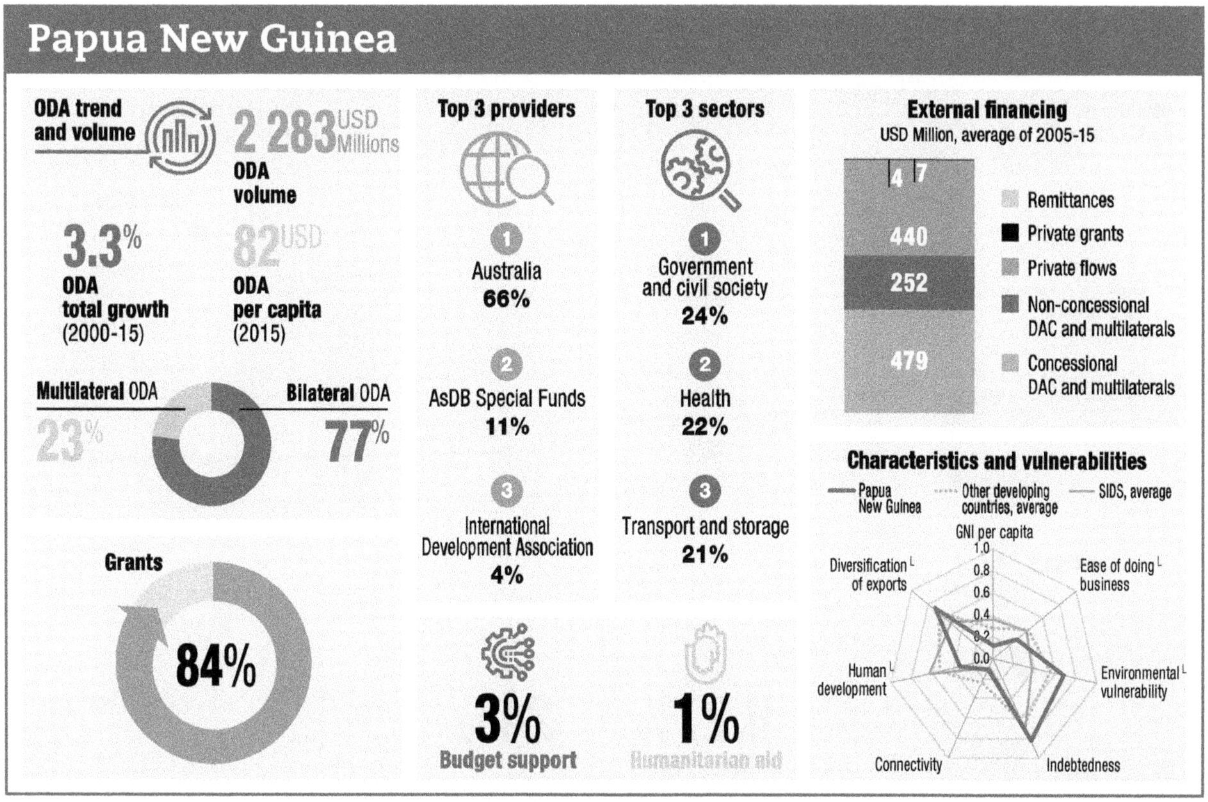

Figure 4.25. Saint Lucia

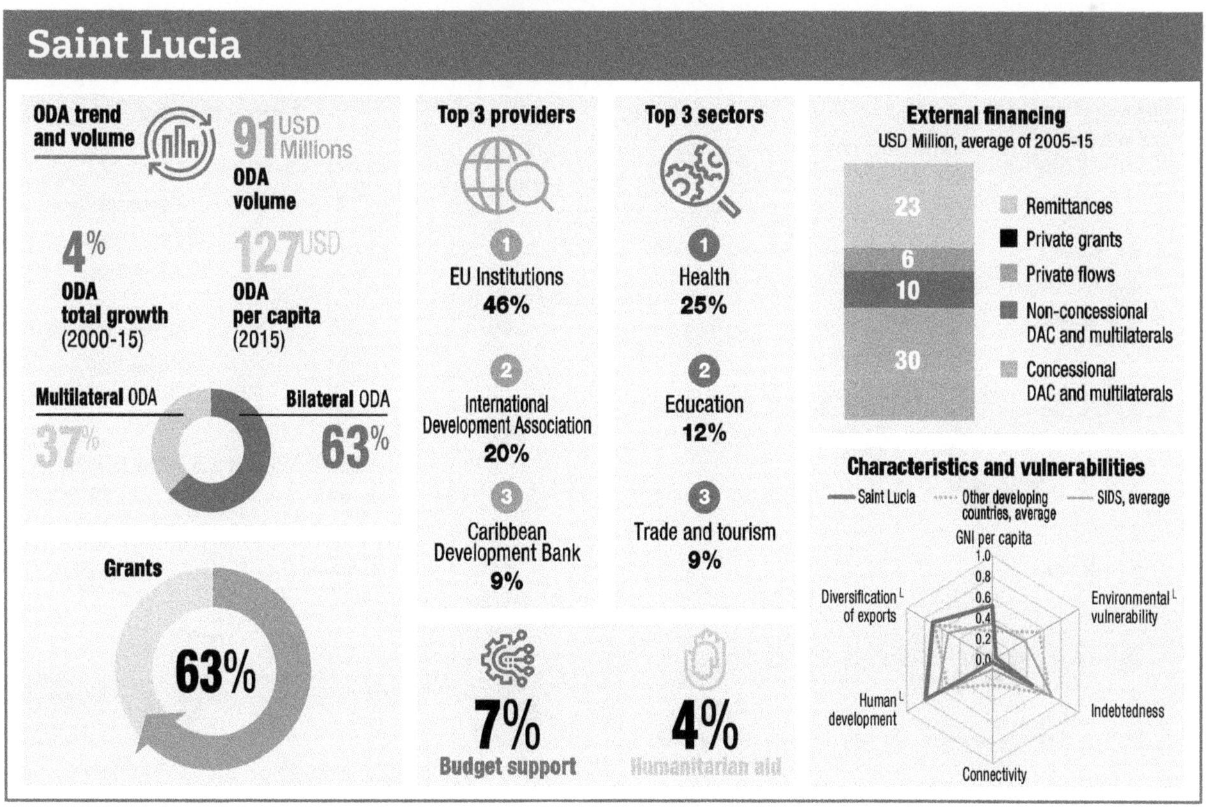

Figure 4.26. Saint Vincent and the Grenadines

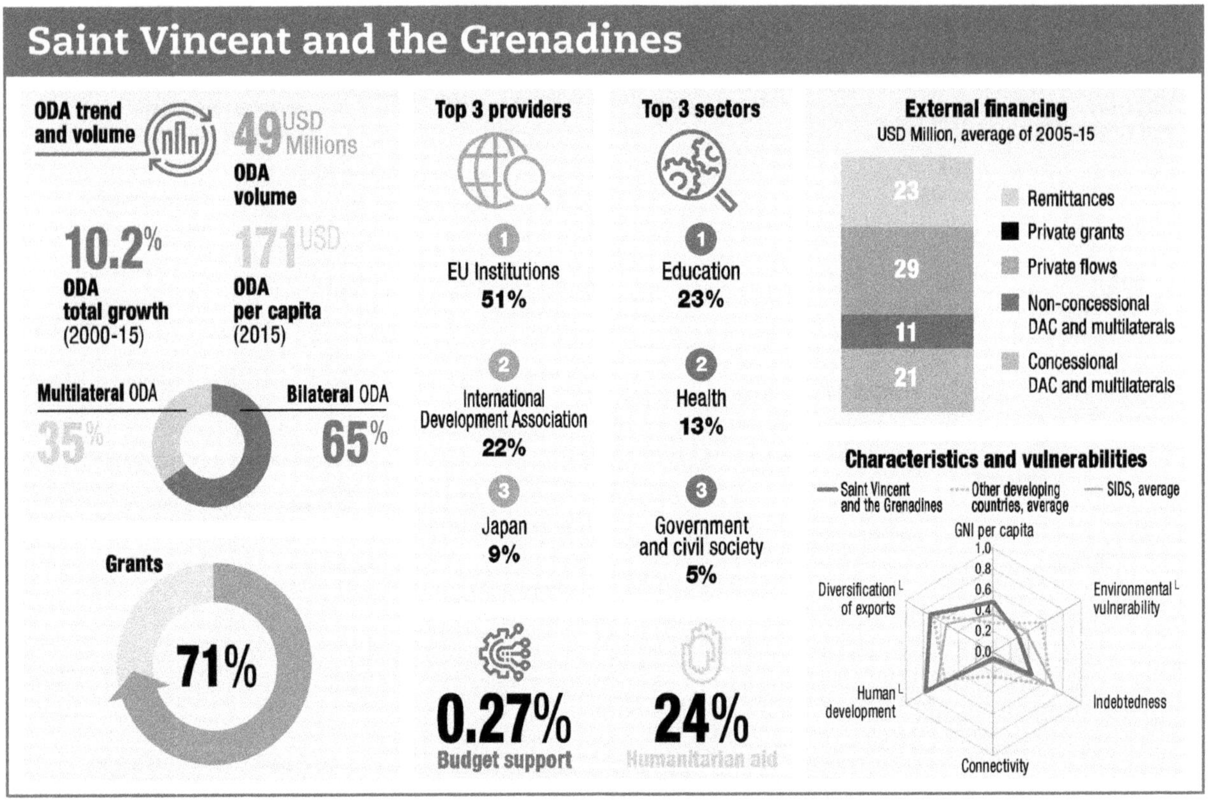

Figure 4.27. Samoa

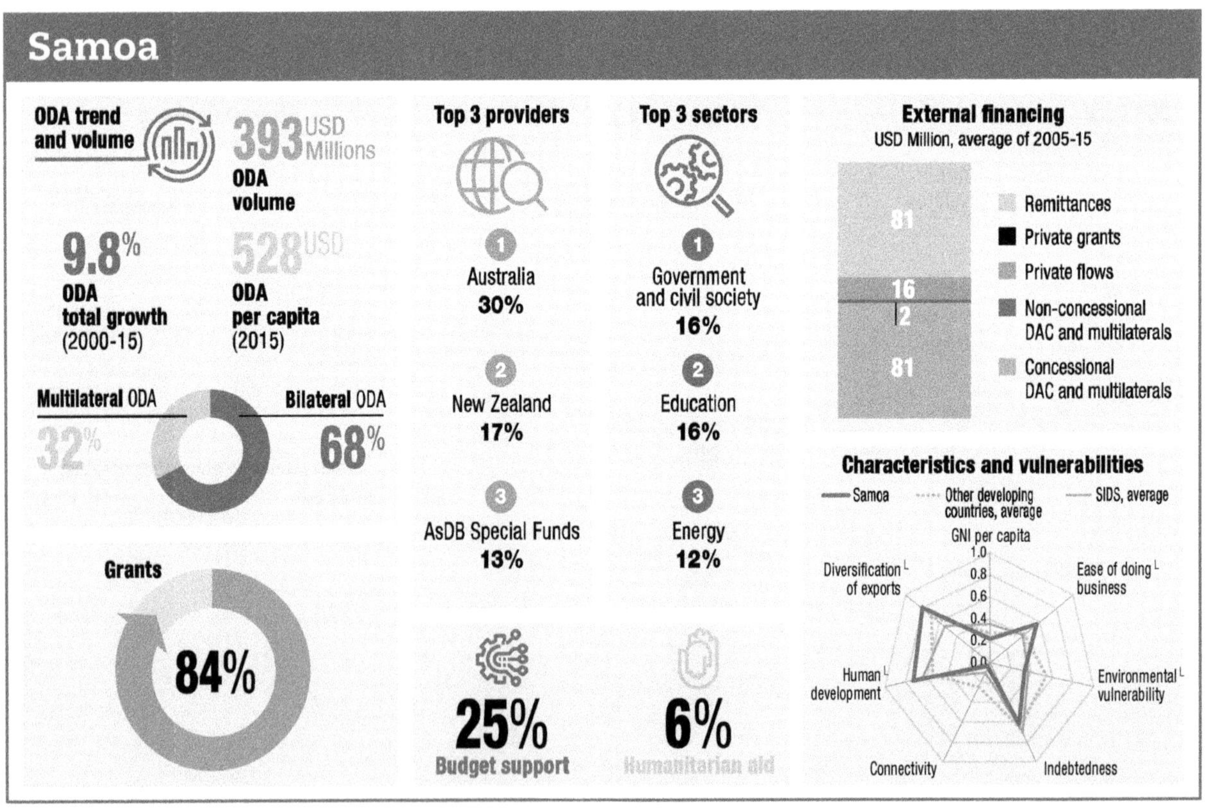

Figure 4.28. Sao Tome and Principe

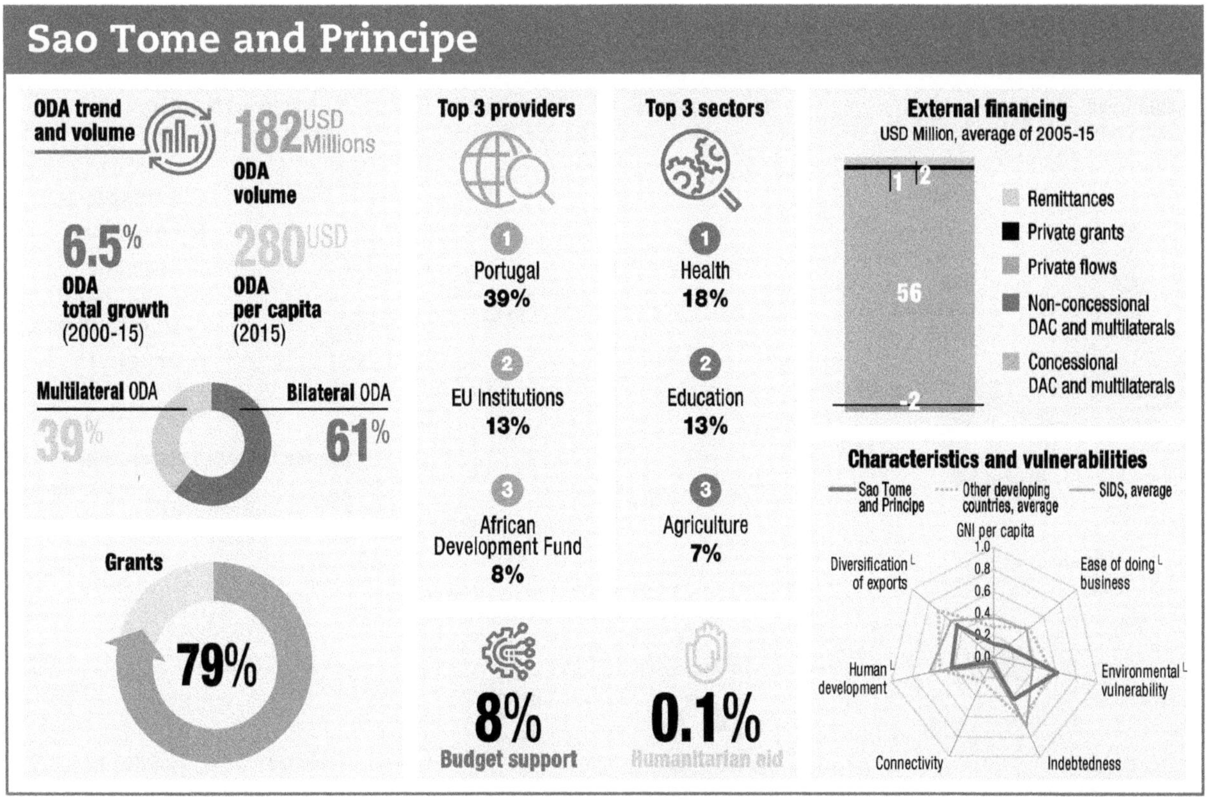

Figure 4.29. Seychelles

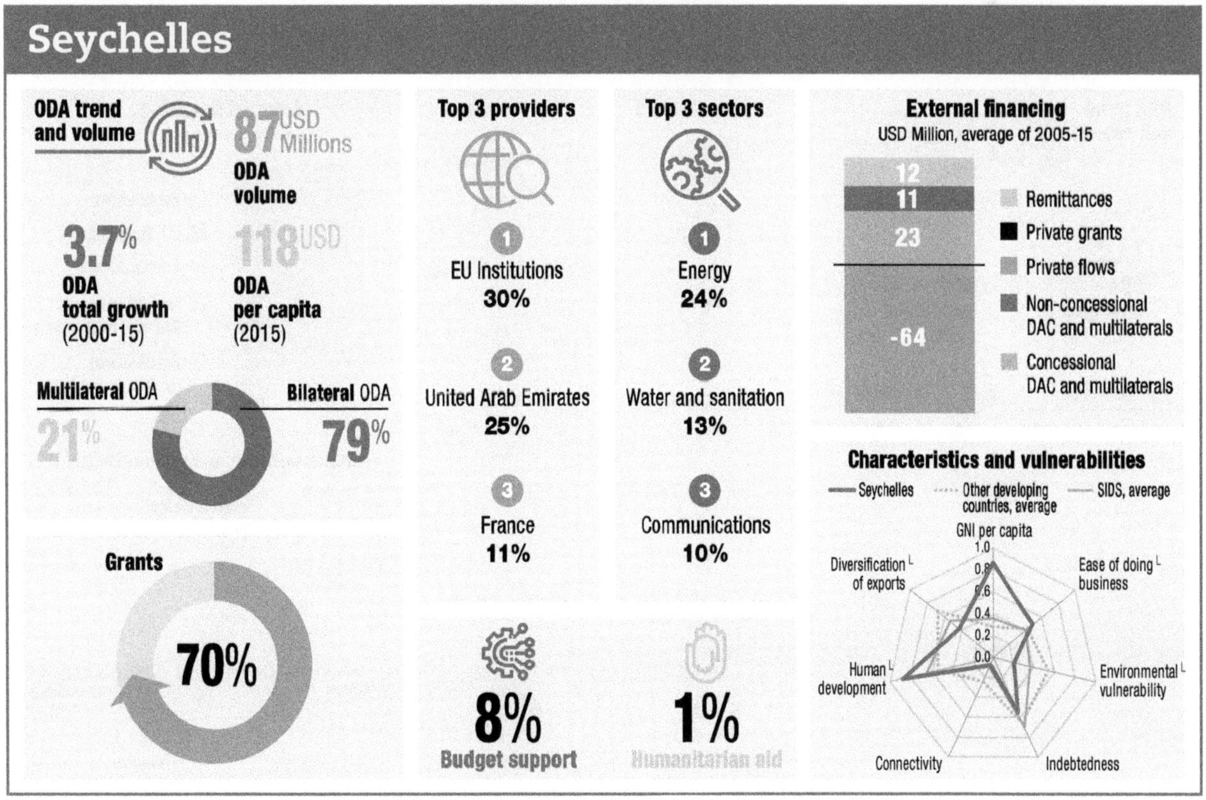

Figure 4.30. Solomon Islands

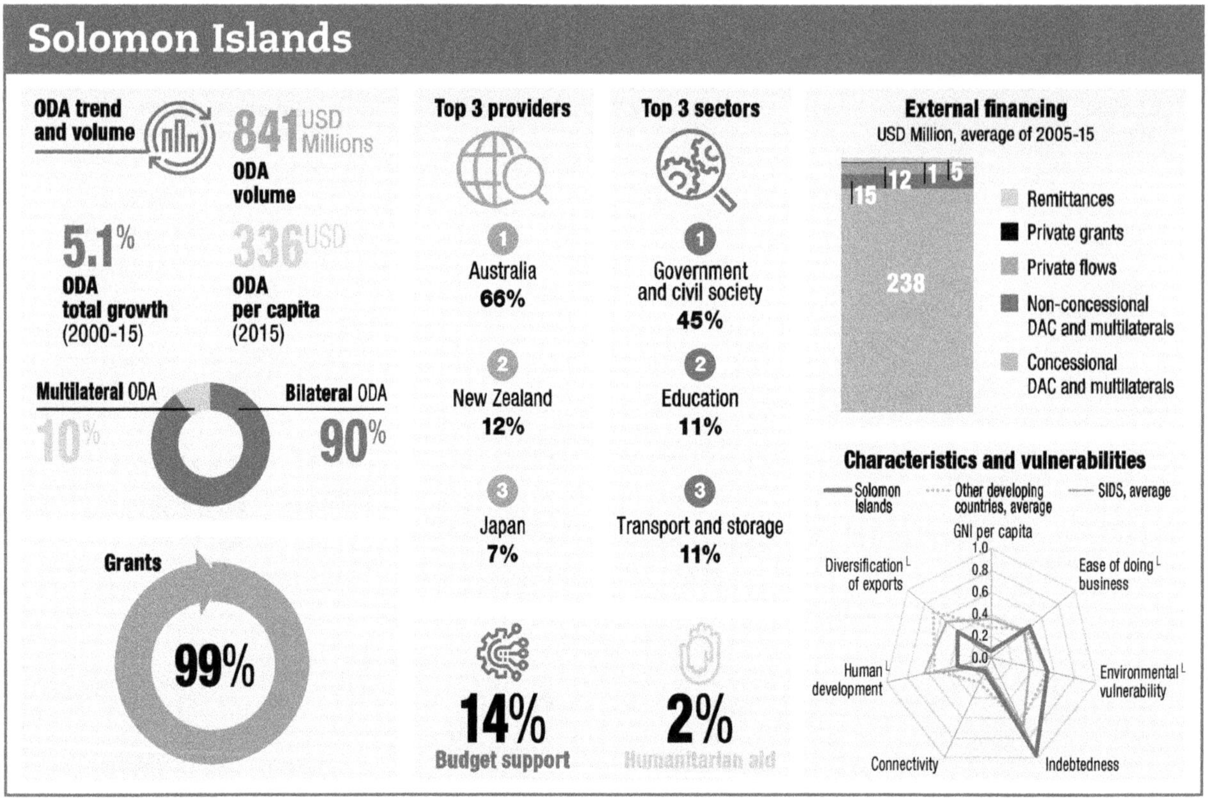

Figure 4.31. Suriname

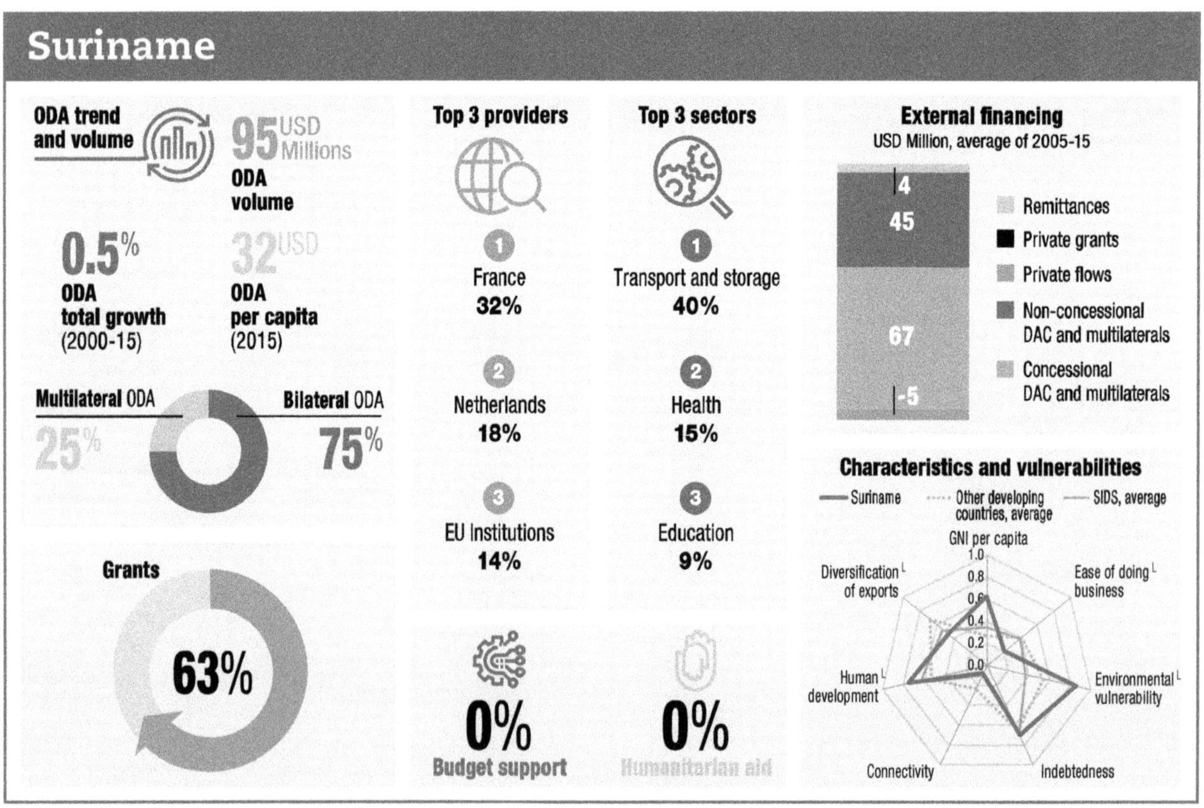

Figure 4.32. Timor-Leste

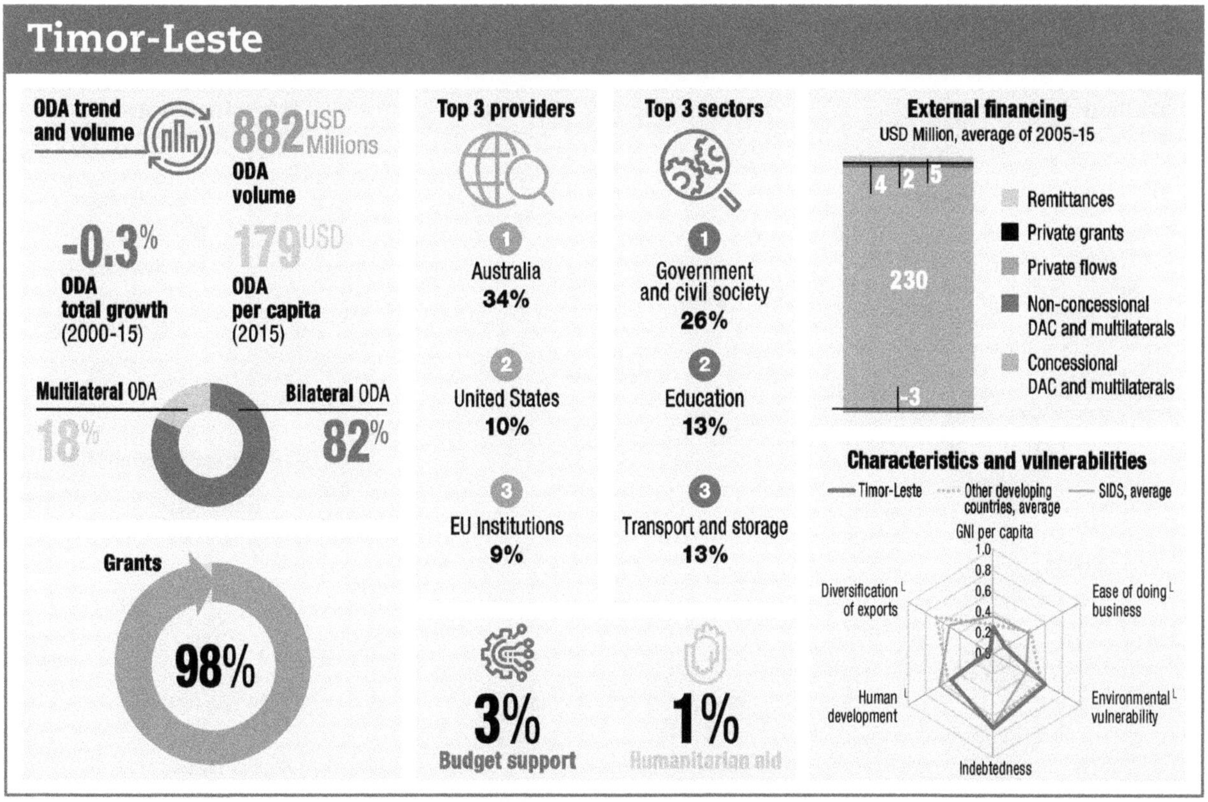

Figure 4.33. Tonga

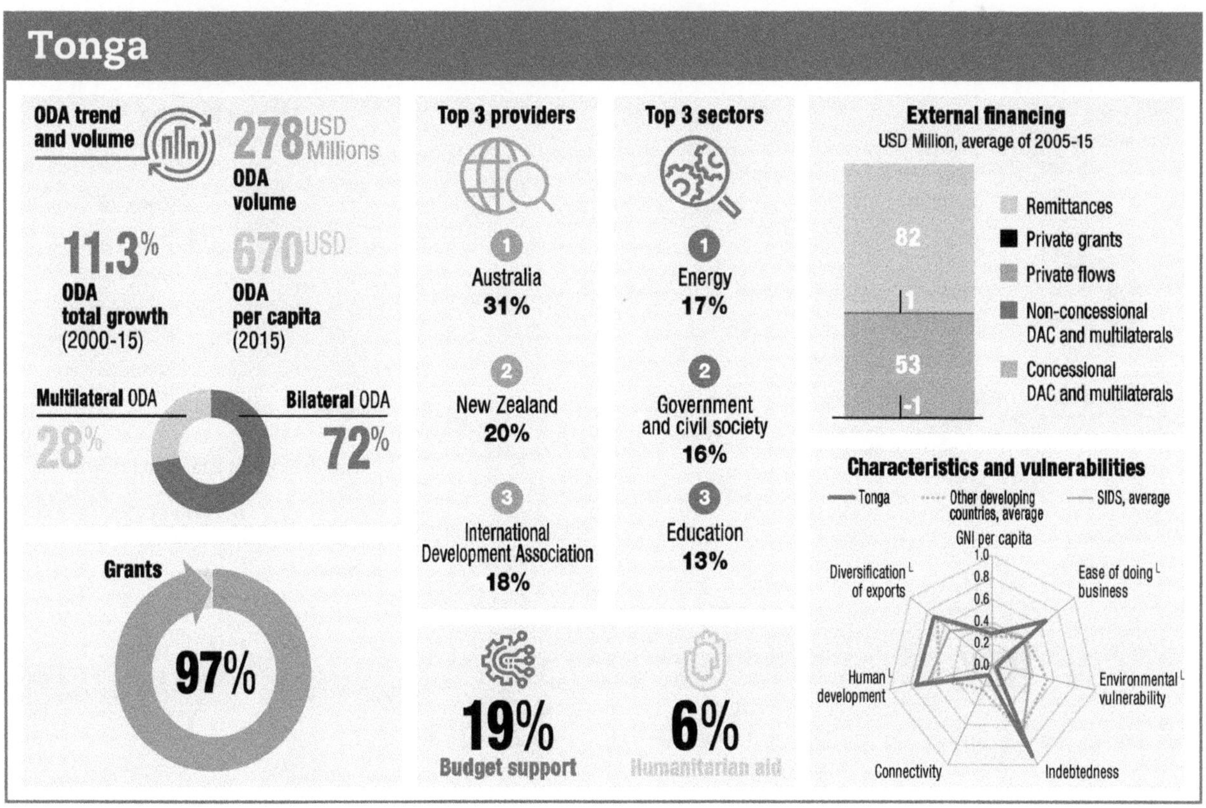

Figure 4.34. Tuvalu

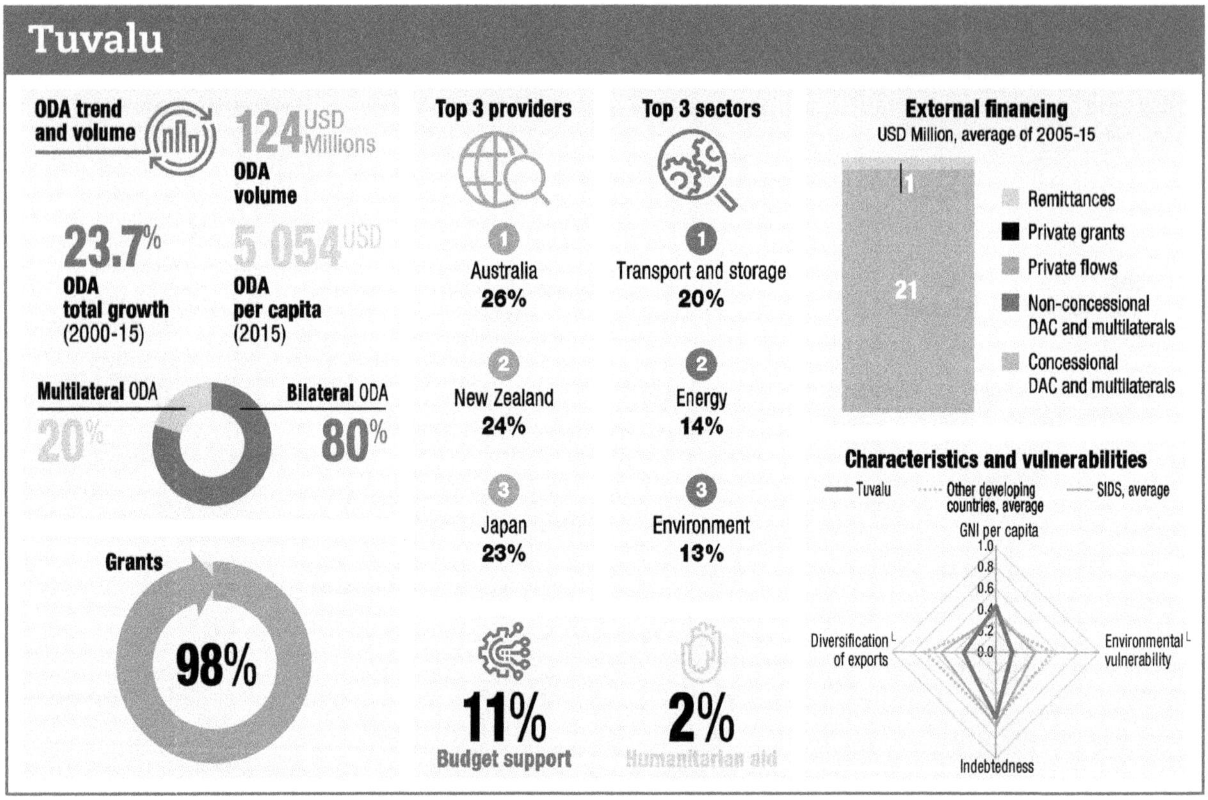

Figure 4.35. Vanuatu

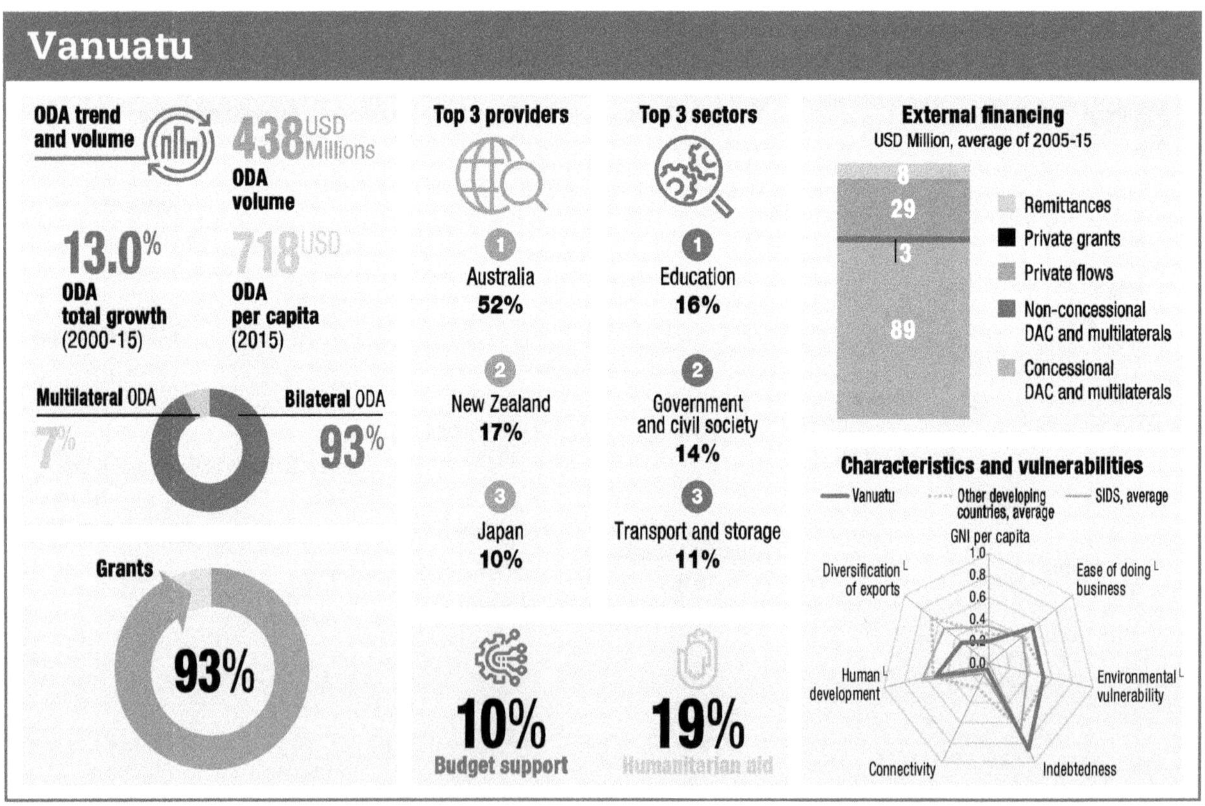

Methodological notes

The snapshots of small island developing states (SIDS) in this report present key statistics on SIDS' financing for development landscape as well as on key elements of socio-economic and environmental vulnerability (as represented in the spidergram).

The spidegrams are based on the following data:

- Gross national income per capita, atlas method, World Bank;
- Ease of Doing Business Index, World Bank;
- Connectivity, as measured by the 'Liner shipping connectivity index', UNCTAD;
- Human development, as measured by the 'Human Development Index', UNDP;
- Diversification of exports, measured by the Herfindahl-Hirschman Index (Product HHI), UNCTAD;
- Indebtedness, or debt over GNI. IMF data and IMF estimations for Timor-Leste, Tonga and Palau.
- Environmental vulnerability refers to the Environment Vulnerability Index (EVI), developed by the South Pacific Applied Geoscience Commission (SOPAC), the United Nations Environment Programme (UNEP) and their partners.

Data and indexes were normalised to obtain values between 0 and 1, where 1 reflects the best position/situation. For indebtedness and environmental vulnerability best performers are countries with the lowest debt over GNI and the lowest EVI score. Data are from 2015 (or last year available, but not older than 2012).

The following data was not available for the following countries:

- GNI per capita and Ease of Doing Business Index for Cuba;
- Connectivity data for Timor-Leste;
- Ease of Doing Business Index, Connectivity and Environmental resilience for Tuvalu;
- Human development for the Marshall Islands;
- Ease of doing business index for Saint Lucia, Saint Vincent and the Grenadines and Micronesia.

Glossary

Blue economy: Development paradigm which leads to improved human well-being and social equity, while significantly reducing environmental risks and ecological scarcities, endorsing low carbon, resource efficiency and social inclusion. The report also makes reference to the "ocean economy", which refers to the sectoral and cross-sectoral economic activities related to the oceans, seas and coasts, without including an explicit sustainability dimension. Projections for the ocean economy are used in this report as proxy for the potential of the blue economy.

Budget support: Finance that is extended by development agencies in order to support to macro-level policies and to augment government budgets to assist the recipient through a programme of policy and institutional reform and implementation that promote growth and achieve sustainable reductions in poverty.

Concessional finance: Official resources extended by DAC members, other bilateral providers, and multilateral providers – grants and concessional loans – which meet the ODA definition. In this report, the terms "concessional finance" and ODA are often used interchangeably. Not all concessional resources to all countries count as ODA. For details about the ODA-eligibility criteria, please refer to: www.oecd.org/dac/stats/daclist.htm.

Creditor reporting system (CRS): The OECD/DAC statistical database recording individual aid activities.

Development Assistance Committee (DAC): The committee of the OECD which deals with development co-operation matters. Currently there are 30 members of the DAC: Australia, Austria, Belgium, Canada, the Czech Republic, Denmark, Finland, France, Germany, Greece, Hungary, Iceland, Ireland, Italy, Japan, Korea, Luxembourg, Netherlands, New Zealand, Norway, Poland, Portugal, Slovak Republic, Slovenia, Spain, Sweden, Switzerland, United Kingdom, United States and the European Union.

DAC List of ODA Recipients: The DAC list of ODA Recipients shows developing countries and territories eligible for receiving official development assistance (ODA). The list is designed for statistical purposes, not as guidance for aid or other preferential treatment. In particular, geographical aid allocations are national policy decisions and responsibilities. The list is revised by the DAC every three years.

Domestic resource mobilisation: Generation of savings from domestic resources and their allocation to economically and socially productive investments. Such resource allocation can come from both the public and private sectors.

Fragility: Measure determined by a country's exposure to risks and insufficient coping capacity of the state, system and communities to manage, absorb or mitigate those risks. This is expressed in the following five dimensions: economic, environmental, political, security, societal. There are currently 56 states on the OECD list of fragile states including six of the SIDS considered in this report.

Official development assistance (ODA): Grants or loans to countries and territories on the DAC List of ODA Recipients (developing countries) and to multilateral agencies which are: (a) undertaken by the official sector; (b) with promotion of economic development and welfare as the main objective; (c) at concessional financial terms (if a loan, having a grant element of at least 25%). In addition to financial flows, technical co-operation is included in aid. Grants, loans and credits for military purposes are excluded. Transfer payments to private individuals (e.g. pensions, reparations or insurance pay-outs) are in general not counted.

Public financial management: This builds on the development community's efforts to strengthen developing countries' capacity to better manage their public finances.

Sustainable Development Goals (SDGs): Officially known as Transforming our World: The 2030 Agenda for Sustainable Development is a set of 17 "Global Goals" with 169 targets between them.

ORGANISATION FOR ECONOMIC CO-OPERATION AND DEVELOPMENT

The OECD is a unique forum where governments work together to address the economic, social and environmental challenges of globalisation. The OECD is also at the forefront of efforts to understand and to help governments respond to new developments and concerns, such as corporate governance, the information economy and the challenges of an ageing population. The Organisation provides a setting where governments can compare policy experiences, seek answers to common problems, identify good practice and work to co-ordinate domestic and international policies.

The OECD member countries are: Australia, Austria, Belgium, Canada, Chile, the Czech Republic, Denmark, Estonia, Finland, France, Germany, Greece, Hungary, Iceland, Ireland, Israel, Italy, Japan, Korea, Latvia, Luxembourg, Mexico, the Netherlands, New Zealand, Norway, Poland, Portugal, the Slovak Republic, Slovenia, Spain, Sweden, Switzerland, Turkey, the United Kingdom and the United States. The European Union takes part in the work of the OECD.

OECD Publishing disseminates widely the results of the Organisation's statistics gathering and research on economic, social and environmental issues, as well as the conventions, guidelines and standards agreed by its members.

OECD PUBLISHING, 2, rue André-Pascal, 75775 PARIS CEDEX 16
(43 2017 11 1 P) ISBN 978-92-64-28761-7 – 2018

www.ingramcontent.com/pod-product-compliance
Ingram Content Group UK Ltd.
Pitfield, Milton Keynes, MK11 3LW, UK
UKHW051504290926
15471UKWH00008B/1411

9 789264 287617